FAR FROM ZION

far
from
zion

In Search of a Global Jewish Community

CHARLES LONDON

wm

WILLIAM MORROW

An Imprint of HarperCollins*Publishers*

HarperCollins books may be purchased for educational, business, or sales
promotional use. For information please write: Special Markets Department,
HarperCollins Publishers, 10 East 53rd Street, New York, NY 10022.

FIRST EDITION

Designed by Jamie Lynn Kerner

Library of Congress Cataloging-in-Publication Data
London, Charles.
Far from Zion : in search of a global Jewish community / Charles London. —
1st ed.
p. cm.
ISBN 978-0-06-1561061
1. Jewish diaspora. 2. London, Charles — Religion. 3. London, Charles —
Travel. 4. Jews — Identity. 5. Jews — Civilization. I. Title.
DS134.L655 2009
305.8924—dc22   2009006568

08 09 10 11 12 \ OV/RRD   10 9 8 7 6 5 4 3 2 1

For Gram Bev

CONTENTS

ONE

Belonging

ooo

TWO

Caretakers:

The Jewish Community of Burma

ooo

THREE

Newcomers:

The Jewish Community of Bentonville, Arkansas

ooo

FOUR

Rebirth:

The Jewish Community of New Orleans

ooo

FIVE

Siege and Survival:

The Jewish Community of Bosnia

ooo

SIX

Converts:

The Jewish Community of Uganda

000

SEVEN

Imperiled?

The Jewish Community of Iran

000

EIGHT

Revolutionaries:

The Jewish Community of Cuba

000

NINE

Zion

000

EPILOGUE:

Home

000

ACKNOWLEDGMENTS

000

FAR FROM ZION

one

Belonging

By the rivers of Babylon we sat and wept, when we remembered Zion . . . If I forget thee, O Jerusalem, may my right hand forget its skill. May my tongue cling to the roof of my mouth if I do not remember you, if I do not consider Jerusalem my highest joy.
—Psalms 137:1, 5—6

THEY KEEP ASKING ME:

Are you Jewish?

Outside the death camp at Sachsenhausen on a snowy morning just before my sixteenth birthday, the guard sighed the question over his morning paper. That's my first memory of being asked. He wanted to see if it was worth getting up and unlocking the gate. The Memorial (that's what he called the place) was technically closed, but if I was Jewish, well, exceptions could be made . . .

In college, walking in and out of campus, the Lubovitch with their black hats and palm fronds and their Mitzvah Mobile accosted me

1

with the question. They wanted to perform a mitzvah on me—a good deed—but only if I was really Jewish. *Was your mother Jewish? Your father Jewish?*

In a market in Mbale, Eastern Uganda, a young man crossed four lanes of dusty traffic to shake my hand, to say shalom, to ask if I was Jewish. He wore a knitted *kippah* on his head and smiled broadly. I was asked outside the cemetery in Guanabacoa, Cuba, the nexus of the island's Afro-Cuban religions. The director of the Jewish hospital in Tehran asked, a university dean in Nablus in the West Bank asked, and an Orthodox soldier at the Western Wall smirked the question at me. I could have sworn he was flirting. The fringes of his tzitzit dangled near the butt of his gun.

The same question all over the world with the same intention: to find out if I belong. Did I belong in that death camp? Was I a friend to the Ugandan Jews on the hill outside Mbale? Did I have a right to visit the Jewish cemetery in Cuba? Did I belong with the Palestinians in Nablus, with the devout at the Western Wall? Was I a member of the tribe?

I certainly didn't think of myself as a member of the tribe. I hadn't been raised with a strong sense of ethnic identity, and my family was not religious. My upbringing was more Don DeLillo than Phillip Roth (except for the masturbation guilt), and I didn't have any great desire to be Jewish. My grandmother—Gram Bev we called her—would have dinners at her apartment on the Jewish High Holidays, but they were more about family than about Judaism. She didn't say prayers or even cook her own brisket. She was, in fact, a terrible cook. She was far more comfortable at cocktail parties than at synagogue, and my family followed her lead. No one in my family could read Hebrew or Yiddish or had any interest in learning to do so.

When I asked Gram Bev about where she grew up, she would tell me, simply, Virginia. She painted a picture of a grand southern plantation. I imagined her as Scarlett O'Hara, wearing giant hoopskirts and going to balls. She fancied herself a bit of a southern belle, even though she'd moved to Baltimore when she was young. She married a business-man with a German-Jewish background, joined the country club, and played the role of the socialite, a role for which she felt she had been raised. In one of my strongest memories of her, she stands in a black Oscar de la Renta cocktail dress, leaning on the piano in a banquet hall, singing along to "My Way." She had a love for crooners, and Frank Sina-tra was her favorite.

"I'm just a thoroughly mod Gram," she would say, smiling. She was an art lover, and could perform hours of exegesis on the works of Matisse or Basquiat, but she only ever mentioned being Jewish when she talked about the time she met the Cohn sisters at their Baltimore apartment. They were two of the most notable art collectors of their day, and Gram raved about their fabulous collection, most of which now belongs to the Baltimore Museum of Art. She spent decades as a docent there, studying and teaching. She simply loved beauty and good taste, and that was how I imagined her. Even after she had a stroke, which impaired her speech and movement, she would go out to dinner at least once a week. I never saw her with less than impeccable hair and makeup. Her temple was aes-thetics; her religion, art. It struck me as odd that she had the High Holi-days services piped in over her phone after she had her second stroke. I'd always assumed she went to the synagogue in order to be seen. I couldn't imagine what she gained by listening in from the yellow armchair in her living room. But I didn't ask either. I was more interested in talking with her about Miro than Moses.

I never knew her first husband, my grandfather. He died long before I was born, and his death pushed my father away from organized religion.

"It just wasn't a comfort to me," my father said. "It seemed like a show; I didn't want to be part of that. It just didn't have any meaning. I didn't know the Hebrew and I didn't want to know. I'd feel like a hypocrite if I pretended to pray." And then he added, "But I am proud of being Jewish." I wasn't sure what he meant by being Jewish then. If there was no religion in it, no ethnic food, no cultural events, no involvement in any Jewish organizations or studying of Jewish history, what could it have meant to him?

My mother did serve on the board of the National Council of Jewish Women, because she believed in the progressive agenda for which they advocated, but when the NCJW ladies would come over in December, we would frantically take down the Christmas stockings. There were no Jewish writers on the bookshelves and there was no Jewish music on the CD players. The news sometimes talked about Israel and the Palestinians, but I didn't imagine that had anything to do with me, and I didn't talk about it in my family.

My first memorable encounter with being a Jew sent me running to hide my tears in the bathroom. No one called me "kike" or drew a swastika on my locker or pelted me with stale bagels. My tormentors were studious young Jews at the Baltimore Hebrew Congregation, where my parents had sent me to get my Judaism from the professionals.

I was twelve years old and preparing for my bar mitzvah with an introductory class at the synagogue. A private tutor would come later. The classroom itself was unremarkable, looking like any primary school classroom anywhere. Paper cutouts from arts and crafts projects hung on the wall. A map of the Holy Land stood sentinel by the door, its deserts stained a pleasing pink. A poster of the Ten Commandments hung by the blackboard, and the teacher, aware, I'm sure, of the authority it gave her, stood in front of it, flash cards in hand. In my mind, she wore the same robes as Charlton Heston in the movie.

There were only four of us in this class, and I provided the only masculine element, such as it was. I had gone to an all boys prep school since first grade, so I already felt a little off guard in the classroom presence of girls. The circumstances were cruel—putting me in my first real contact with the opposite sex just as the awkwardness of puberty was taking hold. The entire custom seemed designed to embarrass me. One of the girls had been a regular in Hebrew school for ages and could already read the language with some proficiency. I could hardly recognize the letters, let alone divine their sounds. What words I knew, I knew only from their English transliteration. My mother went to synagogue twice a year in the fall for the High Holidays of Rosh Hashanah and Yom Kippur, and I always went with her, reluctantly. My father and my sister never did. We held a Seder at our house for Passover, where I, as the youngest, would ask the Four Questions in English. And now my parents had sent me to the professionals, the Hebrew school teacher, the synagogue staff, to fake my way through the language and prepare to become a Jewish man.

The flash cards went up in the teacher's hand, each one more mean-ingless to me than the one before. At twelve, I was an eager reader of novels but I became suddenly reacquainted with illiteracy. The girls all seemed to know, all seemed so comfortable with this strange alphabet. One of them even mentioned that she had gone to kindergarten in this very room back in ancient times, seven years ago. The girls terrified me, not just for their unfamiliar femininity, but because they were *so* Jewish. My regular school was an old Baltimore bastion of WASPishness, deeply tied to the good old boy network that ran up and down the East Coast corridors of power and finance. There were other Jews in my class, of course, but we were small in number and highly assimilated, country-club Jews. Our Jewish identity was hardly visible on the surface. I had only one Jewish friend, and Judaism was not the basis of our friendship. We'd been neighbors until I was six.

But these girls went to coed schools that were dominated by Jews. They had Purim celebrations in class and came dressed as Queen Esther. I'd never in my life been to a Purim celebration, although my sister had, and my parents still tell the story of that ill-fated fete. The tradition calls for the adult men to get drunk and the children to dress up as characters from the biblical story of Queen Esther, who saved the Babylonian Jews from genocide at the hands of the royal vizier Haman. My sister went to the party dressed as Peter Pan. My father didn't attend, and even if he had, he doesn't drink. It would be a number of years before I learned the story of Purim, taught first by a Ugandan on a commuter train and then by a left-wing rabbi among the ruins of Persepolis.

My family celebrated Christmas for reasons that were, at the time, not entirely clear to me, though I enjoyed it all the same. When my friends at school talked about what they got for Christmas, I could join right in. Not even my name brought me closer to the tribe: Charles London? It sounded like an Anglican estate lawyer's name. And I never, until that day in class at age twelve and a half, felt the lack of any of it.

For the girls in my b'nai mitzvah class, names like Kleinberg and Grossbaum and Mendelsohn were not exotic. All three of them lived in the Jewish part of town: Pikesville—a name that made me cringe whenever I heard it, given the unfortunate rhymes it brought to mind. In this class I felt like I was on foreign soil, and, by the third letter I couldn't name, let alone pronounce, my lip began to quiver. I ran to the bathroom and burst into tears, cursing at my mother for dropping me off in this accursed place, for making me Jewish, for not making me Jewish enough. I didn't fit. I was a bad Jew, and these girls and this teacher could see it. I cried with the shame of not belonging in a community to which I'd never before wanted to belong.

When I came back to the classroom, I excused myself and told that old journeyman lie: "My stomach hurts."

My mother was called and I was picked up early.

After that humiliating episode, I steeled myself for the remaining bar mitzvah lessons, bit my lower lip, and got through the ritual. At the same time, on the other side of the world, Sammy Samuels, whose Burmese name is Aug Soe Lwin, was preparing for his bar mitzvah, which would be the first in Burma in over thirty years. And in Israel, Ivan

Hrkas, also thirteen years old, was arriving from war-ravaged Sarajevo in one of the first convoys to escape the city, arranged by Sarajevo's small Jewish community.

The portion of the Torah I read is known as "Parshat Bo." *Bo* is the command form of the Hebrew word for "go" and it is the first word God speaks to Moses in that Torah portion, telling him to visit Pharaoh and bring him the final three plagues. It is also the passage where Moses leads the Israelites out of Egypt and into the desert, into freedom. The first commandments of the Torah are here, turning the book from a story of a nomadic and then enslaved sheepherding people into a book of laws.

The whole idea of "going" has always been central to the story of the Jews. The Torah begins with God expelling Adam and Eve from the Garden, and Abraham going forth into Canaan, and Jacob going forth into Egypt, and the Israelites, named for Jacob, going into exile in Babylon and going back again under the Persians, and, of course, the big Go, from my little *parsha*, the Israelites going forth from bondage in Egypt, that Exodus that is the essential condition of Judaism. Without it, there would be no Torah, no commandments, no Jews, just a tribe of Israelites that was once scattered around the Middle East.

The Jews became Jews as refugees. Fleeing slavery in Egypt, crossing the desert, so the national myth goes, they became one people by receiving a book, *the* Book, the Torah, given by God to Moses and by Moses to the Hebrews at Mount Sinai. The Hebrew people took this Torah and vowed to obey it and to understand it, and upon taking that vow, they became Jews. They had long had a covenant with God, ever since the circumcision of Abraham, but they were not one people until Moses brought the Torah down the mountain.

When Moses presented the Torah to his people, they all cried out in response to each of the commandments, "We will do and we will hear!" And by crying out, they bound themselves under the yoke of those commandments and to each other as one nation. "We will do and we will hear," they said. Doing first, hearing—*understanding*— only later. The most important part, the first duty, was simply to do whatever it was God asked of them. This mixed multitude pledging their obedience to the law Moses had brought down was probably the most unified group of Jews there ever was and ever will be. A crowd of refugees granted freedom and celebrating law, even if they didn't obey it for long.

Among those fleeing Egypt, we are told, there were those who were not Hebrews—Exodus 12:38 reads "a mixed multitude also went up with them." Did those not of the tribe of Hebrews become Hebrews? They were in a crowd of over a million in the desert; they suffered the same journey, fleeing under the awful grace of God. But there is no mention of this mixed multitude later in the journey, wandering the desert for forty years. After receiving the Torah, they were transformed into one nation.

To be a Jew, then, is to be born of those two escapes: into the desert and into the Book. Exile and text created us far more than genealogical descent from Abraham or the high priests, and throughout our history we have always turned back to these two concepts for strength, inspiration, and rebirth. There is no convincing archaeological evidence for the flight from Egypt. Evidence that the Hebrews were even enslaved in Egypt is scarce. But the Exodus story doesn't need to be true to serve its purpose. Whether divinely inspired or written by a series of editors over hundreds of years, the Torah narrative has its normative function, summed up succinctly by my bar mitzvah portion: you owe a debt to the God who sent you wandering, who made you into a people, who promises you won't wander forever.

At the time, I didn't really understand my Torah portion and I didn't give it much thought. I recited it phonetically, and in so doing, I became a man. Then I did my own going forth, and left organized Judaism behind, I thought, for good. My big Go. I heard and I didn't want to do or obey. Once the ritual was complete, my parents appeased, I became just like so

8

many others of my generation in America—to use a word so feared by so much of the Jewish establishment: *assimilated*.

And, like many of my generation, I took an active role in forming my identity while in my early twenties. I constructed layers of meaning, rather than operating only from those labels I had inherited. My friends and I built our identities around other factors—educational background, career, sexuality, the shifting ground of taste, political affiliation, and geography, whether real or imagined. We defined ourselves by our commitments—to causes and ideas rather than ethnic groups and institutions. While attending a synagogue or going to a Jewish community center never entered my mind, I happily went to gay rights rallies and Amnesty International meetings and cleaning days in parks in Harlem.

Thanks to social networking websites like Friendster and MySpace and Facebook, I could tag myself with all the multiple, overlapping definitions I wanted, and do or undo them publicly with the click of a button. Never has identity been so fluid as it is now, so easy to make up or delete. So groundless.

In virtual space, I could connect with the town of my birth or the borough where I lived or the university where I studied or everyone who had ever worked with me at any job. The multitude of nations that fled Egypt with Moses was at my fingertips; I could join it without leaving my apartment, I could leave it again in an instant. Check boxes on the computer, I reasoned, were a hell of a lot better than Yellow Stars pinned to my clothes, yet I never checked off the religion box on any of those websites. I was more comfortable telling a world of strangers that I was a gay writer/librarian who live in Brooklyn, likes Nina Simone and the works of Italo Calvino, and has a dog named Baxter, than saying I was Jewish. I didn't feel Jewish. I used to tell people that I felt guilty claiming my Jewish identity when so many "better Jews" had died for theirs. That reasoning made me sound far more thoughtful about Judaism than I was.

I did believe in God, and felt I had a spiritual life, but it was deeply personal, and not something my partner, Tim, and I talked about. He had been raised in a fundamentalist Christian home, but had grown distant from religion. We talked about the curiosities of faith communites— lavish bar mitzvahs vs. bible camp—but we never really discussed our own faith. My religion, in that sense, was more like an inner monologue mixed with a moral code. I believed in God, argued with God, and prayed when I felt the need, but I didn't like to admit any of those things. My conception of God was still very Old Testament, while everyone around me was into more abstract spiritual conceptions of the divine. I couldn't shake the idea of a God who could be moody, who could be vengeful, and who could love to chat. But I didn't like to publicize our relationship.

My story is certainly not unique among American Jews. A 2007 study by sociologists Steven Cohen, professor of Jewish Social Policy at Hebrew Union College's Jewish Institute of Religion, and Ari Kelman, professor of American Studies at the University of California, Davis, sug-gested that feelings of attachment to Israel among younger Jews—those born after 1974—were decreasing substantially. The study asserted that younger Jews, Jews in my age bracket, were less likely to draw on positive memories and associations with Israel. We were more likely to recall the first Lebanon war in 1982, the First and Second Intafada, and the second Lebanon war or the ongoing violence in Gaza and the West Bank, when we thought about Israel, than to consider the earlier, and, the authors as-serted, less morally ambiguous wars between 1948 and 1974. Of course, another institution of Jewish thought, the Steinhardt Social Research Institute at Brandeis, published its own report on the heels of the Cohen-Kelman survey, which argued that attachment to Israel remained a con-stant and that as people aged, their attachment tended to increase, thus negating the effects of any age cohort that the data might suggest.

Cohen, however, insists that his data holds up to scrutiny. In the report, "Beyond Distancing," he argues that the main cause of this dis-connection from Israel is intermarriage, which goes along with a general decline of Jewish ethnic identity. Jews have left the shtetls and the ghettos and become part of the mainstream. Young American Jews want to marry whom they want; they exist in an open society with choice and freedoms that their parents and grandparents didn't have. And once they do marry, it seems, they become less attached to the Jewish state.

"The connection to Israel is a piece of a larger sense of the collective Jewish identity," Cohen explained to me. "Not just part of a religious faith, but also part of an ethnic group, a tribe, frankly, a nation. Intermarriage and its antecedents and its consequences—the things that lead to intermarriage and the processes that flow from intermarriage—are associated with and certainly incompatible with deep commitment to Jews as a collective nationlike entity. They're more in keeping with a sense of Jews as a religion, a personal faith rather than collective identity. So in that context, among the things that fall down as identification with Jews as a collective identity is involvement and identification with Israel."

So I found myself part of a statistic, part of a trend. I was indeed in a situation akin to intermarriage: I am in a same-sex, interfaith domestic partnership, which complicates my relationship to the Jewish establishment even more. I didn't feel there was much room in the organized Jewish world for me and had certainly never seen outreach that spoke to my concerns and needs. And I wasn't interested in looking for one.

When I thought about Israel, I did indeed think with revulsion about all those wars and the uprisings Cohen mentioned. If young people were thinking beyond nation states, beyond ethnicity, I considered it a good thing. Sixty years after the founding of Israel, the world remained anxious about the Jews, the Jews remained anxious about each other, and these two anxieties animated a great flurry of activity out of all proportion to the size of the world's Jewish population. There are about thirteen and a half million Jews in the world. Some estimates put the number of Muslims in the world at about one and a half billion. I couldn't understand why the Jews got so much press.

Historically, there's no denying that the Jews have been embattled, persecuted, and hounded to near extinction. But Cohen's data indicates that fear about Jewish survival is no longer an animating anxiety for the next generation of Jews. The idea of Jewish extinction didn't make me reach for my wallet or for my prayer book. I never gave it any thought. Perhaps I was too comfortable in America.

Zionism simply could not be the sine qua non of my Jewish existence, and I saw no reason to jump into an identity so tied to that particular nationalism. Jewish values—service, study, faith—these are potent notions, and ones that, living in America, I rarely associated with Israel or with those Jews who argued so vehemently in its defense whenever they felt the smallest criticism directed toward the Jewish state. Alan Dershowitz, arguing in defense of Israel, defended torture. I didn't want any part of a Jewish people that felt the need for such arguments.

I could have remained happily distanced from any sense of Jewish identity and certainly from Israel were it not for a few events that awoke me to the unavoidable reality that I was a Jew and that that meant something.

During college, I started to work with children in war zones around the world, traveling to Africa, Asia, and the Balkans. In the summer of 2004, I stumbled upon the Jewish community of Bosnia. They showed me a kind of Jewish life alongside Muslims and Christians that I had not before had the capacity to imagine. As the Security Barrier began to go up in Israel, turning the West Bank into a kind of giant prison, separating neighbors from each other and farmers from their land, I saw a community in Sarajevo that was tearing down walls and forging lasting relationships with all faiths and ethnicities. They were doing so in what had very recently been one of the most violent cities on earth. The tiny group of Jews, I was told, managed to save thousands of lives during the siege, and got supplies into the city when no one else could. I started to get the idea that there might be something to this three-thousand-year-old culture, something worth knowing about, some part of my identity I needed to find. Even with high unemployment and instability, the Jews were staying in Bosnia, not going to Israel, and they were proud to be Bosnian. I found very few Zionists among them. Rather, I saw in them a community that had disavowed ethnic nationalism and had found purpose in caring for their neighbors. I liked the idea of a humanitarian Judaism rather than a nationalistic one.

After that visit, I didn't think much about getting "more Jewish" or about my relationship to Israel for a few years. The closest I got to an acute awareness of being Jewish in that time came thanks to a patron of the library where I worked for a year. I hadn't noticed she was drunk when I offered to assist her in finding whatever it was she needed. She took one look at me and started shouting about how she knew my kind, knew that I was a Jew, and that Jews were the cause of most of the world's problems, that we were racists and greedy and evil.

"Why don't I call my people and you call your people to meet outside. Then we'll see," she threatened.

My people? I thought. Who would that be? Whom would I call? How had this become a conflict between peoples? I just wanted to help her find a reference book.

She ranted at me for a bit longer, something about her brothers and the FBI and the CIA and a bit more about the perfidy of the Jewish people, until my boss calmed her down and sent her on her way. I had been rattled, however. I felt vulnerable and very much alone. What if she did have "her people" waiting for me outside? Apparently I looked like Jew, and in her eyes that was the worst thing to be.

No matter what my complicated postmodern multicultural queer-theory-saturated hypernuanced identity told me I was, there seemed to be a biological or historical fact of my Jewishness that meant something to that angry woman, but meant almost nothing to me. I began to see a lot of anti-Semitism the moment I started looking for it. I saw videos about French youths in the suburbs of Paris, Muslims who blamed all their problems on Jews. I heard complaints that the Jews were buying up Harlem and kicking out the residents, that the Jews had, Svengali-like, manipulated the war in Iraq into existence, or caused 9/11. In 2006 I heard from the Iranian president that the Holocaust was a lie, or if not a lie, exaggerated, or if not exaggerated, then it was caused by Jews, whose Zionist fervor compelled them to sacrifice millions of their own in order to force the international community to create a Jewish state.

Regardless of what I thought about what it meant to be a Jew, the world seemed to think a lot about it for me. On the other side, supposedly my side, I saw irate settlers claiming land in contested territory, undermining the peace process with the Palestinians. I saw missile assassinations and collective punishment, and I saw terrorism. There was always collateral damage: dead civilians, dead children. I saw the Security Barrier being built to cut off the Palestinians from the Israelis. If I was going to be labeled a Jew, I didn't want walls built with a Jewish imprimatur, assassinations undertaken by a Jewish state, no matter what the strategic need. But I didn't want Jews, or anyone, killed by rocket fire or suicide bombers either. I began to think more about Israel in a vague, anguished way. I didn't want that brutal, unending, morally ambiguous conflict to have anything to do with me, and yet I couldn't escape that it was, somehow, part of my identity. Even though Zionism was born as a nineteenth-century nationalist movement, it had tied itself to Judaism, and I couldn't relate to one without relating to the other. This contradiction kept me from both of them.

IN THE SUMMER OF 2007, MY grandmother, Gram Bev, passed away. She bequeathed to me her collection of books and monographs, whatever art I wanted from her apartment, and a mystery about her roots that forced me to reconsider my own. As I rummaged through her library, I found yearbooks from the Jewish country club with her picture in them, looking slim and elegantly dressed at parties, a highball glass held delicately in her hand. I found books about the "strange sexual practices of exotic peoples" and books about the founding of the Baltimore Hebrew Congregation. I found books like *The Jewish Mystique* and odd tracts about early Zionism and Jewish renewal in America. Scattered throughout the thousands of art books and museum catalogs, I saw the literary grapplings Gram Bev had gone through with her Jewish identity. Though she never spoke of it, her reading habits suggested that there was more to her Judaism than membership in the country club. I thought again about how she listened to High Holidays services over the telephone after she became too ill to attend synagogue.

While my family gathered to mourn, I hungered to learn more about her, and I asked everyone who knew about her life before she was my Gram. She did indeed come from Virginia, as she had always told me, but not from the type of place she had always implied. Her childhood was far more *Fiddler on the Roof* than *Gone with the Wind.*

She came from a town called Berkley, across the Elizabeth River from Norfolk, in a spot George Washington had once considered a potential site for the nation's capital. Around the turn of the century, Berkley had a Yiddish-speaking Orthodox Jewish community that numbered over four hundred people. Now, the independent town of Berkley is gone, incorporated into Norfolk in 1909. Gone, too, are the Jews, who had scattered across the country by the late 1940s and left Orthodox practice behind. My grandmother moved with her family up to Baltimore when she was a little girl, and in Baltimore she reinvented herself, keeping the southern part of her identity but leaving the shtetl behind.

When I learned that my "thoroughly mod" Gram Bev came from Orthodox Jews in an Orthodox town, I was shaken. She had a childhood that was rich in the stuff of faith and ethnicity, which she had not told me about, even though we were close. When I asked my father about it, he didn't know a thing. She never spoke about it to anyone. Her brother didn't remember much either; he was just a baby when they left Berkley.

I wanted to know more than the scant details I had. Those stories were my grandmother's stories; they were my stories. I wanted to know them. The few facts I had explained nothing.

They didn't describe how Lena Goodman wooed her future husband with homemade *rugelach*, how the back room of the Mace Sack's Candy Store was the neighborhood hideout where Jewish storekeepers played cards, or how Eastern European songs poured forth from the Mikro Kodesh Shul onto Liberty Street every Saturday. They didn't tell of the camaraderie of the first Jewish families to arrive in the late nineteenth century—the Glassers, the Legums, the Salsburys, the Zedds—or the bustle of the stores and saloons after the Sabbath ended each week, when everyone seemed to be out in the street.

And these facts certainly did not explain why, over a weekend in the fall of 2007, 250 descendants of the town returned to remember and share stories about the days of a self-contained Jewish community in Virginia, or why I hadn't known about it.

"I grew up listening to Berkley stories," says Amy Ostrower, a California writer whose book, *Nana Lena's Kitchen: Recipes for Life*, recounts her grandmother's tales of Berkley with memories and recipes. "Berkley stories were my fairy tales," she says.

"This was a Yiddish-speaking shtetl in Dixie," Stephen Baer explained to me. He is my uncle through marriage, and, oddly, his grandparents and my great-grandparents were founding families of the Berkley Jewish community. "The families were extremely close. The Jews who settled here did not want to assimilate. They were Orthodox Jews [who] brought their Litvak shtetl with them." Baer, now in his sixties, remembers visiting his family in Berkley on weekends, driving down or taking the Old Bay Line south from Baltimore, where his family had also settled. Baer, a musician and retired businessman, had taken it upon himself to preserve and pass on the town's Jewish legacy. He was one of the key organizers of the Berkley Reunion.

"My mother had such a strong feeling about her neighbors and the people that she grew up with; her influence was grounding to me," he told me. "She had ten brothers and sisters in Berkley, and her parents still lived there . . . Because of these frequent visits and my mother's love for the place, I always had a Berkley feeling."

I never knew of Berkley and my family history until Stephen Baer described it, and it saddened me that I didn't know about the reunion until after it had happened. I knew my grandmother's maiden name had been Legum; I knew her grandfather had been named Abraham and that she came from Virginia, but I never saw a photo of Abe Legum until Stephen showed me one.

The saga of Berkley begins in the Pale of Settlement in Lithuania. During the vicious pogroms of the 1870s and 1880s, life in the shtetl of Ligim became almost unbearable for the Jews. Two young men, Abe Legum and Dovid Glosser, made their escape, embarking by ship to Baltimore, a place where many Lithuanian Jews had settled before them. Moses Molin, who was from a nearby village, took the same path. At the time, Jacob Epstein, one of the most prominent members of the Baltimore Lithuanian Jewish community, was looking to expand his wholesale business into more rural areas, and in these Yiddish-speaking new arrivals, he found the entrepreneurial spirit he needed.

He dispatched Molin to a farming community in Salisbury, Maryland, to go door-to-door selling goods. "When Moses first arrived in Salisbury, he would knock on the doors of the various farmhouses and the person would open the door and then slam it in his face," Baer relates. "He went to another farm and got the same treatment. In each instance, the person would shout, 'Scarlet fever!' Moses didn't understand what that meant and he was very distraught. He had traveled all this way in his wagon and no one wanted his goods. All they wanted was 'scarlet fever.' So he got word back to the Baltimore Bargain House: 'Send me some scarlet fever. You gave me the wrong stuff!'" In time, however, Molin's business found its way, and, as an homage, he changed his name to Moses Salsbury.

Dovid Glosser, who became Davis Glasser, was sent off to Pendleton County in West Virginia, where he opened a small store selling Epstein's merchandise to the coal miners. His English was limited, but he eventually met with modest success.

And lastly, at the request of the Chesapeake Knitting Mills, based in Berkley, Epstein sent Abe Legum to supply its workers with staples. The main product coming out of the mills was high-quality underwear, and with 175 employees, business was booming.

Things went well for Legum in Berkley, and he suggested that Epstein send down his *lantsman* friend Glasser. Epstein did so and also sent Moses Salsbury. As business flourished, the men sent for their brothers and sisters and parents to join them. New families came from Baltimore and from Lithuania—Zedds and Goodmans, Zacks, Krugers, Galumbecks, and Jacobsons. All the families, with their complex web of marriages, lived within a one-mile radius of each other, much as they had in Lithuania.

They opened grocery stores and delis and hardware stores and furniture and dry goods retailers. Baer's research showed eleven Jewish-owned saloons in the neighborhood, which mostly served gentile customers from the mills and the shipyards. Horses and cows needed to eat too, and Abraham Berman made a business selling hay, grain, and feed. The town kept growing to the point where Norfolk's financial institutions opened Berkley branches and were glad to do business with the Jews.

They were still, however, missing a place to worship. Three times a day they held services in a store owned by the Salsburys. Finally, in 1892, they built the Mikro Kodesh Shul, named after the shul in East Baltimore (and perhaps after the synagogue they had left behind in Lithuania, though those records are lost to history). In 1893 the first Jewish wedding in Berkley took place. A local paper noted that the service "was enjoyed on account of its novelty, especially by the Gentile portion of the assemblage, which was quite large." As the community grew, construction began on a larger Mikro Kodesh to replace the original; it was completed in 1922, with a price tag of fifty thousand dollars. The original cornerstone is still in place.

Times changed in Berkley. A bridge was built to span the river to Norfolk. A streetcar brought Berkley's children to school in the city, where they interacted with the assimilated Jews—who nicknamed Berkley "Herring Town," even though the Berkley Jews had built fine homes in the southern style with wraparound porches on tree-lined streets. Still, their religious piety, old-fashioned closeness, and continued use of Yiddish phrases marked them as different.

Though the assimilated Jews of Norfolk sometimes looked down on them, the Berkley Jews did not hide their heritage or attempt to blend in. They learned to do business with the good ol' boys of the South. Everyone knew the Berkley Jews came from good, tight-knit families that valued education and honor.

"World War II changed a lot of things," said Ted Kruger, who grew up in Berkley but left for college in 1946. "After '46, I never really came back. Most young people didn't come back for more than Sunday visits."

After World War II, the returning young men had been exposed to the wider world. They expanded their businesses into Norfolk and beyond. They intermarried—that is, they married Jews from outside of Berkley.

"By the late forties, it was evident Berkley had had its day in the sun," Baer notes with a touch of regret. Ellie Lipkin, who moved from Berkley to Norfolk in 1942 when she was just thirteen, remembers that the younger generation were no longer learning Yiddish. By the 1960s, most of the Jewish residents had moved away to more cosmopolitan environments—Norfolk proper, Philadelphia, New York, even Los Angeles—to establish businesses or practice their professions. Shtetl life in Dixie had come to an end.

When I asked him why he organized the reunion, Stephen told me, "It was time to bring the community back together again. This was a unique place with a unique character. They safeguarded their cultural heritage and their *haimishe* values." To prepare, he dove into the records in Virginia and Baltimore, reconstructing the Jewish narrative. He collected photographs and newspaper articles, studied ship manifests, and created a 102-slide PowerPoint presentation to show to the descendants of the Berkley Jews.

"For me, sharing this story verified the reason I'm here, justified it, because I didn't grow up in Berkley. Bringing everyone together was, for me, a public statement. *Hineini*, in Hebrew. You know *Hineini?* It's what Abraham and Moses say when God asks for them. It means 'I am here.'"

During the three-day reunion, the local social hall, used as a lunchroom, was renamed the Nosh Shop; in its earlier incarnation, it was Pincus Paul's Furniture Store. On Saturday night, members of the African-American community told their own stories about Jewish Berkley—how welcoming it was, how people looked out for each other when money was tight or times were hard. The Church of Jesus Christ of the Apostolic Faith, which now occupied the old shul, opened its doors to the visitors and was once more alive with Jewish song. Sitting on the same wooden pews their ancestors had used, members of all the old families soaked up 120 years of their history as Baer presented his slide show. For many, this was the first time they had ever heard the story of their lineage. Families walked through the streets on a tour, visiting the old houses and addresses that held so many memories. People told each other stories that they had heard from their parents and grandparents.

"It is an amazing thing," Kruger said, "this natural camaraderie that was never lost. In Lithuania, in America, these were the people you were comfortable with."

It was also fascinating, said Ostrower, who brought her mother with her, "to see that many people descended from eight or ten people who came from Lithuania."

On Sunday, the final day of the gathering, they went to the old cemetery, established in 1890, for a memorial service. A retired rabbi from a temple in Norfolk gave a dedication, and a cantor chanted Yiddish songs.

As Baer described the event, "I made it real for [the descendants]. I connected the dots. I became a historian of our common heritage and became part of Berkley by telling the story."

I will never hear my grandmother's childhood memories of Liberty Street or Mace Sack's Candy Store or the great fire of 1922. Before talking to Baer, I never would have thought to attend this reunion had I known about it and, given how far Gram Bev had drifted from her Litvak roots, I'm sure our family's absence at the reunion was not noticed. I would never become part of the story the way Stephen had. As much as it could have been my story, it wasn't my story, because my grandmother chose to close off that part of her past to us.

The Berkley community and its way of life are gone from America: the unlocked doors, the idyllic summer picnics. These are the American dreams that the Litvaks of Virginia embraced, embodied, and passed on with a Yiddish flavor. As Ellie Lipkin told me, "No matter when you left Berkley, you took something with you that you cherish. It was a special place."

This idea of a place to which all your longing goes makes me think of Psalm 137, that passionate lamentation for Zion that was written during the Babylonian exile after the First Temple was destroyed and the Jewish people scattered from their Promised Land: "By the rivers of Babylon we sat and wept, when we remembered Zion . . . If I forget thee, O Jerusalem, may my right hand forget its skill. May my tongue cling to the roof of my mouth if I do not remember you, if I do not consider Jerusalem my highest joy."

I had never felt such longing for a place, such a connection to anywhere. Stephen Baer knew that high joy in a place, having found in Berkley his own Jerusalem. When I thought of Jerusalem, of Zion, all I could
conjure up was the problematic word *Zionism*, and suicide bombers, mas-
sacred Palestinians, colonialism, uprooted cultures, a constant refrain
about the Holocaust and past wrongs, and all the opposing claims to
victimhood.

And as I lamented my own lack of rootedness, I thought once more
about Bosnia. I remembered how the children at the interfaith summer
camp played with each other. I remembered the convoys Bosnia's Jewish
community had organized to get women, children, and the elderly out
of the city through the front lines of the war. I remembered the respect
with which Muslim and Christian citizens of Sarajevo spoke about their
Jewish neighbors. I remembered that theirs was a Jewish story that I
wanted to know more about. Theirs was a Judaism rooted in a place
from which they could easily have vanished, but did not. If some lost
community in Virginia that I had never seen and would never see was a
part of me, then why couldn't a real Jewish community growing under
extremely challenging conditions be part of me too?

I began to wonder if there were other communities like that, places
where the Jews stayed to create something meaningful in spite of all the
pressures to leave, where they built their meaning out of whatever soil
they had. Places where the Jews gave back to the culture in which they
lived whatever lessons their history had to teach. The Jewish community
from which I had come was gone, and now that I knew it, I wanted to
find others. I wondered what Jewish communities would look like where
they were not in constant struggle with their neighbors. I wanted to
find places where another narrative was being lived out, a narrative that
is just as true as the violent conflict in Israel, if not just as publicized.
I wanted to find the stories of peaceful coexistence, and of longing for a
place that was a home that wasn't Jerusalem. Didn't Jews have a gift for

building sacred spaces wherever they found themselves scattered? Didn't they always, in a great history of wandering and exile, manage to influence a place without exerting political control over it? I wanted to find a Judaism that was meaningful without politics, and grounded without dominating the ground.

I thought if I could seek out Jewish communities in challenging circumstances that had found paths other than confrontation and violence, I could perhaps find a model for my own Jewish self that went beyond nationalism but didn't collapse into navel-gazing.

I also thought I could touch something like the community in Berkley and see a little of the life my grandmother might have had, or the life I might have had if she had remained part of the place from which she came.

So I set out for a year of searching for these communities around the globe, without a clear idea what I would find, just a voice in my head telling me to keep moving, to keep looking, to go. I had been a traveler for most of my years as a writer, and it seemed fitting that I would find myself by traveling more. I also realized I could spend the rest of my life looking for interesting Jewish communities but only touch on a small number. This journey led me to Southeast Asia, the Caribbean, rural Arkansas, East Africa, Iran, back to Bosnia, and inevitably to Israel. And though I set out on a personal journey, I became, ultimately, tied to the journey of a people, a variety of peoples, all connected by a label, a religion, a history. I didn't find any one answer to what it was. Like any worthwhile travel, the journey raised more questions that it answered.

two

Caretakers:
The Jewish Community of Burma

For whatsoever soul it be that shall not be afflicted in that same day,
he shall be cut off from his people.
—LEVITICUS 23:29

A MONSOON SEASON SUNSET OVER Rangoon is an unremarkable thing. The sky simply dims, then darkens over the wet city. There are few visual cues to the impending night. On a Friday evening at the start of the dim, I trudged through the leafy boulevards, up to my ankles in dirty water. Side streets were flooded, nearly impassable. Water poured from the balconies of the squat concrete apartment buildings, and the decaying fin de siècle architecture disappeared behind sheets of rain and mist.

I waded past Sule Paya, a 150-foot-high golden shrine in the middle of a traffic circle, which supposedly contains a hair of the Buddha. This is the sort of country I was in: they built massive shrines of solid gold in homage to a single hair. The rain came down so hard that the usual band of peddlers, money changers, and con men were not lurking around the shrine's base watching for tourists. This was also the sort of country I was in: con men and informants and prostitutes linger around even the holiest of places. The sacred is so commonplace in Burma that the profane feels no need to steer clear.

I made a wrong turn down Thirty-first Street and the water came nearly to my waist. I smiled with self-satisfaction because I'd had the forethought to put my money, passport, and camera in a plastic bag in my pocket. A well-prepared pilgrim.

A group of monks passed, radiating purpose, engaged in a political drama, preparing their now daily march against the junta that seized control of the country in 1962. Their protest had gone on now for over a month and was the largest sustained protest in Myanmar in nearly twenty years. They were protesting the poor living conditions the junta's policies imposed on the people, nearly starving the population to death. The monks believed that they would be safer from government reprisals than average citizens. At the time, no one could have predicted the bloodshed that was to come, though the tension in the air was as heavy as the rain. The threat of a violent crackdown by the junta, as much as the downpour, kept a large crowd away from the protest that Friday night. I'd been warned that violence was coming. Everyone I met told me that Burma was a wonderful country, "except for politics . . . " They always let their voices drift away. It was nearly impossible to have an open discussion of the political situation. The government had spent the last forty years creating such a terrifying image of itself that even if one in ten people were not informants, they were believed to be. "The government does not care about the people," an old monk near Mandalay told me. "But what can we do? Someone must try to . . ." He didn't finish his thought. This was a country of unfinished sentences.

Muslim men and women hurried to be in the right place when the muezzin called for the sunset *salat*. Buddhist and Hindu businessmen in the markets carried on as usual, trying to make a living in a stunted economy under a military government. Burma, which the junta renamed Myanmar in 1989, is the poorest country in Southeast Asia, and the act of making a living is a constant struggle. In spite of the rain, merchants called out the fruits they had to sell, vendors pushed lottery tickets, and old women tended their shops and their shrines. The mundane, the holy, the political, and the wet swirled together as the light faded.

I couldn't spend too long watching the scene. I didn't want to be late. I nearly squashed a tray of fruit sitting in the mud at the feet of a sopping market woman. I jumped at the last moment to avoid it and caught an angry glare from the woman and what I assumed were her daughters, but I kept hurrying forward. I was trying to beat the sunset so that I could do something I had not done in years: I intended to atone for my sins.

This Friday night in 2007 was the eve of Yom Kippur and marked the end of the Days of Awe in the Jewish calendar, the ten days between Rosh Hashanah and Yom Kippur when it is believed that God weighs our deeds of the past year and decides whether or not we should again be inscribed in the Book of Life. The Holy Day of Yom Kippur was called for in the book of Leviticus, chapter 23. The Lord commands Moses to tell the Israelites to make this day a day of atonement, to "practice self-denial" and to do no work. The commandment goes on to say that anyone who does not practice self-denial on the Day of Atonement will be "cut off from his kin," and "whoever does any work throughout that day" will "perish from among his people." I had brought a copy of the Old Testament with me to use as a reference. Whether it was a true account of anything historical or not, it was the normative Jewish text.

I didn't want to be caught running through the streets when Yom Kippur services started. This night was to be the start of my own journey toward a spiritual awakening in the Jewish faith, and I had traveled to the other side of the world to participate. It would not bode well to perish from among my people just as I was beginning to find out who, exactly, my people were.

From the corner of Maha Bandoola and Twenty-sixth Streets one can see the Star of David high atop the Musmeah Yeshua Synagogue. The sight startled me when I first saw it. It's surrounded by crumbling concrete apartment buildings and open market stalls that look like storage units. Along the same block, a few relics of the colonial era still remain, but black soot and grime mar most of their surfaces. The clean blue walls of the synagogue stood out amid the faded facades of the other buildings and the heavy gray sky. There was an ornate Hindu temple visible from the same corner where I stood looking at the synagogue, the minaret of a mosque, and of course, the golden stupa of Sule Paya. To say it was an exotic inter-section for a secular westerner like me is an understatement. In spite of the stench of fish, sweat, and car exhaust, I felt for a moment as if I were on the first steps toward something holy, or at least enduring. How should that Star of David find itself here on this corner of this Southeast Asian city? Was it not a testament to the endurance of a people and of a faith?

I was perhaps straining the moment and searching for revelation where there was none. The dizziness that travel induces, the cultural whiplash, tends to provoke overly poetic sentiments in me. I can watch the most mundane scene of a child splashing in a rain gutter by the road and believe I am unlocking a nation's secrets. I have to keep my poetic, pseudophilosophical musings in check. They will not serve me well on this pilgrimage. Real meaning isn't found so easily.

Looking at the Star of David again, I realized that my inner stir-ring had been 99 percent relief at having arrived in time. And I was also happy to be getting out of the rain. My journey was just beginning and I was too wet to have any revelations. What did the Star of David mean to me, really? I didn't know where it came from, or why it was connected with King David. I was a religious and cultural illiterate. What the hell, I wondered, was I doing in Rangoon on Yom Kippur during a time of political unrest? What was I hoping to find, and how would I even know it when I did? I laughed at myself as I stood in the rain silently fabricating epiphanies. I was far from home at the start of a journey that I didn't understand. The Star of David on the high wall reminded me that I had a long way to go.

The muezzin began the call to prayers from the mosque, his voice echoing from the loudspeaker, praising praise. I was eager for the spiritual, but I had more practical matters to attend to. I had to take my life into my hands and cross the street.

There is a vast literary tradition describing a street crossing in the developing world. Lawless traffic, regulated by a mixture of hostility, mutual surrender, and cacophony, has provided many travelers with the opportunity to reflect on mortality, faith, and power. What does it mean when a government cannot or will not provide the simple service of a well-regulated intersection? What does it mean to risk death every time you want to go to the market or the synagogue? The only reference I could recall at the time was Bruce Feiler's admonition about crossing the street in Tehran: if you wake up on one side of the street, he writes, stay there.

I did not heed his advice here, and I crossed the street. Visibility was poor because of the rain, but the water slowed the cars enough that I could dodge and rush through with surprisingly little difficulty. I had learned my first lesson: confidence, when combined with putting one foot in front of the other, will take you where you need to go. The idea also sounded like a definition of faith.

I had arrived at the synagogue and needed to muster that faith now. I took a deep breath, tried to remember even the most basic prayer so that I would not look like a total fool to the community on the Holy Day, and ducked inside.

Moses Samuels, the fifty-seven-year-old caretaker of the synagogue, sat in his chair by his office waiting for visitors. I was the first. The synagogue courtyard was quiet, though the rain beat a tattoo on the roof. Moses greeted me warmly and we sat together while we waited for others to arrive. He had thick black hair and wore a tidy yellow shirt and slacks. He chain-smoked while we waited and listened to the rain falling. A Hindu man worked tirelessly around the tiled enclosure in front of us, sweeping water away with a broom so the filth of the wet city didn't collect in the small courtyard. Moses and the man exchanged brief snippets of conversation every few minutes.

"He has worked here for years," Moses said. "It is much work to maintain this place in this climate. You are enjoying your time in Burma?"

"It's a beautiful country," I told him.

"Beautiful, yes . . . ," he said, letting some secret thought take his mind elsewhere with a chuckle.

I reminded Moses that I knew his son from New York. He smiled and told me that Sammy would be coming shortly. The traffic was bad because of the rain.

"Will others come to prayers tonight?"

Moses shrugged. "They don't often come," he said, and took a drag on his cigarette.

Moses and I had met a week earlier, when I visited the synagogue for Rosh Hashanah, the Jewish New Year, and we shared in a muted and brief celebration with some passing Israeli tourists. They said the blessing over some juice and apples with honey, tried to blow the shofar, failed, and went off to have some curry and beer. They had no intention of returning for Yom Kippur. On the way out, Moses made sure to show everyone the sign he'd posted just outside the sanctuary. It read: "A tree may be alone in the field, a man alone in the world, but a Jew is never alone on his Holy Days."

The weather and the recent rise in fuel prices were keeping most of the locals away. And of course, the protests, which further clogged traffic, had everyone a little nervous.

"In '88, the streets around here ran with blood," Moses told us as we stepped outside. "If the marching starts, don't come around here."

I had come back anyway, after a week touring the Burmese countryside, digesting my fill of curries and dust from ancient temples. When I asked a hotel clerk in Mandalay about Jews, he said that Israeli tourists often came to look at the castle in the city, to see the U Bein Bridge and the surrounding pagodas and the large monastery in Amarapura. He hadn't seen as many tourists lately, though, because of the political troubles, which had started among the monks in Mandalay. And of course all the rain.

When I asked in the ancient city of Bagan, a place of ruined temples and palaces that was once the capital of an empire, no one knew what a Jew was. Bagan was a city where all the holiness had gone out centuries ago. Even the people had been evacuated, though more recently. The government didn't want locals messing up the ancient ambience and had relocated them to New Bagan, an unremarkable little town. Tourists now have free reign in Old Bagan, undisturbed by the reality of life in Burma. Ancient ziggurats rise up from the jungle canopy, still and silent as graves.

I was eager to get back to Rangoon to connect with the Jewish community once more, and I hoped I would find more people. I was getting desperately lonely bumbling around Burma, feeling like a complete outsider everywhere I went. Moses didn't seem to mind my return or remember warning me away because of the protests. Politics wasn't really my interest at the moment. The Jews were, and I wondered where the rest of them were on what was, arguably, the holiest evening of the year.

Even if the rain had not been so intense or the politics so fraught, there weren't that many Jews left in Burma, and those that were did not live in the center of town like Moses and his family. As we listened to the falling rain, Sammy arrived, neatly dressed and impossibly dry. My hair was dripping and my cargo pants and white shirt were soaked through. Sammy looked as if he had just stepped out of a Brooks Brothers catalog. His black hair was trimmed close and he wore a small goatee and a big smile. He was very thin and looked far more like a native Burmese than did his father, who in spite of a paunchy belly could have passed for a Middle Eastern Al Pacino.

"I took a cab" was all Sammy said by way of explanation, laughing a little at how much I resembled a drowned cat. A few moments later, our third guest arrived: Michelle, an American who had just begun teaching journalism classes to eager Burmese students at the American Center. The sun dunked below the horizon and we decided not to delay any longer.

Michelle knew a little Hebrew and the vague outlines of the Yom Kippur service. She was, like many Americans, a High Holidays Jew: she went to synagogue twice a year, for Rosh Hashanah and Yom Kippur. Having heard there was a synagogue in Rangoon, she couldn't miss the opportunity to attend. She'd make her parents happy and she'd do something novel. Who goes to synagogue in Burma, right? I, on the other hand, was totally useless in this situation. I wasn't even a High Holidays Jew.

I hadn't been to synagogue in more years than I could count. I certainly couldn't read Hebrew. I didn't know the prayers or the ritual. I was also soaking wet and dripping on the stack of prayer books piled high in the hope that other visitors might arrive, but no one else came. It was just us three. Sammy's father wasn't a religious man. He wouldn't be taking part.

"We could do *something*," Michelle suggested. "You could lead us."

Sammy nodded. We picked up the prayer books. When I noticed the moisture on their old leather covers, I wiped my hands on the dry part of my shirt. Something felt profane about rainwater on a prayer book. Sammy told me which part I should open to. The rain outside muted all other sounds, and Sammy's voice, quiet but poised, filled the room. We could still hear traffic and the occasional shout from the street, but they didn't seem to be in the same world as we were.

We began, as Jews all over the world were doing, with the Kol Nidre, a problematic chant but one whose melody can't help but move a person. The Kol Nidre, which means "All Vows," is supposed to be performed before sundown and the start of Yom Kippur services, and the entire evening service is called the Kol Nidre service. Jews have debated and fought over the meaning of the words of this chant, changing and excising them from the services from time to time, but they've always insisted on retaining the melody, which is haunting and rousing, and transformative.

In the Kol Nidre, the congregation asks that all the vows we will swear in the coming year, all those well-intentioned or ill-conceived promises we'll undoubtedly make, be forgiven in advance. The prayer is an acknowledgment of our weakness: of the inevitability that we will make vows we cannot keep, that we will fail to live up to the ideal we have set for ourselves, and that we will need forgiveness.

The Vitry Machzor, a prayer book for the High Holidays completed in the late eleventh or early twelfth century in Vitry, France, gives instructions for reciting the chant in terms of the political supplicant, which most Jews of the time would have understood. "The first time he must utter [the Kol Nidre] very softly like one who hesitates to enter the palace of the king to ask a gift of him whom he fears to approach; the second time he may speak somewhat louder; and the third time more loudly still, as one who is accustomed to dwell at court and to approach his sovereign as a friend."

Sammy chanted in Aramaic and I read along in English: "All vows, prohibitions, oaths, consecrations, vows, or equivalent terms that we may vow, swear, consecrate, or prohibit upon ourselves—from the last Yom Kippur until this Yom Kippur, and from this Yom Kippur until the next Yom Kippur, may it come upon us for good—regarding them all, we regret them henceforth. They all will be permitted, abandoned, canceled, null and void, without power and without standing. Our vows shall not be valid vows; our prohibitions shall not be valid prohibitions; and our oaths shall not be valid oaths."

Just reading the words, I could see how easily they could be misunderstood and used to condemn the Jews. The chant—really a legal formula turned prayer—applies to vows we make to ourselves or to God, yet within Judaism there has been vigorous disagreement about its validity as a religious instrument. Even those rabbis who thought it worked as a method of atonement questioned the wisdom of including it in the liturgy because of how easily it could be misunderstood, abused, or used to defame the Jews. Non-Jews could assume that the Kol Nidre freed Jews from any promises they made, so that essentially any vow a Jew made was a lie. The Kol Nidre wasn't included in the Reform movement's prayer book for the High Holidays until 1945.

The anti-Semitic *Protocols of the Elders of Zion*, a forged document published in Russia in 1905, which claimed to be the secret minutes of a group of Jewish leaders plotting to control the world, discussed the Kol Nidre for several pages. The chant was presented as evidence that Jews could be trusted and that they were outside both the rights and responsibilities of society.

"It requires no argument to show that if this prayer be really the rule of faith and conduct for the Jews who utter it," the *Protocols* author wrote, "the ordinary social and business relations are impossible to maintain with them . . . Kol Nidre is Talmudic and finds its place among many other dark things in that many-volumed and burdensome invention."

Throughout the Middle Ages in Europe, the Kol Nidre was used as an example of Jewish otherness, and special oaths were created for Jews to take when giving testimony, if they were permitted to testify at all. This chant had long been used by anti-Semites and those with an anti-Jewish agenda to show that the Jews were not part of the same society as others, that they saw themselves as outside the law and therefore could be treated that way. The Kol Nidre was a powerful weapon in the arsenal of those who sought to push Jews out of public life.

A theory in vogue among Jewish thinkers for a time, but now largely discredited, explained that the Kol Nidre was created as a response to the forced conversions of the Inquisition, allowing Jews who denounced Judaism and converted to Christianity to nullify their conversions before

God. The Kol Nidre was a defensive measure for the soul against unjust religious persecution, this theory argued. But mentions of the Kol Nidre as part of the Yom Kippur service have been found in documents that predate the Inquisition, putting an end to that theory and to the ease with which the problems of the Kol Nidre could be dismissed. Jewish scholars and public figures have gone to great pains to demonstrate that the chant applies only to spiritual matters and does not have any effect on Jewish obedience to secular legal authorities.

I didn't think of court politics while Sammy intoned the words, nor of the vast history of anti-Semitic canards. At first I didn't think of anything at all. My mind was blank, hanging on every sound that passed Sammy's lips. I tried to follow the chant by watching his mouth move, a sacred kind of lipreading that most assuredly fooled neither Sammy nor God.

When I was thirteen years old and having my much-dreaded bar mitzvah, Sammy Samuels was preparing for his. Israel's ambassador to Burma, Ori Noy, conducted the service.

"Representatives from the Israeli embassy came and from other communities—the Muslim, Buddhist, and B'hai communities. Our big celebrations have to be interfaith celebrations"—Sammy smiled—"if we want to have anyone there at all."

"Do you remember the Torah passage you read?" I asked him.

"Yes," Sammy told me. "It was Parshat Bo."

Bo was the same portion I had been assigned to read for my bar mitzvah, which meant that he and I had had our bar mitzvahs in the same week sixteen years earlier. I don't remember much about the service I had, save for the exquisite theatrical power of leading the congregation, commanding them to rise and be seated over and over like a sacred wave at a Mets game. I know that the synagogue seemed crowded to me. Baltimore Hebrew Congregation has around two thousand member families, most of whom only attend for the High Holidays. I tried to picture Sammy's service when he was thirteen: the old synagogue crowded with people, the tropical heat barely mitigated by the ceiling fans, and the secular gov-ernment official acting as rabbi. In truth, I couldn't imagine it.

Yet this Torah portion linked Sammy and me, separated as we were by a gulf of culture and geography. By participating in that Jewish tradition, we had created a common thread between us, even if we wouldn't know it for sixteen years. Trying to determine what it is that we share, what it means to be part of this narrative, was what had brought me to Burma in the first place. The Kol Nidre was a clue. In reciting it we reproduced an ancient moment, a moment that Jews had shared for millennia. The prayer itself brought history to life through us, made us a part of it. It was not only about our relationship to God, but about our immediate connection to each other.

Unlike me, Sammy had remained deeply committed to studying Judaism after his bar mitzvah. There were few opportunities in Burma to do so. When he was nineteen, he was given the opportunity to go to Israel for a year to learn Hebrew and experience a broader scope of Jewish life. It was his first time outside of Burma. He fell in love with Jerusalem and the ease with which a person could live a Jewish life there. There was kosher food available everywhere and an entire culture that respected the Sabbath. Freedom of thought and expression that were un-imaginable in military-ruled Burma were the norm. People in Israel criti-cized their government openly, sometimes just for sport. They discussed and debated religion. And all of them were Jews. Sammy may have been a minority, but of a very different kind. In the most important way to him, he was no longer alone. He was a Jew among Jews.

I TOO FOUND ANOTHER HOME AFTER my bar mitzvah. I went to Germany. I was fifteen and living as an exchange student in Berlin. My grandparents couldn't understand why I would want to live in Germany, why I would dream of learning the German language. They remembered all too well the horrors that Germany inflicted on the Jewish people, despite the fact that my family had already been in the United States for a generation at the time. I hadn't, as far as I knew, lost a single family member to the Holocaust, though much of my grandfather's side came from Vienna just before the turn of the century. And although my grandparents had traveled much of the world, they still wouldn't visit Germany or Austria "because of anti-Semitism."

Germany evoked no emotions in me as far as being a Jew. I certainly didn't think of it as the twentieth century's equivalent of biblical Egypt or Babylon, a site of Jewish destruction, the impetus for Jewish national resurrection. It wasn't a holy place to me, nor was it a graveyard. I wanted to go because of the adventure of living someplace else, of being able to reinvent myself overseas for a while, dye my hair green, get out of narrow little Baltimore. I wanted to be a global person, and so I went to Berlin.

In Berlin, I stayed with a single mother, her mother, and her daughter: three generations of German women. The mother and grandmother were devout Lutherans. The daughter, eighteen at the time, had a nose ring and didn't really give a damn about religion. She wanted an American exchange student because Americans were still cool around the world in the midnineties. Her mother had always wanted a son and in me, had found an opportunity to get one for a little while. And the grandmother, whom I only ever called Oma and with whom I drank coffee and ate pastries at 4 P.M. almost every day, wanted a Jew.

"In Breslau, during Hitler's time, my father ran a bakery," she told me. "He had many Jewish workers." Tears welled up in her eyes. "When the Nazis came and made him fire them all, he was distraught, but what could he do? He continued to sneak bread to them until the Gestapo found out and beat him up. When we fled, he was forced to stay behind and bake for the Germans. I never saw the family's bakery again, or the Jewish workers. I'm so sorry."

She apologized to *me*.

Almost every day she apologized to me for her father's lack of selfless humanitarianism, for her adopted country's moral failings, and for the plight of the Jewish people. Her family had lost far more to the Nazis than mine had, but she felt that by having a Jewish exchange student, she could atone, in some way, for history. She often asked me questions about Judaism and nudged me to think about Jesus, but mostly she just wanted to sit and stare at me and, in the reflection of my eyes, see Breslau and her father and her father's workers before everything was destroyed. I would shift uncomfortably in my seat and sip my coffee and nibble on a Napoleon, focusing on the layers of cream and chocolate, while the woman across from me demanded I carry the history of the wronged Jewish people back to her and accept her apology for it. It was a role for which I was ill-suited, and as my German improved I found more and more ways to dodge the subject of World War II and the Jews.

I did, however, go with my host mother's boyfriend to the concentration camp at Sachsenhausen, near Berlin. It was an icy day in December and the museum was officially closed. The guard asked me the question, the one question that cut through the nuance of whether I observed all the laws in the Torah, whether I knew Hebrew or read Bialek or wanted to live in Israel or attended shul: *Are you Jewish?* Like so many Germans before him, the guard didn't care for the particulars of identity, my conflicted or apathetic relationship to the Jewish people or my inherited religion. His was a practical consideration. If I was Jewish, then it might be worth opening the gate for me, just as it had been in earlier days, when the camp still functioned.

Herr Ekel, the boyfriend, explained to the guard at the booth that I was a Jewish visitor from America and had only this one day to see such an important place. He never outright said it, but he implied strongly enough that I had lost family there. I wasn't just some tourist, Herr Eckel implied—I was a *Jewish* tourist. I had some special claim to this death camp. It was as much mine as the German Parks Department's. The implication worked its magic, and we were admitted to the camp cum memorial as if it were our own private museum.

The cold wind ripped right through my jacket and sweatshirt. Herr Ekel let me walk ahead alone. The ice and snow crunched under my Doc Martens as they pressed the first footprints into the fresh powder. I made a path to the central monument and studied it for any hint of emotion in myself. Nothing stirred, so I turned and made a path to an enclosure where the Jews had been lined up and machine-gunned. The walls had been removed, and one could see right through to the camp fence and, beyond it, right up against it, the houses of the small town. The bare trees along their streets poked their bony branches over the edge as if they were sneaking a guilty peek inside. I felt at that moment a great stirring of emotion, not only for the murder of the Jews, but for the murder of humanity that the whole place stood for.

I still did not feel connected to the Jewish people. Instead, I now felt utterly disconnected from humanity. I strolled through the camp for another hour, my footprints zigzagging in the snow, with my companion following behind at a respectful distance. Sometimes I'd shake my head so he could see I was moved. He wasn't really seeing the camp; he was watching me see the camp. I was a Jewish person connecting with a grim chapter of my history, and he had the privilege, the duty as a German, to witness it. I was performing his patriotic duty for him. But I felt cold and hollow and ready to leave. I stood on the clearing in front of the dormitories where the prisoners were assembled for roll call each day, and I imagined it crowded, tried to hear the sound of the coughing and the foot shuffling, the snarling dogs and shouting SS men. The image was easily conjured, cobbled together from movies like *Escape from Sobibor* and *Schindler's List*. It wasn't real. I was glad when Herr Ekel approached.

"Enough?" he asked me.

"Yes," I answered, and we went back to the car. I felt I'd done my duty to history and was eager to meet up with friends that night and get loaded. I did regret having my own private concentration camp for the day and not knowing the words to the Kaddish, the prayer said at funerals. The regret was fleeting. Had I ever wanted to say the Kaddish before? My uncle had died two months earlier after I'd already come to Germany; I hadn't wanted to say it then. Perhaps, in Sachsenhausen, I craved the sound of something holy to fill the silence made by the snow, or maybe I just wanted to live up to the expectations of sacred grief that I imagined Herr Ekel had of me.

I didn't pray that day, though, or afterward for a very long time. I lived a secular life and did not often associate with people of great faith, at least not Jewish people of great faith. I certainly saw them, living in Brooklyn, but I saw them as an insular group, always going to Israel or Jewish day camps or Jewish retreats or Jewish charity drives, only caring for other Jews and Jewish causes. I associated the Jewish pride that manifested itself in parades, and Jewish summer camps, and Zionism, with the kind of ethnic nationalism that had ripped apart Bosnia and Rwanda, and Israel itself. I saw it as just another way of building walls between people. If I was tragically assimilated, then I thought of these "good" Jews as tragically affiliated. I couldn't imagine longing for that kind of affiliation; I never thought of myself as part of a community any smaller than the entire brotherhood of man.

But when he returned from Israel, Sammy certainly did. He longed for the particular, for the parts of his community that were lost. For his roots. In Rangoon, there were no yeshiva students debating the law, there was no kosher food, and the economic realities made it nearly impossible to observe the Sabbath. On most days, the synagogue sits empty.

"Some days, I was here all alone," Sammy said. "And when I'm away, my father sits here alone."

In Burma, on this Holy Day, Sammy felt very much alone. We didn't have a minyan, the minimum number of Jews necessary to hold a service, so Sammy gallantly guided us through what prayers he could after the Kol Nidre. His father crossed behind us, on his way back to the office to sit and smoke another cigarette. I watched him and thought about the Godfather movies. Rain tapped a rhythm on the roof. The prayers ended and Sammy was quiet, his thin fingers resting on the cover of the prayer book a moment as he set it back on the table. The whole thing lasted about fifteen minutes.

I FIRST MET SAMMY A MONTH before my trip to Burma in a coffee shop on Manhattan's Upper West Side. I'd read about him a few years earlier in the *New York Times*. He was a curiosity, this Burmese Jew, and the *Times* article focused on his efforts to meet a nice Jewish girl. After I decided to undertake this journey through the Diaspora, I got in touch with him. Since the destruction of the First Temple in Jerusalem, Jews had maintained vast international networks for trade and information by arranging marriages, passing messages through merchants, maintaining detailed genealogies, and keeping strong linguistic ties with languages like Hebrew, Judeo-Persian, Ladino, and, later, Yiddish. In this way, they could always find some connection to each other through their shared heritage. Times having changed, I just googled Sammy to get his e-mail address and arranged a meeting.

He didn't look like someone who had the future of an entire culture on his shoulders, nor did he look like a person who would worry about where he would spend Shabbat dinner. He looked to me like many of the other students in the Hungarian Pastry Shop that day. He had a small goatee, more like a soul patch, and neat, short hair. He looked vaguely exotic: had I not known he was Burmese, I would have placed him somewhere in Southeast Asia or the Middle East. His father's side of the family came to Burma from Iraq in the nineteenth century, his mother's came from Iran even earlier, and there had been some mingling with the local Burmese population. He knows that his great-grandmother married a Burmese man. Sammy had the narrow eyes and tea-colored skin of the Burmese. He certainly didn't *look* Jewish.

When he found out that I went to Columbia University for my undergraduate degree, he asked me with excitement in his voice, "Do you know if I can go to the Hillel House for Shabbat dinner, even though I am not a student there?"

He had just graduated from Yeshiva University in upper Manhattan and was looking for other Jews with whom to celebrate the coming Sabbath. He did not want to be alone. I had no idea what to tell him. I'd never been to Hillel House, the Jewish campus association. It is a center for collegiate Jewish life and learning and so totally alien to me.

"I guess so," I said. "I was never really involved in the Jewish community at Columbia." I didn't say that I had never been involved in the Jewish community anywhere. Sammy was planning to attend Columbia the next year to get a business degree. He worked in IT for the American Jewish Congress, and, though he was looking to stay in New York for the near future, he intended to return to Burma one day.

"I'd like to develop our tourism business from here for a while. There are so few economic opportunities in Burma, but it is my home. The people are wonderful, peaceful, and respectful of all faiths. My friends and family are there. New York is great—and it is good to meet other Jewish people—but Burma will always be my home. For me, Rangoon is my Jerusalem. I mean, it is the place I long for."

We sipped our coffee and he pulled out glossy photos of the Rangoon synagogue that he kept in his bag. He spoke with pride about the tourism company he and his father had started to promote Burma to Jewish visitors, Myanmar Shalom. They'd even trained a chef at one of the hotels to make kosher meals for when they had religious tour groups. He had grand plans to keep his community alive, and, as he laid them out for me, I found myself believing them. It came as a shock to face the reality of it in the empty synagogue at the Kol Nidre service.

WHEN OUR SERVICE, SUCH AS IT was, was finished, Sammy and I climbed to the upper floor of the synagogue, where the women used to sit during services. We looked down into the sanctuary at the curtain pulled over the holy ark that holds the one remaining Torah scroll, at the pristine black-and-white marble floor, at the blue and white walls, kept clean by a local Hindu man hired for the task. We looked at the empty bimah, the platform where once a hazan—a lay leader—and a rabbi would lead the community in prayer and Torah study. We saw the rows of benches where families once sat to attend services and, as in synagogues the world over, to gossip. The benches, like the bimah, were empty. The other Jews, mostly elderly, would not be coming tonight or tomorrow. Sammy sighed. I wondered aloud where all the Jews had gone.

"Some to America. Others to England and Australia. Some to Israel," Sammy answered me.

To understand their departure, according to Ruth Cernea, historian of the Jewish community of Burma, one has to understand why they came to Burma in the first place, and how they lived when they were there.

The fate of Jews in the Arab world in the nineteenth century was quite different from that of their harried European brothers. In the Ottoman Empire, Jews enjoyed cultural autonomy and a range of legal rights, as part of the millet system of self-governing religious minorities. In social affairs, like marriage and divorce, Jews and Christians had their own courts and laws. They also had their own tax collectors and bureaucracies under the Ottoman authorities. Jews achieved high positions in the state bureaucracy and, given their extensive international networks of trade and family ties, achieved great commercial success. Perhaps the most notable Jew in the late Ottoman Empire was David Sassoon, who served as treasurer of Baghdad and was a leader of the Baghdadi Jewish community. In 1829, due to increased local persecution and extortion by the notoriously brutal governor of Baghdad, Daud Pasha, Sassoon fled with his family, eventually settling in Bombay and building a vast commercial empire. Other members of the Baghdadi Jewish community noticed Sassoon's success in South Asia, and, given the increasingly corrupt government and ongoing plague, the notion of emigration began to take hold.

As the strength of the Ottoman Empire waned in the late nineteenth century, Turkish reformers began to integrate the religious minorities into the state bureaucracies, building on the millet system to try to create a stronger sense of unified Ottoman citizenship. Their system struggled. A history of self-rule by minority communities was not easily swept away, and the people's loyalty tended to be to their immediate group rather than to the state. The extensive international trade connections of the Jewish merchants had long been encouraged and exploited by the sultans to increase trade. But then, as European encroachment was felt throughout the Ottoman Empire, these connections became a reason for suspicion. The system that had made Jews excellent merchants—often their only legal profession—now made them suspect as spies. Sensitive to the shifting winds of public opinion, which occasionally flashed into violence, many of the Jews decided it would be best to follow the Sassoon example and head east to Asia. India proved a fertile trading ground, especially given growing British strength, and from India it was only a short journey to the ports in Burma.

Like Sassoon, and often with his direct support, Jews established trading outposts throughout Asia. They arrived, as Jews so often had, as businessmen, most of them peddlers and merchants. The earliest settlers even brought their own kosher butchers in order to maintain the basic commandments of their faith in such isolated conditions.

As European Jews struggled under the threat of invigorated fear and hatred, and Russian and Eastern European Jews dealt with pogroms, the Baghdadi Jews established businesses in all the majors towns and ports of Burma, from Mandalay and Rangoon to Bassein and Moulmein. In Burma, they never knew anti-Semitism. In 1879, the same year that the German Wilhelm Marr (whose father was actually Jewish) coined the term anti-Semitism, Mordecai Saul established himself in Burma's royal city of Mandalay and became a favored merchant in the court of King Thibaw, a king with a reputation for brutality. According to Cernea in her book on Burma's Jews, *Almost Englishmen*, King Thibaw's wife loved the perfume bottles that Mordecai Saul had imported from Baghdad, preferring to dump the perfume itself on the floor and use the bottles as vases. Saul traveled back and forth to Baghdad to import this perfume, just so the queen could pour it out on the floor.

Mandalay, at the time, was a violent city. King Thibaw had only been on the throne for a year since the death of his father, and he struggled to keep control. Following two wars with the British, who controlled southern Burma, the internal order of the city had crumbled. Ritual human sacrifice became common; bands of thugs and criminals roamed the streets; pigs wandered between the Buddhist shrines. It was not an easy place for anyone to live, certainly not for a small group of Jews.

When Thibaw tried to sign a treaty with the French, it was too much for the British to bear. They quickly began a propaganda campaign against him—reinforcing the tyrannical image we have of him today—and ultimately initiated the third Anglo-Burmese War, finally deposing the king and forcing him and his family into exile. Burma was annexed as part of Britain's Indian interests and found itself fully a British colony. The Burmese would not rule themselves again in any meaningful way until 1948, the same year Israel gained independence.

The establishment of British colonial rule brought with it expanded trade opportunities, and the number of Jewish settlers in Burma grew rapidly. Now that Burma was essentially an Indian satellite, merchants who had settled in Bombay made their way to Burma, and began arriving in even greater numbers.

Rangoon, or Yangon, as the military junta has renamed it, sits on the Irrawaddy Delta, a fertile and strategic location on the Andaman Sea. I woke early on Yom Kippur and took a walk along the water before going to meet Sammy at the synagogue. Rangoon is a port city, and, strolling by the docks, I could see why the Jewish merchants would be drawn here. I could smell it: The trade in fish and fruit and rice was brisk, and all of it baked under the afternoon sun, mixing with the odors of the living animals—chickens, pigs, and dogs. One smell, however, completed the heady perfume of the docks. Trawlers and ferries and cars spewed exhaust stench, and my tongue tingled with it.

As I walked up and down the banks of the river, I witnessed the docks in action and imagined them a hundred years ago. Men wrapped in sopping sarongs carried loads of dried fish and sacks of rice on their backs, hauling them from trucks onto boats. Children ran messages back and forth. The men with trucks shouted and called out orders. Women sold cigarettes and tea and fried snacks to the workers. Older men stood around watching the activity, their backs long ago broken by the work. The sun churned the humid air, and everything was sticky and smelled like hot fish guts.

The bustle would have been even greater in Mordecai Saul's time. Much of the colony's trade passed through these docks on its way to India and China. Now, isolated by the junta's xenophobia and the international community's sanctions, Rangoon's ports are a shadow of what they once were, as the Jewish community is a shadow of what it once was.

Under the British Empire, the Jews were granted full religious freedom but treated as second-class citizens, like many other groups of colonized elites. In spite of their lower status, they were still a notch above the native Burmese, whom the British considered savages. Burmese Jews were close enough to the British to see their privileges, and successful enough to taste their wealth, and they longed to enter the societal structures reserved for the British. They did not mix with the local population very often, as their language instruction indicates. At the private schools established by the Jewish community, Hebrew was taught for religious purposes and English for public citizenship. The older generation still spoke Arabic and held on to their Baghdadi traditions, but under British influence, the younger generation adopted Western dress and late Victorian styles and manners. Yet the colonial authorities still did not consider them equal to whites.

The Baghdadi Jews of Burma did what Jews all over the world had been doing for centuries in order to survive and to prosper. They assimilated into the dominant culture. Outsider status was forced on the Jews by British chauvinism, and was taken up by the Jews willingly in relation to Burmese culture. They were neither natives nor whites, locals nor colonials, though they strove to become the latter. The physical remove from England did not create a spiritual remove, and they took great pride in being citizens of the British Empire. Generally, the Jews of Burma felt far closer to Westminster Abbey than to Shwedagon Pagoda. Political and cultural loyalty—to the Jewish authorities in Baghdad and to the colonial authorities in London—outweighed any sense of connection they might have had with the local population. They had, of course, never actually seen England.

As religious Jews, they had spent centuries dreaming of Jerusalem as their spiritual center, without any physical relationship to it. They could sing Psalm 137 with great and tearful passion: *If I forget you, O Jerusalem, may my right hand forget its skill . . .* It was an easy leap to singing "Rule, Britannia!" The Jews were prepared by centuries of exile to become ideal colonial subjects, and they embraced London with civic pride, just as they embraced Jerusalem with spiritual pride. Geography was a state of mind.

Learning about the Jews' general remove from the indigenous cultures of Burma during the British colonial period, I'm reminded of a Yiddish joke. An old Jewish man from the Lower East Side, having earned a bit of money in his trade, goes to London and visits one of the best Savile Row tailors to have a suit made. He gets the full treatment—tweeds, vest, a pocket square. When he comes in for his final fitting, he looks at himself in the mirror and starts crying. The tailor asks him if everything is all right with his suit.

"Ja," the man replies through his tears. "But vy did ve haf to lose de empire?"

The second generation of Jews in Burma put on their British identities the way the old man in the joke put on his bespoke suit. They tailored themselves into the empire while holding on to the everyday Jewish mores that sustained them. When religious questions arose, they wrote to the chief rabbi in Baghdad. When questions of political or civic duty arose, they deferred to the colonial authorities.

This psychological adoption of the British motherland is not meant to imply, however, that they did not put down strong roots in Rangoon and the rest of Burma. They prospered under British rule and aimed to be productive citizens of the empire in the country they had made their home. They built factories and social clubs and schools. They established aid societies and, between 1893 and 1896, built the beautiful Musmeah Yeshua Synagogue. In the 1920s, Rangoon even had a Jewish mayor.

At its height, the Jewish population of Burma numbered around four thousand people, most of them in Rangoon, though a substantial community also lived in the former royal city of Mandalay, where they had their own cemetery. Jews were also scattered throughout the provinces, though Jewish cultural, spiritual, and economic life in Burma centered on Rangoon. A prosperous Jewish businessman, Judah Ezekiel, even had a downtown street named after him.

But the prosperity came to an end with the advent of World War II. On Christmas Eve 1941, the bombing of Rangoon began, shocking the complacent population, who had seen the security of the British Empire in Asia as eternal. For weeks, attacks continued, and the city, totally unprepared, lacking bomb shelters and provisions, burned. Hundreds of thousands of people—Indians, Europeans, and Jews—padlocked their homes and fled. The local authorities would not allow the Burmese population to flee, and some Jews who had intermarried with Burmese chose to stay. Others stayed in Rangoon to protect the synagogue. And still others simply lacked the means to escape.

When the Japanese overran Burma during the war, the situation for the Jews worsened dramatically. Nationalist fervor had been growing in the years leading up to World War II, and now, fanned by the Japanese, that nationalism erupted into xenophobia. As Cernea notes with some irony, the Jews had finally been given the status as "whites" that they had so long hoped to receive from the British. Now, though, that status was a liability, and those Jews who had chosen to stay in Burma were viewed with suspicion.

"The Japanese often thought the Jews were spies," Moses Samuel said. "They once came to the synagogue and my father, Isaac, hid his British passport with the Sefrei Torah. He hid the passports under the cover and the soldiers didn't look there, so he was saved." The synagogue was shuttered, and a sign had to be placed outside that it was sealed "as enemy property."

Isaac Samuels and several other leaders of the community were arrested during the Japanese occupation and tortured. When the Japanese were defeated and the British returned, those Jews who had stayed behind felt great relief. The roughly six hundred Jews who returned to Rangoon to have a go at rebuilding their community found burned homes and looted businesses. They received some aid from international Jewish organizations such as the World Jewish Congress, but their situation would never gain priority over the post-Holocaust aid efforts throughout Europe, and they were left largely to fend for themselves. The WJC did compel them, however, to commemorate the uprisings in the Warsaw Ghetto.

The Musmeah Yeshua Synagogue reopened in 1945. Only three years later, Burma became an independent nation. Just as Zionism reached its high-water mark with Israeli independence and the wars that followed, so too did Burmese nationalism burst forth.

An aggressive campaign of "Burmanization" began, and non-native citizens had to decide if they would retain British citizenship and depart or become Burmese citizens, take on Burmese names (as the government had ordered), and try to integrate themselves into the new, officially Buddhist nation. The slogan "Burma for Burmans" that one could hear in the streets had an ominous ring to it after the war years that had seen the Jews officially made outsiders. Still not ready to give up their longing for the glory days under British rule, the Jews held a quiet memorial in the synagogue when King George VI passed away. Postwar nationalism in Burma drove hundreds more Jews away, though the rhetoric was purely antiforeigner rather than anti-Semitic. But the community was not immune to hatred for long. Events in the Middle East found their way to the streets of Rangoon, and for the first time in their history, the Jews in Burma feared for their lives because they were Jews.

In 1956, during the Suez war with Egypt, a group of anti-French and anti-Israeli protesters marched through the streets shouting slogans and working themselves into a frenzy. They grew violent and, finding the embassies of Israel and France well protected, attacked the synagogue and Jewish shops. They posted anti-Israel signs and tried to make their way to the Jewish school, at the heart of what was left of the Jewish residential district. The mob wanted to burn it down, but the police held them back. Things quieted down eventually, but the incident was enough to hasten the departure of still more Jews from Burma. By that time, most of the valuables belonging to the community had been smuggled out lest they be stolen, though several silver-cased Sefrei Torah remained in the synagogue.

In 1962 the hardships increased when a military coup led by General Ne Win took over the government. Two years later, small businesses were nationalized. The meager income from the shops along Twenty-sixth Street, which had supported the synagogue, disappeared. Most of the Jews who could leave did so, moving to Australia, England, the United States, and, a very small number, to Israel.

The community has not had a rabbi since the last one left in 1969. After the death of community president Solomon Joseph, also in 1969, Isaac Samuels was the only trustee of the synagogue. When Isaac Samuels died, he left his son, Moses, in charge. Moses hung the Star of David on the outside of the building in honor of his father, high up, where it could be seen by passersby.

I later learned that the first instance of the Star of David associated with the Jews also commemorates a community whose time had passed. On a bas-relief of the Bablylonian conquest of Judeah in the sixth century, the Judean king has a Star of David on his shield as he yields to the Babylonian king, whose symbol is a winged sun. The Babylonians cast the Jews into four hundred years of exile. Their exile in Babylon produced much of the most beautiful biblical poetry, including Psalm 137, *If I forget thee, O Jerusalem.*

In Burma, Moses alone carried the legacy of his once prosperous community: a synagogue and a cemetery. By government order, the cemetery was no longer in active use. The last body was interred there in 1985. The government had wanted to use the land in downtown Rangoon for its own purposes, but Moses used all the connections and goodwill that was owed him to save it. Now, the synagogue saw little activity outside of Shabbat candle lighting for visiting tourists and Sammy's bar mitzvah in 1993.

"My father swore to my grandfather that he would keep the synagogue open," Sammy told me when we met at the synagogue the morning of Yom Kippur. "He swore that there would always be a place for Jews in Burma. My father is not a religious man, but he is happy when he sees the visitors come here to pray. When he hears the songs and the prayers, he is happy to know that the community continues. The people are his prayers."

"If I didn't do it, who would?" Moses added with a shrug as he took a drag on his cigarette. He found ways to keep the synagogue operating, sharing water and electricity with the Muslim shopkeepers along the block, raising money from passing tourists, and contributing from his own businesses.

Sammy and I took a walk so he could show me a bit of the city where the Jewish neighborhood used to be. We were both committed to fasting for the day. It was the first time I had done so in a long time. My belly was grumbling by noon, but we set off on our walk as the rain continued to pour down on Rangoon. We walked over a wooden bridge and shuffled past a few young monks. Sammy showed me the bland concrete apartment buildings and stores along the street where the Jewish homes used to be. He showed me the government school where the Jewish school used to be. He had gone there, studying on the same plot of land where previous generations of Jews had studied, though in a newly constructed concrete building with a newly constructed, junta-mandated curriculum. Nothing is left of the old Jewish school. In fact, other than the synagogue and the cemetery, little remains to show that there was once a Jewish presence in Burma. In the downtown streets, we passed by a yellow building that had ironwork all over the windows. The ironwork crisscrossed in a Star of David pattern, but Sammy didn't know what the building was, or what it had been. Neither did his father, when I asked him. On closer inspection, it wasn't a Star of David at all, just some decorative ironwork. I was looking for signs where none were.

"People don't know a lot about Jews here in Burma," Sammy told me. "I remember when school groups would come to visit the synagogue and they would look around at the ark and try to see behind it. Puzzled, they would ask me where we sacrificed the animals. All they knew about Jews came from the Old Testament, so they thought we still did that. I had to explain to them that Jews no longer sacrifice animals."

As we walked, we began to see more and more monks rushing through the streets; their saffron robes sopping wet, their flip-flops sloshing through puddles. Sammy had to go to meet some friends and we said our good-byes. I walked back to the center of town, my belly rumbling, thinking about the fast and the history of Burma's Jews.

Outside of Sule Paya, I was surprised by the crowd that had formed. Just the night before, this area had been empty. Now, monks were streaming into the temple from all over the city. City hall stood behind me, its architecture a relic of the colonial era. Police stood behind the fence, their jeep engines humming. An officer unlocked the gate but made no move to open it.

Suddenly, four hundred monks emerged from the temple in rows of four across. They carried flags and upturned alms bowls. When the first group stopped and chanted a prayer, some people in the crowd dared to clap for them. It was timid at first, but as more rows of monks emerged to begin their protest, the clapping grew louder until the whole crowd seemed overcome by it. A Burmese man leaned toward me. "They have never done this before," he said. "They clap for our freedom." The faces in the crowd were excited, part bliss, part terror. A photographer stepped out in front of the monks and snapped a few pictures, then melted quickly back into the crowd. Others snapped photos with their cell phones.

As the monks continued to pour out of the temple, the clapping turned to cheers. The monks walked on, and hundreds of civilians marched with them, in spite of the rain. "We march to University," a man told me, urging me to come. University Avenue is the home of Aung San Suu Kyi, the opposition leader who has been under house arrest for most of the last fifteen years. I did not have the nerve to follow them. I had come to find the Jewish character of Burma and to see how it connected to my own; to see how we, from totally different worlds, were part of the same people. I did not want to become embroiled in the political drama. I had written a lot of critical things about the Burmese junta, and I told myself that it would not be prudent to get involved in this situation. But in truth, I was afraid. As a westerner, I stood out in the crowd. I was afraid the government would find out and not let me leave the country, as I was scheduled to do the next morning. I was afraid they would go after everyone I had met while I was there, if they saw I was engaged in political activity. I didn't want to endanger Sammy or his father, who went to great pains to stay out of politics. But mostly I was afraid of the violence that everyone knew would come. In short, I chickened out. I was in Burma on a truly momentous day, in my religion and in the political life of the nation, and I spent the rest of that Yom Kippur walking the streets of Rangoon by myself.

I learned that the marchers had indeed gone to Aun San Suu Kyi's house, and that she had come out and they had blessed her, an act of bold defiance, an act the government could not allow to go unchallenged. I tried to return to the synagogue, but no one was there. Sammy told me that the Pakistani ambassador, a good friend of his father's, had stopped by to wish Moses a happy Yom Kippur, as had various members of other faiths. I pictured Moses sitting in his chair in the front courtyard of the synagogue, smoking his cigarettes and receiving visitors, remembering the days of his youth, when there were still at least a few hundred Jews left to fill the place on the holiest day of the Jewish year. I thought again about the verse from Leviticus about Yom Kippur, about the punishment for not observing it: to be cut off from your kin and to perish from among your people.

I couldn't help but feel, in spite of Sammy's best intentions, that the Jewish community of Burma was no more. Sammy and his father were carrying the torch for a community that had already turned into a memory. I wondered what the Jews of Burma had done to be cut off, to be a community that had all but perished? Was it cosmic retribution for some past sin by a Sassoon or a Cohen or a Saul? Why had this community lasted only 150 years, when so many Jewish communities around the world, perhaps even smaller and more vulnerable, had survived? Why were Sammy and his father left to keep the tiny Sabbath flames flickering, long after the rest of their people were gone? Why did they want to?

The questions tore at me that last night in Burma, just as military trucks from the countryside were moving into the city, bringing with them hardened troops, veterans of the jungle wars that had been raging along the Thai-Burmese border since the sixties. The Internet cafés were shut down; CNN was scrambled. The military government was sealing off the country, and sealing its people in for the coming retribution.

The morning I left, the monks were preparing another march, and this one had the biggest turnout yet. Thousands of people took to the streets with the monks. I said good-bye to Sammy and boarded my plane. Within three days, over a hundred thousand people had joined the marches against the junta. What had begun in August as a group of monks marching for better conditions for the impoverished civilian population had turned into the largest antigovernment demonstrations the junta had ever seen.

A group of monks and other clergy had come to see Moses Samuels in the days leading up the protests and asked if he or any members of the Jewish community would like to be involved. They hoped to turn the marches into a massive interfaith effort, which would help them garner even more global sympathy. Most of the community, other than Moses's children, were older people and would certainly not want to be involved, so Moses was the go-to guy for Burma's Jews. He turned down the offer to be part of the direct action, preferring to stay out of politics as he always had. His decision proved wise.

On the 27th of September, the government crackdown began. Troops ordered the marchers to disperse, and when they did not, beatings, mass arrests, and gunfire began. With international media access limited and only scattered reports leaking out through blogs, it was hard to know what was happening. A video appeared on the Internet of Burmese soldiers murdering Japanese photojournalist Kenji Nagai. I found another photo of a young friend of mine, a teenage boy I only knew as Che, beaten and bloodied. I heard reports of mass graves, of the crematories working overtime, of disappearances. Monks were fleeing to the volatile Thai-Burmese border. The international community was outraged, but the generals dug in their heels, denied any wrongdoing, and demanded that the world mind its own business. China, Burma's largest trading partner, did not apply the hoped-for pressure, and within weeks the junta had effectively silenced the opposition and sealed the monks in their monasteries. To prevent looting, Moses had hired two security guards to watch over the synagogue, while he and his family stayed in their downtown apartment, trying to avoid entangling themselves in the violence. The last Jews in Burma had survived by keeping their heads down, and Moses intended to do the same thing now. However, given that large gatherings were now illegal, the economic hardship would only grow worse. Moses ran a party supply and catering business as well as the tour company he had started with Sammy. Because of the bad press, tourism was not bringing in a lot of money, and now the catering business would struggle as well.

Sammy returned to New York City two weeks later. He had been worried they would not allow him to leave. He knew people who had been arrested; he had seen the aftermath of the violence.

"The synagogue was not hurt," he told me with relief. "But we had a tour group cancel their visit in November. We've rescheduled, though, so there will still be some business."

Eight months later, just as Burma's tourism industry was starting to recover, another disaster occurred. Cyclone Nargis made landfall on May 2 and battered the country for the next two days. Nargis hit Rangoon with 80-mile-per-hour winds, shaking and soaking the city. The roof and windows of the synagogue were damaged, and Sammy could not get in touch with his family for three days. His mother, father, and two sisters rode out the storm in their downtown apartment, and finally managed to get in touch with Sammy through e-mail at the Israeli embassy.

He remembers his father telling him, "Even though we are here suffering like this, you cannot imagine how the small villages and the small towns and all of these small houses, what these families went though that night. You cannot imagine."

Indeed, Cyclone Nargis was the deadliest in Burma's history, causing near total destruction of the villages of thatch-roofed bamboo houses and leaving at least a hundred and thirty thousand people dead. In Labutta

Township alone, a poor area in the south of the country, estimates put the number of dead at around eighty thousand. Hard numbers aren't easy to find, as the military government's response to the disaster was its usual mix of paranoia and xenophobia. They closed off access to foreign aid workers and the press, and dramatically underreported the destruction through their own media outlets. Westerners with Burmese citizenship were allowed to return, so Sammy worked with campus Hillel associations, the American Jewish Joint Distribution Committee (which had organized a massive response to the 2004 tsunami), the World Jewish Congress, and individual donors to return to Burma and bring thousands of dollars and tens of thousands of water purification tablets.

"My family tried to convince me not to return, but I think they were relieved to see me," he said. Once back in the country, he set about getting the synagogue repaired, aiding the two displaced Jewish families, and figuring out what he could do. "The situation for the Jews wasn't so bad, so my friends and I began to go out to the villages and help them rebuild. People still had no homes, no water or food. We would pull into a village every day with a water tank and supplies and give away what we could. It was unbelievable, like my father said, the devastation. And the government's response was . . . " He hesitated and considered his words carefully. "Frustrating," he chose, though anger flickered behind his eyes.

He stayed in the country for three weeks, and while there he and his father decided to organize an interfaith memorial service at the synagogue. Leaders of the Muslim, B'hai, Buddhist, and Christian communities came and lit candles and prayed for those who were suffering. A choir sang. Some Israeli aid workers who had made their way into the country came. Sammy flipped through his photos of the day, a smile on his face. He described the flicker of the candles, the heat and sweat of the tropical afternoon in the crowded synagogue. I thought about him standing alone in prayer on Yom Kippur, and I looked at him in the photos, speaking to a packed congregation of Muslims in white robes and Buddhists in their saffron, the Israelis in T-shirts, and Sammy and his father wearing their *kippot*.

Disaster had filled his synagogue with song once more. How long it could sustain itself was anyone's guess. How many disasters could this little place endure? How long could Sammy keep things going? He continues to struggle to keep the spirit of Jewish Burma alive and he intends to take over for his father when the time comes. Sammy will do everything in his power to avoid being cut off from his people, to keep the Jews of Burma from disappearing.

"If I didn't do it, who would?" Moses had said. Who indeed?

three

Newcomers:
The Jewish Community of Bentonville, Arkansas

May the children of the stock of Abraham who dwell in this land
continue to merit and enjoy the good will of the other inhabitants . . .
——GEORGE WASHINGTON,
LETTER TO THE HEBREW CONGREGATION AT NEWPORT, RHODE ISLAND

A BLANK STARE AND POLITE smile froze on the teenage waitress's face when I asked her a variation on that age-old question: Which came first, the synagogue or the ribhouse?

"The what?" she eventually mustered.

"The synagogue across Moberly," I answered. She smiled again, blank. "The little shack across the street."

"Oh, yeah," she said, recognition dawning. "That's some kind of church, I think."

"It's a synagogue," I told her.

"It's my first day," she said. "Let me get you that fried okra."

And off she went.

It struck me that I was probably the only person in Smokin' Joe's Ribhouse in Bentonville, Arkansas, thinking about the fate of the Jewish people. This was the Bible Belt, after all, and on a Saturday night most people had better things to do than wonder about tiny synagogues and whether or not violating the laws of koshruth while on a spiritual quest was, well . . . kosher. At least I ordered the beef ribs instead of the pork.

Senior citizens and young families filled the booths along the wall opposite me. I sat at a high table under a flat-screen TV, staring through the football game, enjoying a giant beef rib, and thinking about the intimate Shabbat service I had attended that morning in the shack across the street and the spirited Hanukkah party I'd been to the night before.

Congregation Etz Chaim of Bentonville, Arkansas, is more than a tin shack, but not by much. It has a main chapel room, three tiny classrooms, and a kitchen. Sketches of Jews in prayer hang on the wall near the bathroom, which has plumbing problems. The building used to be a Hispanic Baptist church, until the Baptists outgrew the space and sold it to the Jews, who'd been holding religious services and Sunday school classes in storefronts and living rooms or driving to Fayetteville to attend shul. Once they had a space, they also secured a rabbi, Jack Zanerhaft, and his wife, Debbye, a cantor. The couple drove from Tulsa once a month to lead services and guide the young group as they built the first new Jewish community in the South in over fifty years. Surrounded as they were by churches too numerous to count, I wondered what the Jews were doing here, how they had managed to form a synagogue, and, most pressing for me, why.

These Jews weren't the custodians of a rich history in the region—all of them came from somewhere else—nor were they extremely religious within their own families. Many of them weren't even born or raised as Jews. The Jewish resident who'd lived in Bentonville the longest had arrived twenty years ago. His name was Lee. He had a thick state trooper mustache and the square jaw of a military man. His son, Harrison, was in fact a military man, in the air force. I met Lee after only a few hours in town, and he made sure I felt a certain amount of reverence for the roads, the stores, the synagogue, and the ribhouse.

"When I first came here, there was nothing here. Just cows," he said. "Of course, on the day I arrived, the Ku Klux Klan was having a rally in town, and I thought, really? Is this just for me?" He laughed and his eyes gleamed. Clearly, this was his favorite story. "But really, there's never been much anti-Semitism here. When we moved here there were a few other Jewish families. There was an Israeli couple. And Michael Rosenstein and his wife . . . Michael was the go-to vet for chickens. The Tyson plant is out here, so chickens are big business aside from the obvious one." By "the obvious one," Lee meant Wal-Mart, whose global headquarters are in Bentonville. "Michael passed away about twelve years ago. His widow moved to New Orleans just before Katrina hit."

MY FIRST EVENING IN TOWN, I'D hopped into my rented Ford Mustang and peeled out of the hotel by the airport on a mission. The road wound through an endless expanse of flat farmland. The sky was overcast and I saw few other cars and no pedestrians. The first major structure I passed was the Wal-Mart distribution center, disgorging trucks bound for the rest of America. After that, the farmland took over again, with an occasional plot laid out for new subdivisions, the cookie-cutter homes still gaping and empty. Brand-new shopping centers appeared along the shoulder, like caravanserai along the Silk Road. Their parking lots were empty; the large Wal-Mart trucks rumbled past. Then even more farmland, a rundown farmhouse on each plot, usually with a pickup out front. I could imagine a peaceful life out here in the heartland. As I drove, I felt a strong Americana twinge. I pictured big breakfasts with sausage and bacon, pancakes and eggs. I imagined high school football practices and patriotic rallies and long quiet walks on the hard December dirt, surveying a land of wholesome opportunity. This, I imagined, was how America dreamed of itself, outside the urban Northeast Corridor that I came from.

After about ten minutes the road filled with traffic, and billboards broke the view to the horizon. The density of shopping centers finally overtook the farmland. Traffic lights slowed the flow and I found myself pulled out of my Americana daydreams. I could have been anywhere. Every chain restaurant I could think of was represented. There were car dealerships and motels and churches—dozens of churches—and then still more churches. And more chain restaurants.

I was on a mission to find Hanukkah-themed wrapping paper for the gifts I'd brought to share with Betsy Rosen and her family. Betsy was the president of Bentonville's Jewish community and had invited me to their Hanukkah celebration. I did not want to arrive without a gift for her family, but I'd forgotten wrapping paper. Luckily, amid the churches and chain restaurants on the way toward town, a Wal-Mart Supercenter stood sentinel, ensuring you would never lack for anything on your way into downtown Bentonville. The place sold everything from lawn mowers to avocados, and at 5 P.M. on a December Friday, the parking lot was packed. I rushed in to do my quick shopping, and after wandering in a daze through the cavernous space for a few minutes, I found the gift wrap aisle. I was amazed by the variety of choices I had in terms of ribbon, papers, cards, and bows. I'd always thought of the giant box stores as killing choice, but the shelves and displays in front of me presented the opposite problem, the tyranny of too much choice, though none of it was what I was looking for. Of all the holiday options, there wasn't actually one for Hanukkah. I was in Christmas Land or safely nonethnic, nonsectarian Holiday Land. I missed the mom-and-pop store near my house in Brooklyn that never seemed to have anything anyone would want and didn't pretend to offer more. There were no illusions there. I chose a simple blue and gold gift bag and filled it with decorative tissue paper. I paid in an express line and the high school girl at the counter wished me happy holidays as I left for downtown Bentonville.

The town square boasted a statue dedicated to the soldiers of the Confederacy, draped in festive lights, and a nativity scene that had been erected just after Thanksgiving. Next to the courthouse, off to the side of the square, sat a large Star of David and a menorah, each loaded with tiny bulbs. This would be the place for the evening celebration, the annual outdoor menorah lighting in Bentonville.

When I got to the square, I watched a group of men unloading equipment from a truck. They took out speaker rigs and a large screen. Someone had set up three beach chairs in front of where the screen and the speakers would be. It was the first Friday night of Hanukkah and I was eager to see the miracle of a menorah lighting in the town square of a Bible Belt town, but I hadn't realized it would be such a major event. When I pictured the vast expanses of flat land and the preponderance of churches, though, it dawned on me that perhaps there was nothing else to do. Why wouldn't others come to watch the Jews do their thing? Weren't Evangelicals these days all about Zionism anyway?

The air was crisp and cold and the sky threatened rain, but the men didn't seem fazed by the weather. As I watched them work, I saw people hustling in and out of the hardware store and strolling into the coffee shop and the sandwich place. The square and the lights and the gray sky felt extremely quaint, as if we were all curling up under a quilt together with the colorful lights of the holiday season blinking around us. I was being charmed by small-town America. Used to the pace of life in New York City, I liked the feeling of this slow December afternoon.

I couldn't believe the turnout for the menorah lighting would be enough to demand a large screen and speakers and I was thrilled to imagine what lay in store. I wanted to discover Jews making an impact on their town and I imagined local dignitaries speaking, the visiting rabbi from Tulsa telling the story of Hanukkah to the enthralled masses of

Evangelicals, and a joyous interfaith celebration of all that made small-town America great. I had some time to kill and had already had too much coffee, so I needed another activity to occupy myself. There was a real estate office just off the square, but I wasn't *that* charmed by the place.

One of the highlights of the square, opposite the courthouse where the screen was going up, was Walton's 5 & 10, the site of Sam Walton's first store. It was now a museum to his success. While the men set up the speakers, I went in to have a look around.

A ruddy-faced woman greeted me when I walked in the door. She wore her hair short, which accentuated the roundness of her face. She was big in a way that suited the landscape, generously proportioned. One could tell she had children, and no doubt grandchildren. She looked like a person who gave patriotic needlepoint pillow covers as gifts. Perhaps I read too much into her, but I had an image of small-town America and I needed her to embody it for me. Her Wal-Mart Associate name tag told me she was called Jackie, so I introduced myself and told her where I was from.

"Well, enjoy yourself. Have a look around. The museum is free and it's a self-guided tour. Take all the time you need." Her eyes sparkled and she seemed genuinely pleased to be sharing the history of the world's largest retailer with an out-of-town visitor.

Another man walked in with his wife, who was wearing a sweater with a dog on it. The dog's collar was an actual bow with a little tinkling bell on it. Jackie welcomed them, and the man explained he'd come down to have a look at Bentonville because he'd been transferred by his company and wanted to get a feel for the place. He and his wife wandered the museum quickly, soaking it in. The history of Wal-Mart had a different meaning for them, as every moment in Sam Walton's career—the opening of the first megastore, the expansion to Sam's Club, the honor bestowed by the first President Bush (shown in a video loop)—had led toward this man's arrival in Bentonville, uprooting his life and carrying it from Michigan to Arkansas. In the last twenty years the population of Bentonville has doubled. In a sense the museum of Wal-Mart's rise is a museum of migration. This was what drew me there as well, though my purposes were anthropological and spiritual rather than economic. Wal-Mart has changed the culture of Bentonville in unimaginable ways, from the addition of hotel chains and traffic congestion to the opening of a synagogue and a Hindu temple. Nearby Fayetteville has a mosque.

I told Jackie what I was up to in town, studying the Jewish community and exploring diversity.

"Well, you know," she said with pride, "we get all kinds of people in here from all over the world. Hindus, Muslims, and such. You know we've got a Mormon church in Bentonville now?"

I told her I'd heard about that.

"The Mormon church is a big deal because we're in the so-called Bible Belt," Jackie explained. "That's something different for us. But we've got all kinds of people here from all over the world."

I asked her about the Jews.

"The Jewish synagogue is just up the street, maybe three stoplights—how's that for directions!" She laughed and insisted on taking my picture, in case I ever became a famous writer. She didn't know any Jewish people herself, though they came through the museum from time to time. "Mostly vendors," she explained. "They're curious to see where it all started, just like everyone else."

"How do you know they're Jewish?"

"Well, you can tell." She smiled. "You know, from the beards and the—what's it called, on the head?"

"The yarmulke."

"No, something else, I think."

"The *kippah*?"

"That's it. Yes."

"That's the Hebrew word for it."

"That's the one. We get all kinds of folks. I guess there are other

Jews too who aren't religious like that, and it's harder to tell. It's a melting pot here, just like New York City!"

I wasn't all that curious about the hagiography of Sam Walton anymore, though it was interesting to compare replicas of the two offices he'd had, the first being his cramped enclosure at the back of the store we were in. His guest chair was an apple crate and his accounts payable and accounts receivable hung on hooks on the wall. The second office was a duplicate of the one in his corporate headquarters, a grand and lovely space of milk-chocolate leather, light wood, and the proud statement of his business code of ethics on the wall. A sign told me he spent very little time in this office, as he preferred being out on the road, personally visiting his stores. The reconstructed office reminded me of the reconstructed Temple of Dendur at the Metropolitan Museum of Art in New York, moved stone by stone from Egypt because a dam-building project would have destroyed it. In Walton's case, it was his death and the promotion of a new CEO that would have destroyed his office, redecoration as opposed to a flood. Of course, one can walk into the Temple of Dendur. Walton's office is sealed behind Plexiglas.

I bought some souvenirs (for their ironic value, I told myself), and stepped back out into the gray square. I walked over to the men setting up. They had the screen and speaker towers up now and were checking connections.

"Big turnout expected?" I asked.

"Weather might keep people away," a woman who seemed to be in charge answered. She smiled. "We'll make it fun, though, no matter how many show up. It's for the kids, really."

"Do a lot of children know about Hanukkah?" I asked. She stared at me, blank.

"Excuse me?"

"I asked if the kids know what they're seeing, or is this more of a chance for them to learn about Hanukkah?"

"I'm sorry . . ." She looked lost.

"This is for the menorah lighting tonight, right?"

"This is for the movie," she said. She handed me a flier. It was a holiday movie celebration for all families, the flier told me. They'd be showing *The Santa Clause 3*, starring Tim Allen. I looked off to the side of the screen, where the menorah and the Star of David sat, and wondered if I'd come on the right evening.

"Do you know if there is going to be a menorah lighting tonight?"

"I don't know about that," she said. None of the men setting up had any idea what I was talking about either. The woman reassured me that, even though there was a movie, the holiday lights would be on in the square. She called them holiday lights, deferring to political correctness, even though it was pretty clear they were Christmas lights. The manger scene does not play a large role in the winter holidays of any religion other than Christianity.

As we neared sunset, I grew anxious that I had my dates wrong, so I drove to the synagogue, just up the street as Jackie had told me it would be. Inside, a group of men were frying latkes.

"Nice to meet you," an older gentleman said to me, extending his hand. He wore a yarmulke and a brown jacket. His face was weathered, but welcoming. "Stan Kessler," he introduced himself.

I told him who I was and other men gathered around. They'd known I was coming. Betsy Rosen had sent an e-mail out to their Listserv about the writer who would be arriving. I shook hands all around. It was a very different welcome from the one I'd received in Rangoon. There was a crowd. Everyone expressed an eagerness to share his story during my visit, but not tonight. The Men's Club, of which they were all part, had committed to making latkes for the Hanukkah party after the menorah lighting and they were expecting a big turnout. They had to get to work. The whole place smelled like frying oil. I told them about the screen set up in the town square next to the menorah and the showing of *The Santa Clause 3* that would be starting start at any moment.

"People have set up beach chairs," I said.

"Well, we'll just do our ceremony off to the side," Tom Douglass said. Tom was one of the founders of the synagogue and had lived in Bentonville for seven and a half years. Tom was built like a rugby player, compact and thick, with short hair. He looked like the kind of guy you'd expect to find at a sports bar more than at a synagogue, though I guess the two aren't mutually exclusive. He came from Buffalo, New York, and had come for the same reason as everyone else: Wal-Mart.

"I wouldn't live here if it weren't for Wal-Mart," he said. The other three men in our little circle agreed. Stan was the only one in the circle who didn't work directly for Wal-Mart, though his livelihood depended on the retailer's success nonetheless: he consulted for companies that wanted to do business with Wal-Mart. As the port brought business opportunities to Rangoon, which in turn enabled the Baghdadi Jews to settle and prosper in Burma, so did Wal-Mart bring Jews to Bentonville. It's not a remarkable story, nor is it unique to the Jews. People go where the opportunity is.

"I'm gonna go to the square and meet my wife and kids," Tom said, unfazed by my dire predictions about Tim Allen overshadowing the Jewish holiday. "Why don't I give you a ride?"

Tom and I left the little building and stepped back out into the gravel parking lot. He moved quickly, excitement in his step. As one of the leaders of the Jewish community, this was a big night for him. It had been a great, if not contentious, victory: getting the town to put the Star of David and the menorah in the square. Most of the contention came from secular Jews in Little Rock who didn't think that public property should be used for any religious symbols.

As we drove back to the town square, he told me about all the attention the little community had gotten after the *New York Times* published an article on "the Wal-Mart Jews."

"It's been great," he said. "A lot of communities throughout the South are disappearing as their members get older and the young people move away. The communities are closing. For example, our Torah at Etz

Chaim came from El Dorado, Arkansas, from a community that closed down. After the *Times* article I started getting phone calls from people wanting to donate artifacts, wanting to give things from their communities to a community that was beginning to blossom. A woman called me from Little Rock in tears, she was so moved by what we were doing here. Who else my age can say they've started a synagogue? Not many. I'm very proud of it."

I thought about Sammy in Rangoon and about his father sitting alone, waiting for tourists to come by to light candles, and about my grandmother's hometown in Virginia, the southern shtetl that had melted into thin air.

We pulled into the courthouse parking lot at the same time as Tom's wife in her minivan. Robyn introduced herself with a noticeable Long Island accent, and her sons shook my hand dutifully. We all made our way around the courthouse and could hear the movie before we saw it. At the corner of the square, just to the right of the screen, the Jews had started to gather. People in the crowd watching the movie glanced over as more and more Jewish families assembled, trying to figure out what to do, how to have the ceremony while the movie blared. The menorah was already plugged in and glowing like the rest of the "holiday" decorations. While Tom chatted with the other community leaders, I met Rabbi Jack, who had just arrived from Tulsa with his wife, Debbye, the cantor.

"A Hanukkah miracle," Jack said laughing, gesturing at the crowd of Jews. He had a close-cropped gray beard and delicate glasses. Aside from being a rabbi, he is a practicing attorney. Like so many of the congregation, he had New York roots, having gone to college and studied at an Orthodox yeshiva in Brooklyn. His voice still bent with a slight Brooklyn accent.

"It's a beautiful thing," his wife said, looking over the small crowd of Jews gathered for the Hanukkah celebration and the large crowd of Gentiles gathered to watch the Tim Allen movie.

"What should we do?" I overhead Tom's wife asking him, her sons standing behind her, glancing at the screen. An elf was lecturing Tim Allen about something. "I mean, it's already plugged in."

"We'll just unplug it and say the blessings and sing some songs and plug it in again," answered Tom, ever practical. I pictured Talmudic scholars debating the solemnity of extension cords. We began to cross behind the screen to gather in front of the menorah, when a man came running up to us.

"You gotta go around," he said. "You'll block the projection if you walk behind the screen."

So we Jews in Arkansas turned back, somewhat confused about which way to go, and wandered around the square to the other side of the screen, where we could gather, sing, and pray. As we circumnavigated the statue of the Confederate soldier, children wandered off and had to be collected, and a few adults rushed over to get coffee from the shop on the corner. Finally, the rabbi assembled all the kids in the front, while Tom unplugged the menorah lights so that they could be relit after the blessing. It wasn't forty years in the desert, but below the light-bedecked statue of the Confederate soldier and the roar of the Tim Allen Christmas movie, it did strike me how very far every one of these people had traveled from what they knew in order to make themselves a home in Bentonville.

IF HISTORY IS GEOGRAPHY, THEN THE recent history of Bentonville defies that conventional wisdom. There's not much here, and forty years ago there was even less.

"Nothing but cows and fields," Robyn Douglass observed about her arrival seven and a half years ago, just as Lee had described it twenty years ago. I pictured the area the way Abraham must have seen Canaan—rough, inhospitable land dotted with a foreign tribe. "There was an Applebee's," she added.

Bentonville seems an unlikely place to start an empire, but Sam Walton did not at first set out to start an empire. In 1950 Bentonville was a town of 2,900 people nestled against the Ozark Mountains in the northwest corner of Arkansas. Walton had spent the previous five years running a Ben Franklin Store in Newport, Arkansas, and, when he and the landlord couldn't come to terms on a new lease, he set out to open up his own place, acquiring a five-and-dime from a local man. Walton soon figured out that the key to beating his competitors was price. Rather than buying low and selling high, he chose to buy low and sell low, making his profits on volume. Passing his savings on to his customers served Walton well, and within twelve years he had eleven Walton's stores around Arkansas. He decided to start his own discount chain, opening up the first franchise in neighboring Rogers Arkansas. His assistant came up with the name for it: Wal-Mart.

With a fanatic devotion to lower prices, Wal-Mart expanded rapidly. By 1970, Wal-Mart employed around fifteen hundred people and opened up its home office in Bentonville, a boxy structure that looks more like an overgrown public school than the headquarters of a corporate monolith. A sign outside the headquarters keeps a running tally of how much Wal-Mart has saved its customers. When I passed by on my way to the town square, it totaled $267 billion. Over a hundred million Americans visit Wal-Mart every week, making it the largest retailer in the world. What could people be buying in such massive quantities that the savings alone added up to more than the GDP of Egypt and Israel combined?

One thing they were not buying was giant glowing Stars of David or menorahs to place in front of the courthouse.

"Those don't come from Wal-Mart," Lee told me. "I got them from a place outside Tulsa. It was after 9/11 and Jeremy Hess from Temple Shalom in Fayetteville called me up because I was active in Democratic politics around here . . . I took thirty-five percent of the vote for justice of the peace when I ran, and that's in a pretty Republican area, and I'm a

Jew and a Democrat! Jeremy was concerned about the religious displays in the town square, but I said, listen, Jeremy, this is the wrong time. People need their faith symbols right now. What we need to do is get our symbols out there. I called up Mayor Coberly with a compromise. I told her I have a lot of respect for people's faith and I'd been asked to ask her to remove all the religious symbols from the town square. I didn't want to make her do that, and I can't imagine she would have wanted to. This is a religious area. You see the number of churches? I told her we have a lot of Jews moving here to town and we'd like to be represented too. She let me put those symbols right where you see them in front of the courthouse. When we first did it, the newspaper received a lot of letters to the editor saying how great it was, letters from non-Jews. Though the Anti-Defamation League down in Little Rock wasn't too thrilled with me. They wanted no religious symbols on government property. But they don't live here; they don't know this place. I'm proud of what we did, getting the Jews represented here."

At the menorah, Rabbi Jack led everyone in the blessing of the Ha-nukkah lights and Tom plugged them back in. *Praised art thou, Lord our God . . .* The electric glow lit the area next to the movie screen and drew more glances, some annoyed, toward the forty Jews who'd gathered around. A photographer from the local paper snapped a few pictures and the children sang a few more Hanukkah songs.

Hanukkah didn't really become popular in the United States until the twentieth century, around the same time as the massive wave of Jewish immigration from Eastern Europe. It gained its prominence by provid-ing a Jewish celebration around the time of Christmas, giving Jewish children a way to feel like part of the mainstream festivities. Right now, it seemed, we Jews were interrupting the mainstream festivities, and I imagine the moviegoers were relieved when the group dispersed.

The lighting complete, the songs sung, we piled back into minivans and American-made sedans and returned to the synagogue, where the air still reeked of frying oil. The Hanukkah feast began. The little synagogue quickly filled with at least three times the number of people at the lighting, the temptation of latkes far greater than the temptation of the lights and the cold. As people poured in, it would have been hard to tell we were still in the Bible Belt. A good portion of the members looked straight out of a Long Island synagogue; some seemed to come from a Northern California organic farm. One or two wore yarmulkes. One or two wore state trooper mustaches.

"My first Hanukkah here," Lee told me, "it was just my wife, my son, and I in our motel room . . . nothing like this." He scanned the room. "I'm not really a full member here, though," he whispered to me. "I'll tell you why another time."

I thought of the old joke about a Jew on a desert island. When he's rescued, they find he's built two synagogues. "Why'd you build two?" he's asked. "Well, this one here I go to on the Sabbath," he answered. "And this one here I wouldn't be caught dead in." I made an appointment to meet with Lee another time and continued introducing myself to community members around the room.

"There are a lot of converts here," one of the synagogue board members told me as I watched the arrivals. "And a lot of mixed marriages. We're a small community, so we welcome everyone." Carroll and Paul Stuckey, both converts, introduced me to their seventeen-year-old daughter, Rachel, a passionate Zionist and the only Jewish student at Bentonville High. "When I told people I was Jewish, they asked me what denomination that was," she said. "I'm proud of being Jewish, but some of the other kids, they hide it; they're scared of not fitting in."

"If someone asks, I lie about it," said one of the children standing near us, a skinny kid with a thick mop of dark hair.

"Why?"

"Because they think we killed Jesus," he said. He's home schooled and doesn't really like mixing with the non-Jews. "I might invite one friend who's not Jewish to my bar mitzvah."

"But you'll have a bar mitzvah?"

"Of course."

Steve Crowell, the boy's father, and his wife had also converted to Judaism. They sat on the board of Etz Chaim, and were running the bar mitzvah training program. Their older son, Aaron, was one of the first bar mitzvah in the community, though they were planning nine more for 2008, seven for 2009, and had already booked two for 2010 and six for 2011. None of that accounted for the possibility of more Jews moving to Bentonville and joining the synagogue. They were all excited about their community's growth and eager to bring in anyone who wanted a place for Jewish life in the area, no matter what their Jewish bona fides.

I liked that notion. The smaller the community, the more welcoming. I found it odd, however, that this welcoming of the religious and the secular alike, the Jewish and the non-Jewish, in short, the assimilated, would find such a robust expression on Hanukkah. Very few American children are raised with a conception of the brutality or religious fundamentalism in the Hanukkah story.

Outside of America, Hanukkah is a relatively minor Jewish holiday. In America, it is often called the Jewish Christmas and it has taken on many of the trappings of Christmas, with cards, decorations, lights, and presents wrapped in shiny paper. It is the only Jewish holiday that celebrates an event not in the Torah, and it has evolved into the answer Jewish parents give to their children for Christmas. The way it is now celebrated is an adaptation to the mainstream culture.

But the story of Hanukkah is particularly bloody and ripe with juicy details that are not often discussed: a mad king, parades of martyrs, ritual murders, bribery, betrayal, shame, vengeance, and still more murder. It's a holiday fit for a pulp novel or a summer blockbuster, and perhaps that is why it has found its true home in America. The heart of the story (though not, the rabbis emphasize, the celebration) is the revolt of the Maccabees against the Seleucid Empire.

The Jews, as had been their lot for much of their early history, found themselves stuck between clashing civilizations. The first historically verifiable mention of their existence occurs on a tablet celebrating their destruction in about 1207 B.C.E. by the Egyptian pharaoh Merneptah who, in listing his victories over various states and towns, mentioned the tribe of the Israelites, claiming he had stripped their land bare, ending the possibility of their future. Long after Merneptah became a footnote in history, the Jews persisted in the land of Palestine, although continually subject to conquest by their powerful neighbors, and doing what they could to adapt to the cultures that absorbed them.

Between 300 and 250 B.C.E., the Septuagint emerged—the five books of Moses translated into Greek—for the benefit of Greek-speaking Jews. There is a nationalistic slant to the translation, a moment for the Hellenized Jewish elites to say to the culture around them, "Look, we are just like you." The Septuagint was an adaptation to the dominant culture and a way of preserving Judaism among Jews who sought greater integration into Hellenism.

Three generations after the death of Alexander the Great, Antiochus III came to power. He fought to expand his borders across an area roughly including modern-day Afghanistan, Iran, Iraq, Syria, Lebanon, and parts of Turkey, Armenia, Turkmenistan, Uzbekistan, and Tajikistan. His ambitions ultimately led to a confrontation with the Roman Empire, which did not take kindly to his aggression. Upon invading Greece in 192 B.C.E., his forces were pushed back into Asia once more. His defeat, like that of his grandfather, sparked revolt in some of his outer territories, shrinking the empire yet again. He pulled back, licking his wounds but not defeated. He yearned to become as great as Alexander.

Antiochus III believed that he could reestablish the territory that Alexander the Great had conquered if only he had a unified and *Hellenized* empire behind him. He set about putting up statues of the Greek gods—and of himself—all over his kingdom and demanded that the idols receive the respect and worship they were due. Many regions submitted willingly to the nationalization project, producing a great flourishing of Hellenistic art and culture that survives to this day in Syria. However, the Jews would not submit to the desecration of their Temple, and argued that they proved their loyalty by paying their taxes and defending the borders of his empire. Antiochus followed Alexander the Great's lead and tolerated the Jewish customs, allowing them to keep their way of life. Jewish elites nominated their own high priests, to whom the emperor granted the governorship of Judea. As long as they caused no trouble, the Jews were allowed to exercise a large degree of self-rule.

However, Antiochus IV would not prove so amenable to Jewish exceptionalism. He usurped the throne he was meant to share with his brother and became ruler of the Seleucid Empire in 175 B.C.E. As a matter of policy, he wanted to see every bit of his empire under the influence of Greek culture. Historians note that he had no specific love for Hellenistic culture, but demanded conformity simply to confirm his power.

Some in Jerusalem jumped at the opportunities Hellenization afforded and saw the new emperor's zeal as an opportunity to shake off the ancient ways. Appreciation of Greek culture and thinking aside, many found it politically expedient to assimilate. A Jewish nobleman by the name of Jason understood well that the real power came not from the Jews but from Antiochus, who loved gold, and he bribed his way into an appointment as high priest. To further ingratiate himself with his patron, he built a Greek-style gymnasium and held wrestling matches in the courtyards of the Temple. He introduced pagan rites into the Temple rituals, enraging the pious, but satisfying many of the elites, who hoped an assimilated Judea would give them greater power and prosperity. Resentment among religious Jews grew stronger.

Why had they maintained their culture, rebuilt their Temple after the Babylonian exile, and fought so hard for their way of life, only to be betrayed by one of their own? Jason even passed a law mandating that the young men of the city wear a style of hat that was in fashion at the time.

Then another of the Hellenizing Jews stole Jason's bribe to give it to Antiochus himself, and became high priest. He too continued on the path of Temple desecration and Hellenization. Conflict between the Hellenizers and the traditionalists increased and often turned to violence.

In 170 B.C.E. Antiochus led a campaign against Egypt and removed Ptolemy's heir from power. During this campaign, a rumor spread through Jerusalem that Antiochus had been killed in battle. Euphoric riots erupted. The elites of the city, those responsible for much of the desecration of the Temple, were tossed from the high city walls, with Greek statues following behind. Antiochus, still very much alive, heard about the unrest and, enraged, marched into Jerusalem. He spent three days massacring traditionalist Jews.

Thanks to a betrayal by his appointed regent in Alexandria, who pledged loyalty to the Ptolemies the moment Antiochus's back was turned, Antiochus was compelled to lead another military campaign to take control of Egypt in 168 B.C.E. As he charged forward, however, he met the Roman consul Gaius Popilius Laenas in the desert near Alexandria. Popilius demanded that Antiochus withdraw his forces immediately. The emperor attempted to stall for time, so the consul drew a circle in the sand around him and told Antiochus he must deliver his reply before stepping outside the line. Rather than risk war with Rome, Antiochus retreated, and looked to reestablish his authority elsewhere in his kingdom. But he'd been humiliated and needed to assert himself. He cast his eye on Jerusalem and on the unruly Jews who had always defied his will. He demanded that Judea get in line with Greek culture or there would be hell to pay.

He outlawed circumcision and made the observation of the Sabbath illegal. Women, rather than break their covenant with God, marched their children to death one by one, in order of age, to show their defiance of Antiochus. But seeing the unbreakable will of the pious did not deter his genocidal resolve. He ordered the desecration of every altar, looted the Temple, and made plans to sell the Jews into slavery in foreign lands.

Antiochus invited non-Jews to settle in Judea by the thousands in order to dilute Jewish influence.

As the emperor vented his rage on the Jews, the unexpected occurred. An aged priest named Mattathias could no longer abide the injustice he saw around him. As one of the Hellenized Jews went to sacrifice an unclean animal on the altar, Mattathias slew him on the spot. He and his five sons then fled into the mountains and waged a guerrilla war against the Selucids and the Hellenizers, a war that would last twenty years. They began by killing the agents and officers of Antiochus, but their blood lust could not be so simply satisfied. They had seen the near destruction of their sacred bond with God and saw this war as a chance to purge the Jewish people of sin. They attacked assimilated Jews with merciless vengeance, and indeed, most of those whom they fought and killed were other Jews that the children of Mattathias, called the Maccabees, considered traitors to God. They were unforgiving. Anyone who had embraced Greek culture or norms was a target of their swords. The Maccabees' war against religious impurity might be the first example of a holy war in history, as religion was the driving force behind the violence, and piety was the difference between the clashing forces.

When the fighting was done, the Maccabees had pushed Antiochus out of Judea along with his Greek gods, and the Hasmonean dynasty was established, the first independent Jewish state since the time of King Solomon. During the fighting, the Temple had been pillaged, and the sacred lamp, meant to burn eternally, had been extinguished. Finding only enough oil to last for a day, the Jews lit the lamp and prayed, rededicating the Temple and attempting to purify it from the desecration that had been committed there. And, so the story goes, a miracle occurred. The lamp stayed lit for eight days, the time it took to make more oil to keep the lamp burning. The newly revitalized Jews gave thanks to God for his blessings: the victory of their ragtag force over the great army of an empire, the return of Israelite rule to Judea, and the miracle of the oil.

In later years, when the holiday of Hanukkah was established, the Talmudic scholars pointed out that the celebration commemorates the miracle of the oil, not the bloodshed, as warfare is never a cause for celebration in Judaism. But one thing cannot be denied: Hanukkah is a nationalistic holiday, intimately connected with the defeat of the assimilators at the hands of passionate zealots. The celebration is about the miracle at the Temple, but that miracle involves purification after the Temple was soiled by the assimilated Jews.

AT TEMPLE ETZ CHAIM, AS EXCITED families arrived for the party, I stood by a table covered with trinkets and gifts for sale. Mark Levine had made T-shirts that said Shalom Y'all and Knish My Grits, celebrations of the dual southern and Jewish identities he had adopted after moving from Long Island. Brightly colored dreidels were strewn around the table as if they'd been thrown there in a hurry. A dreidel is a small top with four sides. There is a Hebrew letter on each side. I hadn't played with a dreidel in years and asked a little boy who stood nearby if he knew how to play.

"Of course," he told me as if I were insane. I asked him to explain it to me.

"You need gelt," he said, talking about the chocolate coins that every child expects to get on Hanukkah. "And then you spin the dreidel and wherever it lands you do what it says."

"What does it say?" I asked. "What are these four letters?"

"*Nun, gimel*," the boy said. "Ummm . . ."

His mother was listening by now and prodded him.

"Hey," she said.

"He," he answered, pointing to a letter that actually did look a bit like an *H* to me, which was how I remembered it was the letter *he*. Then the boy was silent.

"And?" his mother kept prodding him.

"*Shin*," the boy said proudly.

"And what does it stand for?" his mother asked him. I felt guilty. My curiosity had led to a quiz for this poor boy who just wanted to play with his friends at the party. We could smell the freshly made latkes and we were both hungry.

"None, all, half, put," the boy said quickly, which described the instructions for the game. Each letter stood for a word in Yiddish that directed you how to play, how much to put in the pot in the middle, or how much to take. You played until one person had all the coins.

"It means something else too," the boy's mother said.

"A great miracle happened there," he said. His mother smiled. She set him free and he ran off to get some food. I examined the dreidels some more. Each of the Hebrew letters stood for a word, and the word had a meaning in both Yiddish—the instructions—and Hebrew—the deeper meaning. *Nes gadol haya sham*—"a great miracle happened there." In Israel, dreidels do not have the letter *shin* on them, but the letter *pe*, which stands for the word "here." *A great miracle happened here.* Even the children's games declare the difference between those living in the Promised Land and those apart. One Orthodox commentary I read asserted that the four letters on the dreidel represented the four great exiles in Jewish history—Babylon, Persia, Greece, and Rome. That particular text imbued each letter with the significance of the threats each of those sojourns presented to the Jewish people. It seemed a bit of a stretch, but I remain in awe that the Jews could make such a complex text out of a top with four letters, and that a simple children's game would reinforce the idea that all Jewish life should cast its eye toward Jerusalem.

When the sanctuary room seemed to be at capacity, Betsy Rosen, the current president of the synagogue, stood on the bimah and thanked everyone for coming. She thanked the Men's Club for handling the latkes, and the rabbi and the cantor for coming up from Tulsa. She introduced me to the room and I said a few words about why I was there. Everyone smiled warmly and laughed at the right moments. Then it was the rabbi's turn to speak.

He welcomed us to the Shabbat and to the fourth night of Hanukkah.

"Do you all know the story of Hanukkah?" he asked the children clustered together in the front.

"Yes!" the younger ones all called out together.

"Good," the rabbi answered. "I want to tell you a different kind of Hanukkah story tonight," he told them. He spoke primarily to the children, only occasionally directing his comments to the parents and other adults in the room, who seemed happy just to watch their kids celebrating Hanukkah together, learning from a rabbi, engaging with their history. It became clear to me that this was a party for the children more than anyone else. It was a younger crowd than I'd ever seen in a synagogue; it seemed everyone had children, and almost everyone's children were with them.

"This story doesn't take place in ancient times or even in the land of Israel," Rabbi Jack said, smiling. "This story takes place right here, in America."

He told another Hanukkah story, one that Jewish children in America know far better than the bloody tale of Seleucids and Ptolemies and Maccabees and murders.

"The year was 1777, and it was winter. A bitterly cold, terrible winter, and General George Washington and his Continental Army made their camp at Valley Forge to wait out the harsh weather before they would continue fighting their war of independence against the British . . . "

Rabbi Jack told us the story of one officer in the Continental Army, a young man named Isaac Israel, who had wandered off into the woods. General George Washington had taken a stroll through the cold forest to reflect on his situation—morale in the camp was at an all-time low and it was Christmas Eve. As he walked, he came upon Isaac sitting alone in the woods, lighting a candle. The general rushed over, alarmed that the candle might be some sort of signal to the enemy. When he came upon the soldier, he saw that the young man was crying.

"Why are you crying? Why are you lighting this candle? What are you doing out here?" Washington asked.

"I'm lighting this candle," Israel said, "because tonight is the first night of Hanukkah, and I am crying because I believe we will win."

Washington was moved that the young man would offer such an emotional prediction and he asked that the holiday be explained to him. Israel told the story of the Maccabees' ragtag rebellion and their victory over much stronger forces. Washington enjoyed the story and found great solace in it, and great cause for hope. It is said that from that day on, he became a great friend to the Jews in America. Some accounts of the story even have the general visiting the young soldier's family for lunch many years later.

"This is a true story," Rabbi Jack finished and winked at me. "Look it up."

I did. What I found told me a lot more about the creation of Jewish identity in America than it did about Jewish involvement in the American Revolution.

Several versions of the story are available, none of them 100 percent historically verified, but all of them sharing certain common themes. There is a Jewish soldier in all the versions, and he is usually an immigrant from Eastern Europe. It is Christmas and Hanukkah at Valley Forge, and the story of the outnumbered Maccabeeans gaining victory over their oppressors inspires General Washington and revives his spirits. America's victory is thus linked to Jewish history, a particularly sunny telling of Jewish history. Whether or not the story is true, it says a lot about the aspirations of Jewish Americans. The pride that rippled through the room in Bentonville when the rabbi had finished, the bursting smiles on the children's faces, told of people who were proud of their traditions and wanted those traditions to be part of America's story, just as they felt themselves fully part of America.

The oral tradition of Hanukkah at Valley Forge, I think, is one of the most important signifiers of Jewish identity in the United States. It speaks to the immigrant experience, while locating it fully in the most patriotic moment of American history, and links the Jews to the most admired of this country's founding fathers. The story of the restoration of the Temple and the destruction of the Hellenizers is not used to celebrate Jewish revival or Jewish national survival but American diversity and loyalty. By telling this tale, Jews reinforce their claim to Americanness. Their Judaism becomes that which makes them more American. Wandering the room, talking to people who had moved to Bentonville from all over the country and come together around this little synagogue, I couldn't help feeling connected to something too. Perhaps it was the latke fumes going to my head, but while the cantor led the children in more Hanukkah songs, I began to see the benefits of being part of a community. It was nice to be so far from home, but in a place so familiar and so welcoming.

The next morning, I went to the Shabbat services. There were about a dozen adults there and about half as many children. As people filed in, Stan Kessler, the older gentleman I'd met the night before, told me that there were often more children, but there was a big soccer game that morning. His children were grown already. One of them had moved to Israel. Stan and his wife were in charge of new membership at Etz Chaim, which is how he knew what was going on with the kids and their soccer games.

The rabbi and his wife arrived and greeted everyone and we began. The service was informal, a large part of it taken up by questions and answers. I'd never been so relaxed at a religious service before. Children were encouraged to sing the songs they knew, as the adults prayed fervently. Steve and Tom wore prayer shawls, bowing and bending and singing loudly. Others were more reserved. Most followed the transliteration in the prayer books. Few of the members could read Hebrew. As the service went on, with clapping and laughing, I began to feel part of it. I hadn't spent enough time in synagogues to know how this service differed from others, though I knew it was far from Orthodox. Men and women sat together; they didn't in Orthodox synagogues. Otherwise, I didn't know much about what was going on around me. But no one made me feel uncomfortable about it. My knowledge seemed adequate to allow me to participate as much as anyone else, and Rabbi Jack made sure I did, sending occasional smiles and winks my way.

I stood when the congregation stood, sat when they sat, and tried to mouth the words to the prayers in Hebrew when I could. When the call-and-response happened in English, I added my voice to the response with everyone else. It was such a small group, my silence would have been noticeable. The intimacy of the experience denied the possibility of disappearing into the background as my instincts screamed at me to do. By showing up, I was part of this community activity, on equal terms with everyone else there.

When it came time to read that week's Torah portion, I was invited, as an honored guest, to make an *aliyah*—to go up to the Torah and say the blessings before and after a section of the weekly portion was read aloud. I hadn't stood on the bimah of a synagogue during services since my bar mitzvah, nor had I said a prayer in public since then. There was a sheet of paper that had the blessings written out in Hebrew and English, with a transliteration of the Hebrew below. Still, I didn't know the tune to the chants, and I was terrified of looking like a fool or somehow insulting the entire sacrament of the Torah reading.

"Because we're small in number this morning," Rabbi Jack said, smiling, "we'll give everyone a chance for an *aliyah*." He called up a few others to read with me, and in groups of three we said the blessings and then stood to the side for the next group. The whole congregation had the chance to read, and several people were just as lost and excited as I was to do this for the first time. Of course, most of the ones who were as lost as I was were children, but still, when it was done, I felt a great sense of pride. I'd participated in something with the community. I was a part of it and I'd learned something new.

"Hanukkah is a time of dreams," Rabbi Jack said during his sermon on that week's Torah portion. "The passage we read this week concerns Joseph interpreting the pharaoh's dreams. It is appropriate that we read this passage here at Etz Chaim, because here too is a place for dreams. These few families dreamed of creating a community where none had been, and look at what they have made." He spoke for a time about dreaming and building and survival and miracles. Afterward, Jack and his wife had to leave quickly because an ice storm threatened to block their way back to Tulsa.

"Happy Hanukkah," he wished me as they left. They would be back in about a month.

"This time of year, it's a struggle," Tom told me when I sat down with him and his wife after services. "With Christmas, I mean. Hanukkah is not just the Jewish Christmas, and we have to let people know that."

"Everywhere you go," Robyn added, "people wish you a Merry Christmas, ask you about Christmas. They ask what church you go to. When we first came to Bentonville, we went to the synagogue in Fayetteville. It was in an old frat house and there were four or five people there. There was some service about the Holocaust. I just started crying right in the middle of it and wondering *What am I doing here?*"

Tom, remembering his wife's shock and agony, put his hand on hers, engulfing her tiny fingers.

"For us, it's a big change, coming from a community of a thousand families and moving out here," he explained. He had moved to Bentonville to be the director of an IT group at Wal-Mart seven and half years earlier. "Out here, there are no professional Jews. Anything we wanted to do, we would have to do ourselves."

I thought of my parents' synagogue, of the handoff to the pros when it came time for me to learn anything about being Jewish.

"There were eleven families in Bentonville who wanted to create a synagogue," Tom continued. "We were all younger people with kids and didn't want to drive to Fayetteville all the time. So we just started our own thing. We grew to fifteen families and were meeting in storefronts and the Boys and Girls Club. We'd haul the Hebrew school supplies around in big Rubbermaid tubs. In 2005 we appealed to the first fifteen families for a down payment on this building here that the Baptist church was selling so they could move into a bigger space. We hired Rabbi Jack and his wife part-time—we can't really afford a full-time rabbi, but we'd been getting rabbinical students as they were available and that wasn't working. They came from all different affiliations, and every week the service was so different, no one could follow along."

I mentioned how I had trouble following along during the service, not having spent much time in a synagogue. If the order of the service and the tunes to the songs changed every week, I would never have been able to keep up.

"It's funny." Tom drummed his fingers on the table. "By putting together this sort of DIY synagogue, I've become much more religious than I was back on the East Coast."

"I make my own challah now," Robyn added, laughing.

"It's funny to think we just started a synagogue. Most people doing this are twice my age. But it's for the kids. We all do it for the kids. That's the future, that's what you hope to pass down. I see it as a spark."

"At first I got a lot of pressure to go to church," Robyn said. "So I just started letting people know right off that I'm Jewish. The kids picked up on that. On the first Rosh Hashanah we were here, I sent my oldest, Michael, to school. I still feel bad about that, but I wanted him to fit in. Now I have it worked out with the school. I explained that it was a holiday and he would make up the assignment, but I didn't want him marked absent for the attendance records. It wasn't like he was just skipping a day. I learned you have to pick your battles. But there's always a battle. I'm a fighter, you see? I'm from Long Island."

"We just need to be consistent," Tom interjected calmly. He was clearly the mellower one in the couple, the peacemaker, whereas Robyn was the warrior. I could see how both could be useful in building a new community. "Transparency avoids ignorance. So much of what we've had to deal with out here isn't blatantly anti-Jewish, it's just ignorance. Though generally, the response to the founding of Etz Chaim has been very positive. People from all the different faiths came to the dedication and some local politicians too. We've got nothing but positive feedback. And people were curious. I speak at schools and at the library about Judaism, especially around this time of year, about Hanukkah. I sometimes get questions at work. People are interested. Some churches even started throwing Seders around Passover, so we have to figure that out . . . It's a tough bridge to cross, but it can be an opportunity. There is definitely a lot of support for Israel among the Evangelical community now, the most since I've lived here. We've never been there—to Israel—but I feel a certain connection, a desire to be there. I guess it's genetic, this yearning for Israel. To be with other Jews, to be around the Jewish people."

Funny, I thought. Living in New York, I'm always around Jewish people. Does that explain why I had never really felt a longing to go to Israel? Would I feel more Jewish if I lived in the middle of the Bible Belt like Tom and Robyn? Would I want more of a connection to Israel if I didn't live in that other center of Jewish life, New York City?

"I always wanted my kids to be around other Jewish people," Robyn added. "It changes the way you react to your own faith, just because you have to make sure that that feeling is there when you need it. Being together at Etz Chaim helps us all find a place out here and gives the kids a chance just to be comfortable, not to have to explain themselves all the time."

"When we came," Tom said, "the big thing was to find a preschool that wasn't praying all the time. Nondenominational still meant Christian. We ended up finding one for Michael that was for army kids. Our youngest just studied at home, because Robyn's a teacher. We did have one incident last year, where a teacher said something like 'Those New York Jews are a different breed.' "

"I was ready to put up the For Sale sign," Robyn interrupted. "But I confronted the teacher and we worked it out. Michael's the only Jewish kid in the fifth and sixth grade. He's become very confident because of it. He wears a Jewish star, and some other kids have said to him, 'I didn't know you were Jewish; that's cool.' " I think the things that bother me don't bother the kids as much because they've become teachers too, teaching their peers. For my kids, this is normal."

"And that bothers her." Tom smirked.

"Educating the community has become a survival strategy."

"It's not survival," Tom clarified quickly, alert to the scribbling I was doing on my pad and not wanting me to paint a picture of isolated Jews under siege in the heartland. "It's about meaningful dialogue. We don't want to be foreign. If I can get people to ask questions, then I've done my job."

"We're always teaching," Robyn said, "giving out dreidels, gelt, and directions for how to play. Now all the kids want the games and Mark's Shalom Y'All T-shirts."

"We want to plant solid roots and to get other families involved. It can't just be the founders who keep it going," Tom said. "We have over sixty-five families now and are always growing. We don't want to be on the board forever. This is a transient community—there are vendors and executives coming and going. We need to create a core that will survive even if we are not here."

WHEN OUR CONVERSATION ENDED, I HOPPED back into the Mustang and went to meet Lee at the coffee shop on the town square. He pulled up in his truck a few minutes late, still looking more like a state trooper than a Jewish community leader. He wanted to tell me the other side of things; the reason he wasn't a full member of Etz Chaim. I felt strange plunging into the divisive politics of a small-town synagogue. I felt strange even knowing there were divisive politics.

"When I came to Bentonville," he told me, "I was going to Temple Shalom in Fayetteville, but there was no structure at the time. I couldn't find anyone to teach my son Hebrew. I met Jack and Debbye in Tulsa and we'd drive over there for Harrison to take lessons from them. When the group here wanted to split off and get their own rabbi, I recommended Jack and Debbye. I go there for them, but I really didn't think the split with Fayetteville was the right thing to do. Though Etz Chaim is not officially affiliated with any of the Jewish movements, they really stayed sort of a Reform/Reconstructionist type place, which is just the kind of synagogue Temple Shalom is. Why do they need two of the same type of congregation in this area? They aren't really far enough apart to justify it."

Lee said it upset him, but he seemed like the kind of guy who would always find something to object to. He had been a talk radio host at one point and I think took great delight in being both an insider and an outsider in the community. For all his strong opinions, he still found what the small group had created in Bentonville remarkable and was happy to have played a role in contributing to its growth.

I wanted to see the scene in Fayetteville, which was a university town and home to the other synagogue. I made plans to go the next day with Mark Levine, the leader of the Men's Club at the synagogue in Bentonville. He too seemed like an odd transplant to Bentonville. He was Long Island through and through, he'd told me when we first met at the Hanukkah party.

The local Chabad rabbi, a kind of Jewish missionary, was throwing his own Hanukkah celebration: a bowling party. The Chabad movement, an Orthodox sect, sends emissaries, called Shluchim, all over the world where there are viable Jewish communities or a steady stream of Jewish visitors. They try to provide kosher food and create circumstances for a regular minyan. They act as teachers and try to engage Jews of all kinds, even "bad" Jews like me. Mendel Greisman was a young Orthodox rabbi who'd made his way to Bentonville, and I was excited to meet him, to hear about life for a black-hatted Orthodox Jew from Brooklyn living in rural Arkansas.

Once Mark and I had finalized our plans to go the party, I had some time on my hands, so I drove back toward the synagogue. It was all locked up and the sun was setting. The gravel parking lot was empty. I drove right past it and pulled into the parking lot of Smokin' Joe's Ribhouse to get myself some dinner and think about what I'd seen so far. And to eat some delicious barbecue.

The synagogue had grown to include over sixty-five families and to host a variety of cultural events. They had brought the Israeli Scouts to perform during the height of the war in Lebanon in 2006 and every year since then. They taught classes on Judaism at the local schools and libraries. The worked with interfaith groups and reached out to new arrivals in town. The local Hindu Association even used the synagogue for its meetings twice a month. By creating a community center, they demonstrated the value that participation in Jewish life could have. Newcomers who had not been involved with the Jewish community in their hometowns were signing up in droves, and the existence of Etz Chaim helped Wal-Mart with recruitment, the synagogue's leadership believed. "We are making Bentonville more appealing to a greater variety of people," Tom explained.

Was it the free latkes? The parties? Or was it something deeper that happens to people when they are far from home, a desire for the familiar that they never knew they had, a desire to pass on to their children something that they hadn't realized was important to them. If this was the case, then perhaps the best thing for organized Judaism in America would be to split Jews up, scatter them in isolated areas in small groups where they would have to fend for themselves. Would they learn how to cure their own salmon, make their own bagels? Would they teach themselves Hebrew? Perhaps a more realistic solution would be to get rid of the professional Jews, make everyone do it themselves the way the Bentonville community had. Take away the two-thousand-seat synagogues with their overly structured liturgy and let spontaneity and the DIY attitude of the American heartland take over. Would it breathe fresh life into American Judaism?

Doubtful. It would probably just lead to more young people knowing as much Hebrew as I do. Zilch. But what would happen if everyone thought like this new and growing community? What would happen if everyone thought about the benefits being part of a community could have, and worked to build one for themselves? These people are Jews because they get something out of it. The converts are converting because they see a reason to be Jewish. It was a question with which I had never seriously engaged before. I had inherited this label, Jewish, and had never gotten much from it. I'd never put much into it either. The community in Bentonville was actively trying to answer the question I had never thought to ask: Why be Jewish at all?

I thought again about Rabbi Jack's sermon, which brought to mind a quote from Theodor Herzl, the father of modern Zionism: "If you will it, it is no dream." He was talking about a Jewish state, but his aphorism was just as relevant here in rural America. These people had found themselves in the Bible Belt, separated from the cultural norms and institutions they had grown to take for granted, and instead of fading away, disappearing into the dominant community, they dreamed up a new community and willed it into being, not as outsiders, but as a piece of Bentonville, a part of the place itself that would endure even after these specific Jews left. As long as the Wal-Mart empire existed, the community would continue to exist.

I thought again of the Jews in Burma, how they nearly came to an end when the sun finally set on the British Empire. Would this community indeed fade if the retail economy faded? Hadn't the community in El Dorado thought of itself as everlasting at one point, only to find its Torah now in Bentonville, its children scattered to the wind? Hadn't my great-grandfather dreamed that Jewish life in Berkley, Virginia, would always endure? As this community in Bentonville was emerging, why did I find myself already thinking about its demise?

I arrived at Mark Levine's the following afternoon to get a ride with him and his wife, Karen, out to Mendel's Hanukkah party. He'd lived in Bentonville for thirteen years. Like Robyn Douglass, he too came from Long Island. Though he'd mostly left his accent behind, he still had his Jets jersey, and he wore it proudly. He echoed what the others said about the effect of this community on their faith.

"I've never been more Jewish than when I moved to Arkansas. This place didn't really feel like home until we opened the synagogue." His son, Evan, was the first to have a bris in Bentonville. I remembered reading about the curiosity of non-Jews in my grandmother's Virginia town when the first Jewish wedding took place. I could only imagine the curiosity of the Gentile citizens of Bentonville when the town had its first ritual circumcision. "It was catered by Katz's deli in New York," Mark laughed. "Some things you can't give up."

While we drove to the bowling alley in Fayetteville, Mark and Karen talked about their unexpected friendship with the Chabad rabbi, about Mark's work with the Boys and Girls Club, his concern about diversity issues for the Muslim and Hindu children in the area, and his concern for the one thing the community lacked: a cemetery.

"That's one thing we're still figuring out: what to do when Jews die here." Mark too was thinking about demise.

An incongruous sight welcomed us to the bowling alley. A white van with a menorah on the roof sat in the parking lot and a sign on the door invited the Chanukah Bowl participants to get their shoes from the counter and proceed to the lanes at the far end. There seemed to be some sort of office Christmas party happening at the other end. When we walked in, I was startled to see men in yarmulkes standing around and little Orthodox children running to and fro. Women in long skirts bustled after them. There were other Jews who blended in, of course, but these Orthodox Jews made no effort to blend. They were the first I'd seen in Arkansas who dressed so traditionally. Holding court over it all was Rabbi Greisman, who stood next to a menorah made out of bowling pins, smiling and urging people to eat some of the snacks. He had the unmistakable accent of a Brooklyn rabbi, and from beneath his thick beard shown a bright, youthful face. The glint in his eyes suggested that this was a religious man for whom the work of Jewish outreach was not just a professional commitment but a wellspring of joy. The crash of bowling balls resounded in the air as Rabbi Greisman cheerfully asked if anyone would like to fulfill the mitzvah of tefillin.

I said I would. Having made an *aliyah* at the Torah the day before, I figured I might as well step in and complete this ritual too. Twenty-four hours in rural Arkansas and I was fulfilling two holy commandments of the Torah, two mitzvoth, three if you considered the fact that I skipped the pork ribs the night before.

Tefillin are a pair of black leather boxes with scrolls inside them containing biblical verses about God's redemption of the Jewish people from bondage in Egypt. They look a little like bondage gear, in fact, and there is a complicated method for wearing them, one on the head and the other on the arm. They are held in place by leather straps. The straps on the head rest above the ears and hang down the back of the neck. The straps on the arm are wrapped tightly with precise positioning all the way from the bicep to the fingers. Scholars of Chinese medicine have argued that the placement of these boxes and the tying of these straps reflect an awareness of acupuncture points and help the flow of mental energies. Jewish thought, Rabbi Greisman explained, asserts that the tefillin were commanded by the Torah in the book of Deuteronomy, where the Hebrews are instructed to "lay these words of mine in your heart and in your soul; and you shall bind them for a sign upon your arm, and they shall be as frontlets between your eyes."

I wasn't sure what frontlets were, but the rabbi gently placed the leather box on my head with the strap hanging behind my neck. I put on a yarmulke. The rabbi told me to repeat after him, and word by word he guided me through the blessings as he placed the other box on my arm and wrapped the straps around my bicep, forearm, hand, and fingers. I continued to parrot him, not knowing what I was saying, but fixing on his sparkling blue eyes. I could feel my pulse beating against the leather straps.

At first I was acutely aware of the people at the office Christmas party looking over and staring. A fat lady in a pink shirt even pointed. I imagined I looked strange to them. I had a black box sticking a few inches off of my forehead and leather straps wrapped around my arm and hand, and I was chanting. Their interest faded quickly, though, and I could hear their cheers as one of their party nailed a spare. After a moment I gave in to the rabbi's intense stare, the feeling of pressure on my forehead and fingers, the strange bowling alley mysticism of it all. I couldn't say why, but for a moment I did truly feel centered.

I looked strange and I felt strange, but why shouldn't I? The unfamiliar sensations forced me out of my normal modes of thought and heightened my awareness of the moment and of the people around me. Didn't yoga do the same thing? Didn't yoga look pretty strange too? Tefillin were ancient Jewish spiritual technology, as yoga was ancient Indian spiritual technology. Judaism, I suddenly felt, was not just a religion of the book. It was physical. That was why the Orthodox rocked and bowed and nodded when they prayed. The mind and body were one, and the prayers were physical as well as mental. The strangeness of the sensation was deliberate. It carved out this moment as different from all the other moments of the day and all the other meaningless physical activities a person does. This was a physical activity, odd, and some might say point-less, that became magical by its very strangeness.

Rabbi Griesman explained it to me: "When you put on tefillin, you are connecting your head, your heart, and your hand, all with one intent. You are binding them to each other and yourself to God. You are con-necting to the divine by fulfilling this commandment, and even if you don't think you are, you are still centering yourself by performing this mitzvah. It can't hurt, right?" He smiled broadly. It would be a sad day, almost a year later, when his friend and colleague the Chabad emissary in Mumbai, India, was tortured and murdered in one of the most shock-ing rampages in the city's history. Watching the violence on the news, I couldn't help but think of Mendel's unassuming kindness when he taught me this ritual.

"That your first time?" a man asked me when I took off the tefillin and Rabbi Griesman moved on to mingle with the other guests. No one else who wanted to do the tefillin needed the rabbi's guidance. Mark picked up the straps and started tying them on. I turned to talk to the man who'd asked the question. He looked perhaps more out of place than the black-clad rabbi.

His name was Yossi. He had a white Santa Claus beard and shocking blue eyes. He was dressed like everyone else in the bowling alley—blue jeans, a sweater—though he wore a knitted yarmulke, the kind I'd seen Orthodox settlers in the West Bank wear on the news. He explained that he was indeed one of those settlers, and that his kippah— "That's the Hebrew word," he told me, echoing the woman from the Wal-Mart Museum—came from the West Bank, though he called it Judea and Sa-maria. He'd been a cop in Arkansas and had, long ago, been assigned to the security detail of the notorious Rabbi Meir Kahane, founder of the Jewish Defense League ("Every Jew a .22" was their catch phrase) and the racist Kach Party in Israel, which has since been labeled a terrorist organization. Yossi became enamored with the rabbi's teachings and militant Jewish ideology and eventually moved from Arkansas to a settlement in the West Bank, where he applied his military and police training to security work and, as he proudly declared, "fucking with so-called Palestinians." He'd come back to Arkansas to visit his sick mother who was, he said, "nastier than a bucket of rattlesnakes."

He saw Israel as the natural home for all the Jewish people and was saddened to hear I didn't know my Hebrew name. He hoped I would continue to study and eventually visit the Promised Land. He believed in the "Greater Israel" idea, which did not recognize any Palestinian claims to the lands of the Bible or even acknowledge that Palestinians were a real people.

"They're just Arabs," he said. "Arabs who hate Jews. In fact, they're the worst of the Arabs. They live like dogs, you know. I keep waiting for one to mess with me. I drive around with my window open and a gun in my hand, just hoping one will throw a rock at me. This one kid almost did, but I made the mistake of making eye contact—never do that if you need to shoot someone, by the way—and the kid dropped his stone and ran. I haven't killed anyone since the seventies."

He was genuinely sad about it. I couldn't believe what I was hearing. The kindly rabbi was just a few feet away. Families surrounded us, laughing and bowling. We were munching on potato pancakes. I had just had a transformative weekend with a Jewish community, and now here I was with the worst sort of racist, redneck, religious fanatic I could imagine as he cheerfully told me about wanting to kill Arabs and invited me to visit his settlement. In his eyes, we were indeed one people, or, with the right guidance, I could become one of his people. Being Jewish, I was at least part of the way there.

"But you've got to learn your Hebrew name," he said, smiling. Then he wandered off to tell some boys playing dreidel how they used to bet on it in the army. The boys looked at him with skepticism and a bit of reverence. He was a fixture at these events. I tried to focus on something else, anything other than the anger his comments provoked in me.

"A good man," Rabbi Greisman told me, seeing me standing alone again. "Though I wish he wouldn't say so much of that violence stuff."

I changed the subject and asked him what it was like for him to live out here in northwest Arkansas.

"It's been great," he said. "My first month here, it was Shabbat and there was some problem with my daughter. I needed to turn the light on, so I went over to my neighbor. I was worried. I thought, What am I going to do? I'm going to have to explain the whole Shabbat thing to him and see if he'll turn the light on for me, and he'll probably be wondering what the heck this strange-looking neighbor is doing. So I go to his door and he says, 'Shalom!' So I smile and start to explain what I need and he interrupts me. 'You need me to turn on your light because it's Shabbos, right?' I was shocked! How did he know? He told me he had a Jewish roommate in college. Generally, everyone out here has been friendly. It's hard to get kosher food and that sort of thing, but the people are really wonderful. And I wouldn't want to be doing any other work than this."

"Stay close to the rabbi," Yossi interrupted. "You might learn something!"

I ended up staying near Mark and his son for the rest of the evening, and never did touch a bowling ball. I wasn't eager to chat with Yossi again, though I would have liked to talk more to the rabbi. But he was busy playing the host, and had his own children to look after. I watched the others bowl. I ate some more of the latkes and the cold salads. I did, at one point, talk to Yossi again, this time about Israeli wine, which had fewer political or moral implications. Eventually I left with Mark and his family and went out for dinner—Chinese food, of course—and then packed to leave Arkansas the next morning.

I'd had some moving religious experiences in Arkansas, and I'd seen the transformative power of building a community. In Bentonville they were looking toward the future with great optimism, building it up as if there would always be a Jewish presence there, which it seemed there might well be. But my interaction with Yossi left me troubled. It brought that elephant back into the room—Zionism—and all the messy contradictions it evoked for me. I knew I would have to grapple with Israel and its policies before my journey was done, but I hadn't imagined it coming up so soon. I also knew I didn't want to be considered of the same people as Yossi's people. I wanted to be as far from his ideology as I could. Yet there was something that united us—I couldn't deny the thousands of years of history that tied us to each other. In fact, he had more in common with the zealous Maccabees of the Hanukkah story than I did. I was far more like the Jewish assimilators of that tale, eager to be part of the dominant culture. But both of us were part of that mixed multitude of the Jewish people, those historical nomads, scattered again and again, and, if community has its benefits, it also has its dark side. Because to be an "us" is to create a "them." For most of Bentonville's Jews, that dynamic is a source of creativity and inspiration. They use differences to make their lives and their community richer. Their success is Bentonville's success, and, unlike Yossi's particular brand of Judaism, theirs makes room for a neighbor. Both are answers to the question of what it means to be a Jew, and I was beginning to see what kind of Jew I might want to be.

four

Rebirth:
The Jewish Community of New Orleans

I will remember my covenant which is between me and you and every living creature of all flesh; and the waters shall never again become a flood to destroy all flesh.
——GENESIS 9:15

I TOOK A DRIVE THROUGH the Gentilly neighborhood of New Orleans the day after I arrived from Bentonville. I saw gaping doorways and dark windows on block after block of abandoned homes. After the Lower Ninth Ward, Gentilly suffered the worst damage from the levee break caused by Hurricane Katrina in the summer of 2005. Two and half years later, entire blocks of residents still hadn't returned. Cryptic graffiti on the sides of the Gentilly houses—big blue Xs surrounded by lines and numbers—indicated that they'd been searched and whether any bodies had been found. "Dead dog inside" needed no interpretation. Two and half years later, and no one had repainted.

My guide through the devastation was Ina Davis, president of the New Orleans chapter of the National Council of Jewish Women, a cheerful redhead and the mother of three boys. She'd met my mother at a convention some months earlier and, in true New Orleans fashion, invited me to stay with her in the city. While we drove, she happily expounded on the unique charm of the Big Easy, but as we passed each abandoned house her mood darkened. Every bit of graffiti reminded her of what was lost, and every empty house made her think of her city the way it was before. When we'd pass a house with the lights on and a generator running out front, she'd shake her head.

"Imagine living out here, all alone," she said. "No city services, no schools nearby. It's terrible. You wouldn't believe this street when we first came back. It was just piled with garbage. There were refrigerators all along the median, lines of them all filled with mold. The smell was terrible."

After an hour of driving around, she was near tears. It was the kind of drive that only served to stir bad memories. The landscape itself battered anyone who looked too long at it. "The emotional damage from the storm hasn't really been addressed," Ina said. "There are so many needs, how do you meet them all?" She wiped her eyes and sighed. "C'est levee, as we've taken to saying." She laughed, because what else could you do? We cruised past vacant lots, more Xs and slashes, more high-water marks on the sides of houses.

We hadn't even been down to the Lower Ninth Ward yet, where the storm had claimed most of its victims. Ina dropped me off in the Garden District, an upscale neighborhood of stately mansions and trendy shops, overflowing with flora. The neighborhood had not been irreparably damaged by the storm, and life seemed relatively normal on its streets. There were some contractors doing renovation work, but otherwise things were quiet. A steady stream of staff from the nearby Touro Infirmary, named for the wealthy Jewish merchant Judah Touro, flowed in and out of the restaurants and sandwich shops.

That day, for the first time since Katrina, the streetcar had begun rumbling along Saint Charles Avenue again. People were still surprised to see it, and turned their heads to watch it as it passed. I hopped on it to ride a few stops to Touro Synagogue, the largest Reform synagogue in the city. It too was named for Judah Touro. He had been one of New Orleans's biggest philanthropists. Founded in 1828, Touro was the first synagogue in the United States established outside the thirteen colonies. It had arrived at its current upscale location in 1909, when the city's Jewish population started to expand beyond the French Quarter in significant numbers. Touro was also the first synagogue in the city to hold services after Katrina. I went inside to meet the young rabbi, Andrew Busch, who had taken leadership of the congregation just two months before the hurricane hit.

"It was not the job I was expecting to have," he said. The top of his head was bald and, I noticed, slightly red, perhaps from sunburn. It made me think of him as someone who spent a lot of time outside. "But we started rebuilding from day one. We were the primary information source many people had in the evacuation and now for returns. We are actually back to ninety percent of our pre-Katrina membership: five hundred and fifty-five families. We've had seventy new ones since the storm. We are a fairly young congregation, which helps. Many of the older people won't return to New Orleans. Though we do have one seventh-generation member."

I'd come to New Orleans from Bentonville with the idea of contrasting a brand-new community living in a thriving area with an old community recovering from a disaster. I'd heard there were miraculous efforts going on within the Jewish community and that it was involved in a variety of interfaith initiatives. Its program designed to encourage young Jews to move to New Orleans had also garnered some national media attention. I wanted to see the situation for myself.

College students were spending their winter, spring, and summer vacations helping to rebuild. The United Jewish Communities and college Hillel organizations sent groups down to gut homes and construct community centers. Hundreds more volunteers came on their own and just started working. A friend of mine from college, Mark Weiner, had come down and set up makeshift emergency communities in the Lower Ninth Ward. He was Jewish, but hadn't come as part of any organized Jewish effort. He just wanted to help, to fill in the gaps where the government had so completely failed. His organization, simply named Emergency Communities, provided children in the Lower Ninth Ward with activities, gave parents a chance to do laundry, served hot meals to familes—basically did whatever was needed. He had, however, started to wind down their operations.

"We have plenty of volunteers. Everyone wants to come down here. But what we need now are specialists: electricians, plumbers, and such. Everyone has goodwill, but now we need a certain knowledge base. There are some things we just can't do with good intentions. There are still so few services on the block I live on."

"I feel like [we're in] Buenos Ares or Kiev sometimes," Rabbi Busch said. "All these aid missions coming down to help us, to see what we need. I suppose there is also that kibbutz aspect of it . . . young people coming to work here because it gives them a sense of purpose, of meaning." The kibbutz is a form of Jewish community—one based on the idea of social and economic equality—that started in the early twentieth century in Israel. They had been essentially rural communities throughout their history, though in recent years the notion of the urban kibbutz has become popular.

"Katrina is our main reality, but it has not shaped who we want to be," the rabbi continued. "It has increased the pastoral need, certainly. There is a lot of trauma counseling, financial assistance, that sort of thing. We provide stability in a very unstable environment. No one knows what the future holds in terms of the economy here, in terms of who will come back, what will happen to this city. What about another storm? Crime? Schools? People need to feel grounded, and we can provide that. We have an amazingly high rate of affiliation. Through the Newcomers program we give free synagogue memberships. We are generally optimistic about the future."

In Bentonville, I saw one constant of Jewish history playing out: a community of migrants forming around economic opportunity, trying to build institutions that would outlast them. In New Orleans, I saw other themes in action: Jews dealing with disaster, saving their neighbors and traditions from destruction, and, of course, returning from exile.

IN OTHER PARTS OF THE COUNTRY, there is a sharp divide between the liberal strains of Judaism and the Orthodox. The Orthodox tend to think of liberal Judaism as overly permissive and overly assimilated—a gateway right out of Jewish life. They do not respect conversions performed by any rabbis but their own, and they tend to look down on the secularism rampant in the Jewish community. Liberal Jews, especially secular ones, generally see the Orthodox as old-fashioned, stuck in outmoded ways of thinking, rigid, and fanatic in their beliefs. There are exceptions to this, but for the most part there is a deep level of misunderstanding, mistrust, and disdain between the Orthodox and the rest of the Jewish community. Not so, it seemed, in New Orleans.

I remembered a picture from the news when the levees broke: a bearded man in a yellow Emergency Responder vest carrying a Torah from a synagogue while wading through waist-deep water. Sadly, the Orthodox synagogue was destroyed by the storm and the heroic rescue of the Torah was for naught. They had to bury it, as is the custom when a Torah is irreparably damaged. Having no place to worship when they returned to the city, the Orthodox community used the liberal Touro Synagogue for its first bar mitzvah after the storm.

"We would have let them do that before the storm too," said Mark

Rubenstein, the executive director of Touro. "Of course, there wasn't a need then."

What I found was a community eager to heal their wounds and their city, working not only with each other, but with other religious and civic organizations as well. Touro had a partnership with an African-American mosque in the Treme neighborhood. They held food and clothing drives together, learned about each other's customs, and prayed in each other's houses of worship. The Jews had been in the city long enough that they were not a community apart; they were central to the life of the city.

Rabbi Busch, I learned, was leaving New Orleans to be closer to his family in Baltimore, where he would be taking over the synagogue at which I'd had my bar mitzvah. We chatted for a while about what he could expect, and I revealed my total ignorance of Jewish life in the city where I grew up. He was excited about the move, though he would miss the city he'd served during its most trying time. There was no way to go through what this community had gone through, he explained, without feeling a sense of loss at leaving. There was still much work to be done.

AFTER MY DISCUSSION WITH THE RABBI, I went to see if I could get a sense of the history of New Orleans's Jews from the resident expert, Catherine Cahn, the archivist at Touro Infirmary and author of a book about Jewish New Orleans.

"My great-great-grandfather came from Alsace in 1832. He wanted to get ahead, and things were not so good for the Jews in Alsace at the time. He spoke French, so he came to New Orleans. There wasn't a Jewish ghetto in the city and he settled on Esplanade Avenue at the edge of the French Quarter." Cathy had red hair and stormy green eyes, typical of Alsatians. "We New Orleans Jews are like the Japanese," she told me. "We eat rice and worship our ancestors."

Jewish history in New Orleans goes back to 1757, when a businessman named Isaac Monsanto settled there in spite of Louis XIV's Code Noir, which banned Jews from settling in the French colonial city. "This is part of New Orleans' dual history of tolerance and corruption," Cathy said, laughing. "The governor of the colony took a liking to young Monsanto and was curious about him. He also probably took a bribe."

When the Spanish took control of New Orleans from the French, times became hard for the lonely Jewish merchant, and he lost his fortune. It would be nearly fifty years before a Jewish presence returned to the city, with Judah Touro's arrival from New England after the Louisiana Purchase. He built his fortune here and, like many of the prominent Jewish businessmen of the city, felt no need to connect with the religious aspects of Judaism.

As Cathy explained it, "In New Orleans, religious indifference was the norm, and that these men settled here shows they didn't have much interest in finding a strong Jewish community. Because of the lack of anti-Semitism, the Jews felt no need to band together."

There were a few religious Jews who'd come from Eastern Europe, and they did establish a synagogue in 1828. However, in keeping with the cosmopolitan reality of nineteenth-century New Orleans, the Articles of Incorporation for that synagogue stated that no Jewish child would be excluded because of his mother. This flew in the face of the matrilineal tradition of Judaism and acknowledged the widespread phenomenon of intermarriage that continues to this day.

Mark Rubenstein, from Touro Synagogue, had even married a non-Jew, though she eventually converted, and it was her involvement that drew him into the Jewish community. Her interest set off his participation in organized Jewish life, though he had always been involved in one important aspect of the city's culture. Aside from overseeing the administration of Touro Synagogue, he was vice president of the Krewe of Orpheus, one of the newer Mardi Gras krewes—private carnival organizations—which puts on a large parade on the Monday before Fat

Tuesday. It was founded in 1993 by Harry Connick Jr., and its parade is one of the most popular parades in town.

"In general," Cathy explained, "Jews were excluded from the four society Mardi Gras balls, which was where debutantes were presented—Momas, Komas, Proteus, and Rex—though Rex has long had a certain number of Jewish members who went to the balls and rode on the floats. Like everything in New Orleans, there are the official rules and there's what really happens. The rules bend."

Though Carnival is technically a Catholic festival, the Jewish community found ways to participate. In older generations it was done by quietly breaking the rules, but the newer krewes—Orpheus and the Krewe de Vieux, for example—have never had policies of exclusion. The parades are about the party, not the faith, and New Orleans loves to party. Ina Davis gave me an excited tour of her closet, showing off the different costumes she and her husband had worn—the bright pink bowling outfit, the Elvis costumes, the lamp shades—and this year's work in progress, an intricately beaded pirate's costume.

The Krewe de Vieux is made up of a lot of miniature krewes, each of which makes its own float. One krewe that has gained notoriety is the Krewe du Jieux, which was founded in 1996 by L. J. Goldstein. Jewish revelers dress as whatever Jewish stereotype they can make into a costume, play a sort of Yiddish-flavored jazz, and throw decorated stale bagels into the crowd instead of beads. They take what history there is of Jewish exclusion and turn it on its head. They would not be kept out of the party.

"One year, I was elected King of the Krewe du Jieux," Hugo Kahn, a prominent Jewish businessman and philanthropist, told me when we met for breakfast in his beautiful home on the water. "I had a bar mitzvah that day, so I rushed home to get out of my suit and put on a Blues Brothers outfit and get to the float and toss some bagels."

I tried to picture him dressed as a Blues Brother. He was an older man with a thin neck and wisps of gray hair. He had a prominent nose. Sitting amid the art and Judaica in his large home, he looked like a serious businessman. But like all good serious businessmen in New Orleans, he loved to party. Being successful, to him, did not mean he couldn't have fun. That wouldn't be very much in the spirit of the city, after all. The theme of the parade that year had been "Souled Down the River," fitting for Mr. Kahn, who had been president of the Krauss Department Store for decades, until it closed because of the influx of the big-box stores, like Wal-Mart.

After Katrina, he and his wife were some of the first people to move back to this upscale neighborhood, just around the corner from Mayor Ray Nagin's house. The Kahns had had four feet of water in their house, but they also had the means to repair it quickly. They'd been encouraging friends to come back, but Hugo explained that many just would not. They couldn't handle the uncertainty of life in New Orleans, the lack of services, and the ever-present threat of another storm. "We lost a lot of friends, our whole inner circle."

Hugo and his brother had escaped from Germany in 1939 and eventually settled in Nebraska. He came to New Orleans to work for the Krauss Department Store.

"After we moved to New Orleans, my father would walk around saying, 'Next year in Omaha' instead of 'Next year in Jerusalem,'" Hugo said, laughing. "But I loved it here. Walking around this city, I can't go two feet without someone shouting out, 'Hey, Mr. Kahn!' The relationships are what make this place special. The African-American community were my customers and employees, and it became my duty to integrate the department store. It gave me an opportunity to put what I believe are Jewish principles into action."

"What principles are those?"

"Fairness. Equality. Justice," he answered without hesitation. "These values are central to who I am and, I think, to who we are as a community. Do you know *Ayeka*? It's Hebrew. It's the question God asks Adam, Abraham, Moses. 'Where are you?' That's the question we have to ask. Where are we, what are we doing with our time? Since the storm, the community has really come together to help, not just each other but the city at large. It's a good question for you to remember while you're traveling. *Ayeka*? . . . Where are you?"

Ayeka? Where are you? It's not a question God needed to repeat after he asked it. Obviously, he knew where Adam was. But Adam, having sinned, needed to be asked. Though the answer he gives, "I heard your voice in the garden, and I was afraid, because I was naked; and so I hid myself," does not admit to his sin. It admits to his shame at being revealed. The question that drives Hugo, the question God wants me to ask myself—*Where are you?*—requires me to take an honest inventory of myself, with no excuses, to look around and see what I have done, see where I really am. What am I doing with the time I have been given? Answering these questions, living up to the questioning, has been the driving force behind why so many Jews came to serve in New Orleans after Katrina hit. *Hineini*, I am here, is one answer. It's the one that both Abraham and Moses give when God asks, *Ayeka*? It's a lot more than an ancient GPS device. It's a way of saying, "I'm ready to serve. I am fully present in this moment."

Perhaps that's what my uncle Stephen meant when he said that telling the story of Berkley, Virginia's Jews was his way of saying *Hineini*. He was ready to embrace the community's story, just he was ready to be embraced by the community. These two statements summarize a kind of spiritual presence and engagement that run through Judaism, a constant inventory of one's physical, intellectual, and spiritual whereabouts.

THE DAY AFTER MY VISIT TO the synagogue and my meeting with Hugo Kahn, I took a long stroll among the fortune-tellers, art galleries, bars, and touts in the French Quarter. There was even a Judaica shop, but it was closed. I had a beignet at Café du Monde, inhaling my weight in powdered sugar, and then I took a cab out to Metarie, where I was scheduled to meet with the man responsible for organized Judaism's response to the storm and recovery from the destruction it left behind.

The drive took me past the notorious David Duke's favorite bar, and the most incongruous of places in Louisiana: Kosher Cajun, a New York–style deli serving corned beef and pickles as well as kosher "shrimp" po'boys. I'd been told that a Friday afternoon at Kosher Cajun deli saw much of Jewish New Orleans pass through its doors, and I intended to spend some time there after my meeting was finished and before they closed for the Sabbath.

A little over a year earlier, the Jewish Federation of Greater New Orleans, an umbrella organization for the city's Jewish organizations, had hired Michael Weil to be its executive director. Weil had previously worked with the Israeli government on absorption programs for immigrants from the former Soviet Union, who numbered over a million. He'd been hired to help revitalize the Jewish community in New Orleans and lead their recovery efforts, which was the just the type of job for which he had spent years preparing.

"The work here is great and very hands-on, which is what I'd wanted after years in a think tank in Jerusalem. It's important that we as Jewish people deal with disasters properly," he told me, speaking rapidly. Conversation with Michael was jolting. Most of the people I'd met in New Orleans spoke slowly and let their thoughts wander. Michael spoke like lightning and remained fixed on his message. He'd talked to a lot of journalists and donors and knew how to keep control of a conversation. "Patterns that disasters follow are very similar no matter the disaster. The recovery and renewal patterns are the same. Which begs the question, perhaps, why New Orleans?"

I hadn't thought to ask him that, but he kept going, without pause. It was a good question and I'm glad he asked it of himself.

"There are plenty of disasters, after all, and from a Jewish perspective New Orleans is numerically insignificant, but it is one of the most important communities, historically speaking, in terms of Jewish immigration. The community has been tied into civic institutions, whether it be the Museum of Fine Art or Touro hospital or the Newman School, which was a Jewish orphanage; Jews have always been very central to the city. Jews create new communities all the time because we're very mobile; we go where opportunity is, and we discard old communities all the time. But we need to keep this one because it is so vital to the city. That's why we started the Newcomers program. Most of the those who are coming are pioneers, idealists who want to be part of history, who are committed to ideas of social justice and *tikkun olam*—healing the world. Social justice and activism are great motivating factors, especially among marginalized Jews who aren't members of other organizations. We can appeal to them in ways that establishment Judaism cannot. This is where you come if you really want to build a city and create history. We've had a good response so far. We're ahead of most other groups in the city in terms of recovering pre-Katrina levels. Why? Because we've had three thousand years of persecutions, disasters, and crises. We know how to come back."

I couldn't help but draw parallels between what Michael Weil was saying and twentieth-century Zionism, when Jews from all over the world, battered and traumatized by the Holocaust and inspired by a new sense of pride, came pouring into Palestine to work the land on a kibbutz, or serve in the military, or build new institutions, to create a nation from the desert. The spirit was the same, but in New Orleans there were none of the politics or the history that so plagued the Holy Land, no violent nationalism or spirit of exclusion that I could see. Jews had strong ties to their neighbors and worked with them to rebuild.

In parts of America, there is still great mistrust between the Jewish and African-American communities, as I'd been reminded by the drunken library patron who'd challenged me to a duel a year earlier, but, as Mark Rubenstein pointed out to me, "someone whose home was rebuilt by Jewish volunteers might have a different opinion of Jewish people." Michael Weil agreed with the idea that interfaith outreach was important both for the success of the reconstruction effort and for the recruitment effort. The young people moving to New Orleans wanted to serve and would not be content with any kind of Jewish isolationism. People who were deeply committed to Jewish tribalism, wanting to serve only Jews, wouldn't be the type of people to move to New Orleans.

"Even though we are still at thirty percent fewer people than before the storm, attendance at meetings and events hasn't dropped," he said. "Except during Saints games. There is only so much the Jewish community can ask of a good New Orleans citizen. The Saints will always take precedence." He laughed, but it was true. Everyone I wanted to meet that weekend avoided scheduling on Sunday with the simple, unapologetic statement "The Saints are playing."

With little more to say, the meeting ended. Michael was a busy man, with a city to rebuild and over two hundred inquiries from young Jews interested in making the move to attend to. He only had one staff member dedicated to the Newcomers program and could not spend any more time answering my questions. "Next week we'll be celebrating two hundred and fifty years since the first Jew arrived in the city," he added, and showed me the door.

THE JEWS OF NEW ORLEANS WERE certainly of New Orleans. They liked their parties, their Saints, and their Cajun food. I was eager to get a taste of that last piece of Jewish life. It took me about ten minutes to walk from the community center where I'd met Michael back to the Kosher Cajun deli. Immediately on entering, I was transported to the Lower East Side. There were Orthodox Jews in black hats, young men in yarmulkes eating knishes, and all kinds of Hanukkah paraphernalia for sale. I ordered a "shrimp" po'boy, which was made from white fish shaped like a shrimp and then fried. It was delicious, and, as I sat listening to two old men at the next table talk about how one of them got the nickname "Bobby" when his name wasn't even Robert—it had something to do with World War II—a young man with long curls, the scruffy beginnings of a beard, and a black fedora came up to me.

"Shalom, shalom," he said. "You Jewish?" That question again.

"Yes, I am."

"You a student?"

"No," I explained, "just visiting."

"You have a place to spend Shabbat?"

He didn't even know my name yet, and he was inviting me to his house. This was the way of the Chabad movement, as Mendel had shown me in Bentonville. This young man was a Shluchim just like Mendel, posted to serve the Jews of Metarie; New Orleans proper had its own Chabad emissaries. It turned out that this young man knew Mendel.

"A good man, lovely family," he said. "Well, you should come see us if you have the time. We have a minyan every day." With that, he said his good-byes, picked up the food he'd been sent for, and rushed out to make it home for the candle lighting. The deli was getting ready to shut down for the day, so I took the opportunity to talk to Joel Brown, its owner.

Joel and his wife, Natalie, founded the Kosher Cajun deli in 1987. It was the only kosher restaurant in the New Orleans area, and seemed to be doing well with the monopoly, meeting the needs of the community and prospering. Kosher food was hard to come by in New Orleans before they opened, and over the years they'd become the go-to people for observant Jewish travelers in the area. Joel told me that before the storm their business was split fifty-fifty between Jews and non-Jews, but with the decline of the community's numbers since Katrina, their customers were now about 75 percent non-Jews.

"We're more of a neighborhood restaurant and grocery, but I'd love to see more of the catering come back and more of the Jewish community return. I came back as soon as I could after the storm. My family fled to Memphis when Katrina hit. Our dog died on the journey, which was pretty upsetting for all of us, but the Jewish schools in Memphis took in our children and the Jewish community took care of us in remarkable ways. I am still in awe of their generosity. Of course, I wanted to come home. When I got back, I saw my house had taken about seven inches of water. When we came in here, back to the business, the smell was terrible. Everything had rotted in the heat and the floodwater. My staff wanted to get back to work, and I wanted to rebuild, so I came back alone, leaving my family in Memphis, and worked to clean and repair and rebuild. It was hard to live here without much for city services, without my family, but it was worth it. It was an example for the community. We've got more and more Jewish people coming to take advantage of the opportunity, the clean slate that this city now presents, with Israeli visitors and Tulane students and newcomers looking for spiritual connection that seek us out. We provide kosher food, but also community. I'm very proud that we are up and running again. I also serve as the *gabbi*—the secretary—for the Chabad house in Metarie."

Looking around the deli, you couldn't tell that they had been flooded. The black-and-white–checked floor was pristine, the chairs and tables sparkling and new. The Friday afternoon rush was winding down. Pickup trucks barreled into the lot, men and women jumping out to load up on supplies, to chat with Joel and his staff, and then to peel out again, racing the sunset. The staff started shutting down the store at three, and I called a cab.

My Shabbat evening wouldn't be spent at synagogue on this Friday. I'd made an appointment with Rafiq Nu'Mann, the imam of the mosque in Treme that worked with Touro Synagogue. All the Jewish leaders I'd met had spoken about outreach and service as their mission, and I couldn't imagine a better activity for a Friday night than meeting with a holy man from the Muslim faith to hear his perspective on the Jewish community. It took the cab about an hour to pick me up. Kosher Cajun was not in an area frequented by people without cars. Joel was slightly concerned that waiting for me to get picked up would make him late for Shabbat, but he was still a southern gentleman and would not abandon a stranger to wait alone on the street. He lingered until the taxi came, wished me a good *Shabbos,* and rushed to his car.

My cab driver, curious why I'd want to go from the kosher place straight to a mosque, had his own views to share on the idea of religion. In Yiddish literature, the wagon driver—*baal agallah* in Hebrew—plays an important role. Rabbi Irwin Kula notes that in mystical Jewish litera-ture, the person who ferries people from town to town is "almost always Elijah," the harbinger of the messiah. So I always made a conscious effort to engage with those who took me from town to town, place to place, nation to nation. I'd been taught that it was bad journalism to quote cabdrivers, or to swallow what they said without a big grain of salt, but taking the *baal agallah* concept to heart, I learned a great deal.

The cabdriver had grown up in Louisiana and been raised a Jeho-vah's Witness, but he'd since left all organized religion behind.

"Religions are all corrupt. Ain't none of them true," he said. "These so-called Jews, for example, they're not the descendants of Abraham, and they're not of the Tribes of Israel. They aren't the chosen people really; they've just stolen the mantle of Abraham. It's like Catholics and Mus-lims, and just about everyone else. They all corrupt fools. I'm sorry I'm not educated, so I can't articulate what I'm trying to say. I don't meant to offend."

I told him he was doing fine. I was curious why he thought they were all corrupt and why he thought the Jews weren't really Jews.

"It's genetic. It's just a fact. There's no why to it. There were the Israelites and then these people who came from Europe and took on the whole Jewish thing so they could benefit, but they aren't really the descendents of Abraham. They ain't from the Holy Land even. How else would they look like they do, and not like, you know, the Arabs? They took the Arabs' land by pretending to be Jews, you know, the Zionists, and they brought God's wrath onto the world for doing it. The Catholics too. Pretending to have the word of Christ and then doing all that idol worship and stealing and molestation . . . They brought the wrath too . . . And Muslim terrorists . . . It's all part of it . . . A reckoning will come . . . You'll see."

He'd drifted into some old anti-Semitic traps before going off on just about everyone else in the world, but I wanted to hear more. He was one of the first people on my journey to speak not only openly but angrily about religion. I was, in a way, thrilled by it. I knew there was anger out there, anger toward religion in general and anger, however misguided or delusional, toward Jews specifically, for Israel's crimes and for whatever other crimes could be attached to them. I hadn't faced much anti-Jewish thought yet, so I wanted to know more about what was fueling it. Sadly, all he could muster was vague nonsense about the Rapture and corrupt Catholic priests.

"The teachings of Judaism are good, sure," he acknowledged, "and I suppose religions have done some work here in New Orleans, but I came from religious people, and I can tell you, they're no good. The Jehovah's Witnesses have the message, but they're all corrupt. The Jews had the message, but they lost it. And some other folks took it. They're not all bad. You seem nice enough, but how do you know you're Jewish? I mean, how do you know you come from Abraham? That's all I'm sayin'."

The discussion of who has the claim on Abraham, and on being the "true" Jews, has been going on for a long time. They argued about it during the Roman Empire, when nationalists and collaborators both staked their claims to the true covenant, right through to the destruction of the Temple, and they argue about it now. Some say that the essence of being a Jew is in the observance of the ancestral laws. By this argument, those who observe the 613 mitzvot are more Jewish than those who don't. As Rabbi Griesman in Arkansas pointed out to me, that's like saying of two different married men that the one who does the dishes and takes out the trash and goes to movies with his wife is "more married" than the one who comes home from work and goes to bed and doesn't do much around the house.

Then there are those who claim that direct genetic descent from the patriarchs defines Jews as Jews. And also those whose commitment to different aspects of different Jewish cultures determines their Jewishness. There's no easy answer to the question of who is a Jew. It seems that, throughout history, only the anti-Semites had a clear understanding of it. The Jews were whoever they needed them to be. They didn't care about the debates within the community. The Jews served a purpose as the Other. For this driver, the Jews were a corrupt group of Zionists. He reminded me of that book *The Protocols of the Elders of Zion*, which had been forged in Russia in an attempt to stir up anti-Semitism. And for over a hundred years it had worked. The book is still, sadly, a best seller in the Arab world. Hearing all the anti-Semitic blather, I couldn't take the driver seriously anymore, and was relieved when he dropped me off at the mosque. So much for the *baal agallah*.

Masjid-ur-Raheem (Mosque of the Merciful) was a bright turquoise explosion of color on a block of run-down single and double shotgun houses. Some were in the midst of repairs, others were boarded up. You could still see the high-water marks on several. The gate to the mosque was locked, and three men drinking on their front steps down the block called out to see what I wanted. I told them I was looking for the imam.

"He went home," one of them told me. "About ten minutes ago."

I was about half an hour late.

I ran after my taxi, which hadn't gotten far. There were no other cabs in the area, and without him I would have been stranded. He waited while I called the imam on his cell and arranged to meet him at a hardware store. We didn't talk about religion again. I steered the conversation toward the New Orleans enconomy (lousy), to the food (great), to the Saints (doing all right, playing Sunday).

At the store, the imam had to buy some lightbulbs and a few other supplies. He was still rebuilding his home. I paid for the cab, and Rafiq and I found a café where we could sit and talk at last. I bought him a coffee and then felt ridiculous when he didn't drink it. I realized how little I knew about Islam. Was there a rule for the very pious about caffeine? I was sure I'd been to coffee shops in Muslim countries, but I began to doubt myself. I'd never sat down with a Muslim religious leader before.

"It's not that," he said, laughing quietly. "It's just not very good. I wanted a cappuccino. I don't know what *this* is. I first met the former rabbi at Touro Synagogue, David Goldstein, over coffee after a program at the cathedral. At the time, in 2004, there wasn't much dialogue between our faiths. It was actually here, at CC Coffee Shop. This is a very special hangout for Muslims and Jews."

It looked to me like a normal neighborhood coffee shop, but when two Jordanians came by to greet the iman, followed by a middle-aged Jewish woman, I saw that, indeed, this was a meeting place of the faiths. They talked about a conference that was under way at Tulane; they talked about joint synagogue-mosque outreach; they talked about music. Of course they talked about music—it was New Orleans. People didn't hesitate to sit down with us and talk about whatever was on their minds, and somehow, it never felt imposing. Something about the atmosphere of the city made it seem that no one was a stranger. It reminded me of Manhattan a few days after 9/11, when people spoke more quietly but more often and to more people. It was a place where no one wanted to be alone. It was another half hour before the imam was able to return to his story of how he formed a partnership with the Jewish community.

"Our first year together, the Jewish people from Touro came to the *masjid* on Friday"—the Muslim holy day. "Then we went with members of the mosque to the synagogue on Saturday for prayers, a dialogue, a food and clothing drive, and dinner. Then we played basketball on Sunday at the JCC. The next year we cut back to only two days, but we focused more on service, giving out food and mattresses at a homeless shelter. Everyone wants to help with the healing process. The biggest effect we have is through our prayers, of course, but we are also playing an active role in addressing some of the people's material needs. Since the storm, most [of the members of my community] are looking for government help for their material needs. They come to us for their spiritual needs."

I was struck by the cultural difference between Imam Rafiq and the Jewish leaders I'd spoken with. They served on the same interfaith committees and advisory councils and they had the same commitment to service, yet in all my conversations with Jewish leaders I heard a lot about the practical needs of the community and very little about their spiritual needs, with the exception of an offhand comment by Rabbi Busch. It was as if the Jewish leaders felt their primary duty was rebuilding institutions rather than interceding with God. Was this because Jewish culture was more secular than spiritual? Was this a result of Jewish history, in which the government could not be relied upon, so the Jews simply took to organizing and looking after their own practical needs? Or was it that the Jews, a far more affluent community than the African-American Muslims, were simply more able to meet the practical needs of people themselves? Or maybe it was the legacy of the Holocaust, a mistrust in prayer to deliver us from disaster?

I asked the imam if there was any sort of effort from the larger Muslim community analogous to the massive mobilization of Jewish groups across America that had come to aid the Jews of New Orleans. The imam, as president of the Islamic Shura Council, a consulting board of all the Muslim leaders in New Orleans, was uniquely positioned to answer my question.

"There was some outside support, but mostly the immigrant community of Muslims was more hesitant to get involved with the Jewish and Christian communities. They coordinated to some extent, but not nearly as much. We in the African-American [Muslim] community never hesitated. For me, it is like a family with Rabbi Goldstein and Busch. And I've hosted volunteers from all over the country in my house. They come from all religions and stay with me and we send them out into the community to work. A group of Christian volunteers gutted and repaired my house, which had taken two-and-a-half feet of water."

The imam's personal commitment struck me, but it raised questions. If there were about fifteen thousand Muslims in New Orleans, why were so many homes still in ruins? Why had so many of the members of the imam's mosque not returned after the storm? Why had they not organized at anywhere near the level of the tiny Jewish community, which was less than half their size? It suggested to me a theme that had continued throughout Jewish history, one that had led some outsiders to admire the Jews' ability to look out for themselves and to rally together in a crisis, and led others to mistrust us as an insular, self-obsessed people. As a teen, I'd been put off by the idea that the Jews only took care of their own. I saw the vast number of Jewish organizations as a sign of cultural standoffishness. I thought of the Jewish community as overorganized and the people as overaffiliated. Ina, Hugo, Rabbi Busch, any of the Jewish leaders could have gone to a different meeting with a different committee every night.

As I'd been traveling and visiting Jewish communities, I'd had my assumptions challenged. With the exception perhaps of the isolationist ultra-Orthodox, Jews tried to benefit the society around them wherever they lived. Their intensive organization and obsessive creation of institutions had served them well. As Michael Weil said, they had three thousand years of disasters to learn from, and perhaps this was the lesson: if you are connected to each other and to your community, connected deeply with time and intelligence and energy, when disaster does strike, you will be able to respond very fast and very well. There was no arguing that the Jews of New Orleans had done both of those things. But Imam Rafiq was certainly organized, and his community committed to their city, yet why had so many not returned? Was there something beyond organization? Certainly the Jewish community was wealthier than the African-American Muslim community. That was part of it. And certainly the Jews were more tied to the city's history than was the community of Muslims, who had immigrated there in more recent years from the Middle East and South Asia. But I wondered if there was something unique in the Jewish heritage that might also explain it. Was it the history of disaster that had prepared them to bounce back? Perhaps Inge Elsas could tell me.

INGE, AT NINETY-TWO YEARS OLD, HAS more energy than most twenty-three-year-olds. She's a tiny woman, stooped with age but buoyant and charming. She practically bounded into the room at the Jewish Community Center where we met. I asked her how she came to New Orleans and why she stayed. We spoke for over two hours, and for most of that time, she did the talking. In a nearly continuous monologue she answered my question, and her answer spanned decades and continents.

"I always feel I've had many lives," she said. "When I was seven years old, I knew I wanted to help people. My interest is still the same. I want to give a positive outlook to whatever people experience."

She told me of her childhood in Germany, in a fully assimilated family. When she was ten years old, she performed as the Virgin Mary in a Nativity play, and one of the girls in her class complained that "the Jew-girl couldn't be the Mother Mary."

"I didn't know that I was a Jew-girl," Inge said, laughing. "We were so assimilated. I cried to my mother and asked what a Jew-girl was and she started to explain. Then I started to study with a liberal religious group and I became observant. I learned Hebrew. There was no more Christmas for us. Sadly, my school became more Nazi oriented, so I had to move to a private school where the teachers were of all religions. I was preparing to be a nurse, which was my goal, but I could not find anywhere that would take a Jewish girl. When Hitler marched into Hamburg and closed down all the schools that taught Jews, I saw the writing on the wall. I didn't want to stay in Germany, which would have been very limiting. I wanted to help the world. So at seventeen years old, with twenty deutschmarks in my pocket, I went to Switzerland. When Switzerland would no longer allow Jews to stay, my nursing school sent me all over the continent for a year, moving me from place to place. It was a scary time, but eventually they sent me to Italy. I fell in love with Italy and the Italian language. I worked as a governess for ailing children of high-class families. I spent winters in Tripoli and summers in Rome when I worked for a count's family. I had my own apartment in Tripoli, right in the desert, and my own camel and donkey. And I stayed in touch with my family for a time, through the Red Cross, but I lost them all . . . I lost them all in the camps . . ."

For a moment, Inge's voice faltered as she remembered the hardest time of her life, traveling in luxury and unable to help as her family was murdered by the Nazis. But then, resolved to share her story, she continued, telling me how she found an American diplomat's family who took her in when Mussolini ordered the expulsion of the Jews, how they took her with them around Europe. She remembered Prague on the gray November day when the Nazis marched in. She left with the diplomat, spent a year in Rio, and then, at last, came to America. After some time in Washington, DC, she decided to strike out on her own and study social work. She'd never been to the South but was admitted to Tulane and eventually earned her master's degree. She also met her future husband, a concentration camp survivor, and they settled down in New Orleans. She worked at an orphanage and volunteered to help the elderly. She opened an association for handicapped children and joined every Jewish organization in the city. Since the storm, she has been counseling people with post-traumatic stress disorder and serving as the only Jewish teacher at a multifaith Bible class. She has been a member of the National Council of Jewish Women since she was a teenager in Germany and continues to participate in their initiatives. After Katrina, NCJW ran a help line for people in crisis to call, to talk, and to get referrals to whatever aid existed, and Inge volunteered on it. In 2006 NCJW recognized her community service with the Hannah G. Solomon Award, their highest honor.

Inge struck me as someone who could, quite easily, have answered Hugo's question. *Ayeka?*—Where are you? She knew the answer both spiritually and geographically. I was traveling around the world, as she had, to find my answer to that question too.

"I can't be Jewish just by being a food Jew or a nationalist Jew," she said. "I believe it takes a commitment to serve, to help people. We have to do something with our lives. That is how I understand Judaism. We have to serve the world. I've been to Israel two times, and liked it. I'm not a strict Zionist, though I believe we need a place. It should exist as a Jewish state, in case we need it, as we have needed it before, but America is my home. I don't want another. There are a lot of similarities between Israel and New Orleans since the storm, in regard to trauma, but in Israel, they have support. Here, the people have no support. So of course I will stay in New Orleans. This is where I live. It is a very unusual city, and I'm committed to it totally. New Orleans gave me my freedom, my education, my honors, and my love. I will never leave it."

ON MY LAST DAY IN THE city, I went with Ina to the Lower Ninth Ward, on what she called a "devastation tour." The idea made me uncomfortable, but she assured me that taking such a tour was essential to my understanding of what happened to the city and how far they still had to go. So many houses were still in ruins. So much of the rebuilding had replaced old unsustainable houses that had been vulnerable to flooding with new unsustainable houses that are vulnerable to flooding. We saw the brightly painted rows of homes that make up Musicians' Village, a program funded by Harry Connick Jr. We saw the site of the green homes funded by Brad Pitt's Make It Right Foundation, and we also saw the crosses marking where people had died, trapped in their homes or torn away by the flood. A New York artist had just finished a run of Samuel Beckett's play *Waiting for Godot* at a nearby trailer, and we studied the grim set amid the devastation that said all that needed to be said about waiting for help from the local government, from FEMA, from God. The area was bleak and ruined. But looking around, there were people working. There were visitors and volunteers and citizens.

"We never saw so many white people in the Lower Ninth Ward before Katrina," a woman next to me joked. The storm had brought people together, and it was not just the Jews. Those who stayed in the city and those who returned are finding allies everywhere and, lacking outside support, coming up with creative ways to survive and rebuild together. Muslims and Christians and Jews are gutting houses together for total strangers. People like Inge and Rafiq and Hugo are doing what they can to help, giving time, money, and energy to repair their city and its residents.

Ina didn't say much while we looked out over the devastation. We could see the levee, and it was a strange sensation, watching ships pass above street level on the canal. Of course my thoughts turned to the biblical images of the flood and, staring at the cross that marked where a young boy was torn from his grandfather's arms by the floodwaters, my anger flared. If there is a God, and that God is just, then how could this have happened? What kind of God lets this happen? It is one of the oldest theological questions: why do the good suffer?

I couldn't answer the question, and the desolate landscape couldn't answer it for me. The imam and his prayers can't answer it for me, nor can the rabbis, nor can Inge Elsas or Ina Davis. But they are not trying to answer it. The question with which they struggle is not why, but what do we do about it, how do we answer that suffering? Their answer is to come together. They come together as Jews, and they come together as people of faith, and they come together as citizens of New Orleans, and they come together as people in need. The lesson is one the Jews have long known—*tikkun olam*—repair the world—but it is one that does not belong to them exclusively, and they are trying, in myriad ways, to share that lesson with their city. And perhaps that is also the answer to the why. Disaster is an opportunity to care for each other. Suffering gives the members of a community the chance to ease each other's pain. What use would compassion be without suffering? What use would service be with no one to serve?

Looking at that cross in the Lower Ninth, I stopped thinking about Noah and the wrath of God, and I thought of Ernest Hemingway's line "The world breaks everyone and afterward many are strong at the broken places," and I thought that must certainly hold true for the Jews. I pray it's true of New Orleans. And then I think of W. H. Auden's line "We must love one another or die," and then, because it's New Orleans, I go out for a drink with a friend at a bar on the edge of the French Quarter, and I raise a glass and we give a toast. "*L'chaim,*" I say, which means, so simply, "To life."

five

Siege and Survival:
The Jewish Community of Bosnia

*And seek the welfare of the city to which I have exiled you and pray
to the Lord on its behalf; for in its prosperity you shall prosper.*
—JEREMIAH 29:7

THE FEBRUARY SKY TURNS red over the hills surrounding Sarajevo as the sun collapses, exhausted, for the day. Muezzins chant the call to prayers, slightly out of sync with each other by just a fraction of a second, so that the city sounds like a round-robin of the faithful, echoing one another in praise of prayer. In Arabic, the prayer one performs five times a day is called *salat*. In Bosnian, they call it *namaz*. In Burma, I'd seen men rushing to prayers at this same time on a Friday night. In Sarajevo, there are a lot of people on the streets, seemingly unconcerned with the business of *namaz*. They sip cappuccinos and chain-smoke Winstons in outdoor cafés.

It is surprisingly warm for February, and everyone seems happy to shed layers. The women wear tight sweaters and lots of makeup, the men, not to be outdone, squeeze into tight jeans and drench their scalps with hair gel. Everyone is pale from the typically sun-starved Bosnian winter.

In the old city, the beautifully restored Ottoman-era market is alive with men selling everything from pastries to watches. I catch sight of a few Muslim women wearing head scarves and a few with the full black chador covering them from head to toe. Mostly, the people all look the same: young, smoking, and trying very hard to appear cosmopolitan.

I head past the old city, through a downtown area of grand Austro-Hungarian—era structures mixed with massive concrete blocks from the Communist era. The diversity of architecture suggests the rich history of Sarajevo, the constructive mingling of aesthetics, commerce, and ideas, but graveyards pop up unexpectedly, crossing a park or rounding a corner, grim reminders of the recent civil war.

I cross the Miljacka River, which flows through the city center, and cut through the back of a giant utilitarian apartment building built during the Communist era, which someone had decided to paint a cheery green. It didn't cheer the building up at all. Satellite dishes pop out of its facade like zits, and laundry hangs to dry on just about every balcony. Though it is on a prime piece of Sarajevo real estate, with views over the river to the grand Sarajevo library and the old city, the building gives off the feeling of a gulag.

I cut around the corner and find myself on a narrow street with a restaurant and another café, both full and loud and dense with cigarette smoke. The hills around the city rise sharply behind the next buildings, and in the fading light I can make out a repetition of that peculiar pattern—the soviet-style apartment blocs, the minarets of mosques, and the cheery glow of a bar or a café. The loudspeaker of a nearby mosque crackles nearby, reminding those within earshot that it is time to give God his due.

While the café crowd chatters and the muezzin chants, I slip into the synagogue at the end of the block on the south bank of the Miljacka River to observe the Friday night services that welcome Shabbat. The Jewish Community Center has been repaired and repainted since I was here in 2004. The outer wall facing the hill had been pocked with bullet holes and torn by a mortar shell. Now, four years later, the evidence of those wounds is erased; the Moorish architecture, with its grand arches and ornate domes, recalls a far greater past than the ignoble ethnic strife of the midnineties. I pause for a moment of thought before stepping inside, as has become my way in synagogues all over the world, collecting myself before I meet "my people," and I can't help but smile. It was this community of Sephardic Jews and this very building that had worked their way into my thoughts and would not let go. The story of these Bosnian Jews and this building on the river had inspired me to take this journey through the contemporary Diaspora, and I felt a great sense of relief to be back with them, even if only one or two of them knew who I was.

The hazan who led the services was a music teacher from the conservatory, whom the community paid. He was one of the few Bosnian Jews who knew the melodies, and he guided us through the prayers rhythmically, though at a breakneck pace. Not many of the Jews in Bosnia could read Hebrew, and not many were religiously observant. In that, they mirror most of their half a million Muslim neighbors, who prefer the cafés to the mosques.

The prayers were held in the lunchroom. There were about twenty people at the service, most of them older. A group of French tourists had come to take part, mostly out of curiosity, though a few were Jewish. Next to the rows of folding chairs, a table had been set up for the party that would follow the service. I noticed that there were twice as many chairs around the table as there were worshippers. Just as at the Hanukkah celebration in Arkansas, people came for the party, not the prayers. For most of the members of the Jewish community, being Jewish was about being connected to each other and to their history, not so much about the connection to God. But I hadn't come just to meet people. I truly wanted a spiritual experience, as I had sought in Southeast Asia and in rural Arkansas. By observing the arrival of the Sabbath in the way Jews all over the world, and throughout history, had done, I intended to feel a connection and to gain some insight into Jewish survival. So I joined the small group of worshippers and followed along as best I could, standing when others stood and sitting when others sat. I still didn't know the proper way a Jewish service should go, so I wasn't sure how what I was seeing conformed or differed. I just followed along and did what everyone around me was doing. I cursed myself a bit for not having studied up on the Jewish liturgy before embarking on this journey.

The pantomime of religious observance that I performed on Friday nights around the world did have a spiritual purpose, though. It connected me to that moment in the desert described in my bar mitzvah Torah portion when Moses reads the commandments to the Israelites and after each one they shout out, "We will do and we will hear!" The first part is always to do, to perform the commandments, and hope that through doing them and studying them understanding will come. But the doing comes first. Understanding is not a necessary condition of faith.

It reminded me of a Buddhist teaching by an eleventh-century Japanese monk named Ryonin. He practiced the *nembutsu*, which is a meditation on the Buddha of compassion. The worshipper chants the name of the Buddha, petitioning him to grant perfect enlightenment to all beings and an end to all suffering. Ryonin asserted that one person chanting the Buddha's name one time with perfect purity of intent was enough to benefit the entire world, so his school of thought called on practitioners to chant the name of the Buddha of compassion over and over and over, with the hope that in doing so, just once they would say the name with complete selflessness and clarity. The chant was a tool to arrive at the faith. That was how I experienced my Friday night services. I didn't fully understand the prayers, but I knew that without performing them, I certainly wouldn't gain understanding.

No prayer in the Jewish liturgy better illustrates this than the Amidah. When it came time to do it, everyone in the congregation stood, and I stood right along with them. Everyone took three small steps forward, so I took three small steps forward. The Amidah is arguably the central prayer of Judaism, and it is performed in near silence. The idea is that you whisper it just loud enough for you to hear and no one else. You are meant to be speaking directly to God, with no hazan or rabbi or anyone else interfering. It is every Jew's direct line to the holy. Like the *nembutsu*, the prayer should be performed with absolute sincerity and concentration. Though ideally read in Hebrew, some Orthodox authorities have argued that it should be read in a transliteration so that the reader understands, in order that no barriers stand between the worshipper and the prayer.

The Jews of Bosnia originally spoke Ladino, which was a mixture of Spanish and Hebrew, but few speakers of it remain, and the liturgy is now in Hebrew. I wasn't sure why, when so few of the community read Hebrew. Why let Ladino pass away in favor of another language none of the community members speak? Was it because Jewish authorities had long ago made Hebrew and its northern European cousin, Yiddish, the dominant languages of Jewish life, another example of Ashkenazi culture steamrolling over the unique perspective of Sephardic Jews? Or was it simply that communities evolve and Ladino just wasn't necessary anymore? These were Bosnian Jews, after all, and they no longer saw themselves as exiles. They had Hebrew for religious purposes and the Bosnian language for civic life. Still, I was sad not to hear a prayer service in Ladino, just for the novelty of it.

Some of the worshippers chuckled at how long the *Amidah* went on at this particular service.

"It's because he doesn't read Hebrew," a man next to me whispered, laughing. "Our hazan. He likes this part because there's no pressure."

The prayer consists of nineteen blessings, eighteen of which were codified after the destruction of the Second Temple in Jerusalem as a way to preserve Jewish ritual in exile. The nineteenth was added against heretics in the second century C.E. It was meant to combat breakaway Jewish sects and, later, converts to Christianity who informed on faithful Jews to the authorities.

The prayer contains a logical structure. The first three blessings are in praise of God. The next thirteen are petitions to God: six of them are for personal needs— knowledge, repentance, forgiveness, redemption, health, and prosperity—and six of them are for the needs of the Jewish people—ingathering of the exiled, the restoration of justice, destruction of Israel's enemies, reward for the righteous, the restoration of Jerusalem, the arrival of the Messiah. An entreaty follows that God hear our prayers. The last three blessings ask for a return to the Temple (which must have appealed to the newly exiled priestly caste), offer thanksgiving to God, and plead for peace. During the prayer, there is an opportunity to insert one's own private prayers and needs in any language one wishes. There are also traditional movements, bowing and bending, that one performs throughout. In the Reform tradition, from which I come, the prayer had been adjusted to be both gender neutral and more disposed toward the Diaspora condition and the messianic age rather than an individual Messiah. The differences in the prayer that exist within the sects of Judaism are differences in interpretation rather than need. The prayer is universally performed, and going through it in every country I visited, I could see how clinging to it helped to preserve Judaism. The entirety of the religion—the covenant, the laws, and the blessings—are contained in its words.

I just wish I could have read them. I had to look all of this up later. At the time, I just stood there moving my mouth like a fish. After a few minutes of bending and bowing and whispering, I stopped reading the transliteration of the Hebrew words, accepting that I couldn't possible pray with any pure intention if I had no idea what I was saying. I still wanted to believe in my revelation about the *nembutsu* and the holiness of going through the motions, but I was committed to entering into this moment of prayer in some immediately meaningful fashion. I stood in silence, thinking about this place I was in and why I had come. Reflection seemed to me a valid form of spiritual exploration, and I figured there would be other nights to mouth the words of the Amidah, maybe even memorize them. I'd have plenty of time to explore the divine workings of repetition. In truth, I'd always been more drawn to narrative, which was why I'd never made a good Buddhist. Almost as soon as I'd connected Ryonin, from my college Buddhism classes, to my Jewish awakening, I left him behind. I owed far more of my spiritual revival to Bosnian war criminals than I did to eleventh-century Japanese monks or rabbinic authorities.

I FIRST CAME TO BOSNIA TO do research about children recovering from the civil war that erupted after the collapse of the Soviet Union. I had spent time with war-affected children in Africa and Asia who were struggling with the reality of ongoing armed conflict, and I came to Bosnia to examine how individual children healed when the violence stopped, and how their healing contributed to the larger recovery of a society. I hadn't intended to learn anything about Jews or Judaism. I was interested in universal concepts of human rights and childhood development, which meant that any interest I had in the Jewish people tended to be limited to the actions of the Israeli Defense Forces in the West Bank and the state of Palestinian children. Before coming to Sarajevo my first time, I had met many people in Kosovo who spoke with admiration about Israel, as Kosovar Albanians were in their own struggle for independence at the time. They saw in Israel a model for their own state. I would shrug or nod or smile and change the subject. I just wasn't interested. I didn't want to touch the Israel issue with a ten-foot pole, and I wasn't comfortable talking about my own ethnicity lest I be linked with the Jewish state and all that that implied.

In France and Germany, in fact all across Europe at the time, violence against Jews was on the rise. During April of 2004, just months before I visited the Balkans for the first time, there were four hundred attacks against Jewish people and institutions in France—double the number that had occurred in 2002—and 2004 saw further attacks on Jews in Brussels, Strasbourg, Lyon, and Marseille. French police attributed the violence to North African youths acting out of anger toward Israel and the situation in the Middle East. If I had thought about Jews in Sarajevo before I arrived, I would have assumed their situation was the same, if not worse. Sarajevo is 90 percent Muslim and was a known transit point for Al-Qaeda operatives from Europe. I didn't, however, think about it.

I had been invited to spend my first week in Bosnia at a summer camp on Mount Igman, where Serb, Croat, and Muslim children played together as they had done since the camp's founding during the siege of Sarajevo in 1994. I was shocked to learn that not only were there Jewish children at the summer camp, called Club Young Friends, but that the program was founded by the humanitarian arm of the Jewish community of Sarajevo, La Benevolencija, at the height of the war. A group of volunteers, eager for something to do, had decided that the children should have an opportunity to learn and play and escape for a few hours a day from the terror of survival under siege.

In the country where the term *ethnic cleansing* had been coined ten years earlier, I never would have imagined a place where Muslims, Croats, and Serbs all came together to play and to learn, or that the Jewish community would be responsible for it. I hadn't imagined there were any Jews left in Bosnia after the Holocaust and decades of Communist rule. As I would come to learn, the Jews did more than survive in Sarajevo; they gave their gift of survival back to the city.

On my first visit to Sarajevo, I stayed with Dada Papo, a secular Muslim woman and one of the two leaders of the camp. The other, a child psychologist named Giselle, was Jewish. That a Muslim and Jew should run an interfaith, multiethnic camp for children seemed natural to them, but for me, it was a revelation. The Jewish narratives I had grown up on involved ever-increasing hostility between Muslims and Jews, rising anti-Semitism in Europe, and, of course, vitriolic Zionism.

The Jews hadn't planned specifically to become a lifeline for the city of Sarajevo, though perhaps their history had done the work of preparation for them. The first Jews to arrive in Bosnia were Sephardic Jews, who had come originally from the Iberian peninsula (the word *Sepharad* means "Spain" in Hebrew) but were expelled by the Inquisition and other persecutions and sought refuge in the Ottoman Empire. Ashkenazi Jews, primarily from central and northern Europe, came to Bosnia later, mostly during the period of Austro-Hungarian rule. Some of the early Sephardic arrivals brought the iron keys to their homes in Spain and Portugal with them. The keys were passed down through generations, as reminders of their second exile. Jerusalem was an abstraction. *Sepharad* was the real home they had lost. Many Bosnian families still have the keys to those long lost homes in Spain.

In Bosnia under Ottoman rule, the Jews prospered as merchants, government advisers, and doctors, as they did throughout the Ottoman Empire. They never lived in a Jewish ghetto in Sarajevo, though a sixteenth-century sultan did build a settlement for them in the old city because a visitor had complained that much of the Jewish quarter was a fire hazard. Not all of the Jews moved to the housing the sultan built, but today the area is prime Sarajevo real estate.

At the end of the Ottoman era, when things were becoming more difficult for Jews, one of their leaders, Rabbi Moshe Danon, was arrested in Sarajevo. The pasha—the Turkish noble in charge of the city—demanded a huge ransom that the Jewish community couldn't pay, and he threatened to execute the pious man. It was the Sabbath, and the community gathered to pray for their rabbi's release, but in spite of their prayers it seemed that the pasha's heart could not be softened. That evening after sunset, while most of the Jews were observing the Sabbath, a member of the Jewish community walked from coffee shop to coffee shop, buying a cup of coffee at every one and paying with one gold coin. Not only was he in violation of the Sabbath, which forbids doing business from sundown to sundown, he was overpaying for coffee and breaking a law that forbade Jews from patronizing Muslim coffee houses. Needless to say, he caught the attention of most of the market. When the shop-keepers asked him why he was doing something so crazy, risking conflict with the religious and secular authorities, he explained how the pasha had arrested Rabbi Danon. The Muslim shopkeepers grew so enraged at the injustice against their Jewish neighbor that three thousand of them surrounded the pasha's house and demanded the release of the Jewish citizen. Facing insurrection, the pasha had no choice but to acquiesce. This spirit of interfaith cooperation was a hallmark of Bosnian life, though it would come to be sorely tested in the twentieth century.

When the Nazis took over Yugoslavia, they deported nearly fifty thousand Jews and exterminated most of them. Some survived by fleeing to the partisans and fighting the Nazis. Others found refuge with their non-Jewish neighbors, who concealed them until the end of the war. Of the fourteen thousand Jews in Bosnia before World War II, only four thousand survived, and many of them went to Israel rather than return to the embers of their community in Europe. Their businesses and institutions had been destroyed. Their old synagogue had been turned into an ammo dump. But some two thousand did come back to the city. Under Tito's Communist government, religious instruction was banned and knowledge of Jewish customs waned but did not disappear. Jews participated fully in public life, and privately they continued to pass on what traditions they could.

"I remember our neighbors bringing us matzo at Passover," said Elma Softic-Kaunitz, the current secretary general of La Benevolencija. She's a heavyset woman with searching eyes and a sharp wit. I rarely saw her without a cigarette. "My grandmother was Jewish, my father was Muslim. We were a very mixed family, like most everyone in Sarajevo. I was close with my grandmother, so even though she died when I was young, I always knew I was Jewish. I didn't know the traditions, but I felt the historical meaning of being a Jew.

"In 1983, when the Sabra and Shatila massacres occurred in Lebanon, there were protests here against Israeli policy. I thought it would be good to join these protests because it was a horrible thing that happened. When I was marching, I saw a placard with a crossed-out Star of David and the words Alle Juden Schiessen written on it. That was the moment I realized that I was part of *that* people, the Jewish people, and I left the march."

Yugoslavia officially cut ties to Israel in 1967, though it never took an anti-Semitic stance. Tito suppressed religion and ethnicity in general. Jews, as long as they were Communists, rose to high ranks in his government. The antiethnic policy no doubt increased the rates of intermarriage, helping to bolster the cosmopolitan atmosphere of Sarajevo, though intermarriage and intermingling had been the historical norm in the city since Ottoman times.

When the Soviet Union collapsed, latent ethnic tensions between Muslims, Catholic Croats, and Christian Orthodox Serbs rose to the surface, and Yugoslavia began to crumble along ethnic lines. In June of 1991, Slovenia and Croatia declared their independence. The Jewish community watched anxiously as nationalism increased. With memories of the Holocaust still lingering among the older generation, the community began to fear the worst. On all sides, loyalties were divided between Jewish unity and national identity. Later that summer, arguments over the question of independence broke out between the Jews of Serbia and those of Croatia at the annual meeting of Yugoslavian Jewish leaders, who had met since the end of World War II. And if there were tensions between the tight-knit Jewish communities, it was clear that the atmosphere was dangerous for everyone.

The leaders of Sarajevo's Jewish community—Jakob Finci, then head of La Benevolencija, and Ivan Ceresnjes, the community's president—knew that trouble in Yugoslavia meant trouble in Sarajevo. Bosnia was the most ethnically mixed of the former Yugoslavian republics and integral to the "Greater Serbia" that Slobodan Milosevic aspired to rule. Radovan Karadzic, leader of the Bosnian Serbs, had warned that if Bosnia declared independence, its citizens would find themselves on a "highway of hell." So when they returned from that 1991 meeting, Finci and Ceresnjes began to prepare for the worst. They met with local doctors to figure out what supplies would be most crucial, and sought help from the New York–based American Jewish Joint Distribution Committee—known as "the Joint"—a humanitarian organization founded in 1914 to serve as the overseas arm of the American Jewish community that sent stockpiles of medicine, bandages, and body bags. For the first time since World War II, the community packed up the Sarajevo Haggadah, an illuminated manuscript from the fourteenth century, and sent it to a secret location known only to Ivan Ceresnjes.

The following April, the Bosnian parliament passed a referendum declaring independence. Barricades went up around Sarajevo, and on April 6 Serb forces clashed with the Bosnian police, starting the civil war. One night soon afterward—the first evening of heavy shelling—Ivan Ceresnjes arrived at the community center for work. To his surprise, he found about five dozen people asleep on the floors and benches. He didn't know who they were, but since the building was open to the public, he assumed that they were "frightened people from the neighborhood," who did not know where else to go. Ceresnjes didn't turn them away, and after that, the Jewish Community Center was open to all who needed it.

The center became a base of operations for the community's aid programs, which were vast. Through a two-way radio provided by the Joint, they passed messages between members of separated families. The community opened three pharmacies—according to Finci, "the best in town"—created a clinic in the community center, and arranged for doctors to pay visits to homebound patients. Under the Jewish community's aegis, Muslim and Croat nurses, doctors, and volunteers took to the streets, rushing through mortar blasts and sniper fire to treat the wounded. A psychologist who worked with the community immediately after the war told me that if not for the Jewish community's arrangements, many more residents of Sarajevo would have died, and if not for the work the community provided for people, many more would have gone mad. She didn't use those exact words, but madness is what it was. The city had become an insane asylum. Mobsters controled food and medical supplies, had rank in the army, became political leaders. Death touched everyone, and struck at random. One young man's family even sent him to a mental institution to protect him from conscription. In an insane time, the Jewish community provided a place of stability and sanity, as well as historical perspective. Many Holocaust survivors still lived in Sarajevo and knew all too well the patterns of death and destruction. They'd seen it all before.

At the start of the war, in coordination with officials in Belgrade, the Jewish community arranged for two airplanes to evacuate women and children. The Bosnian government insisted on clearing the passenger list, but once that hurdle was overcome, many families flew their loved ones to safety. When the fighting grew more intense, air transport was no longer an option, so the Jews persuaded the Serbs to authorize bus convoys out of the otherwise-sealed city to evacuate "their people." Jewish Sarajevans had first priority on the buses, but given decades of intermarriage and the many non-Jewish community members, it was natural to extend the invitation further. In the end, over one thousand non-Jews left Sarajevo in the convoys—nearly half the total number of escapes the Jewish community arranged. Finci, Ceresnjes, and the Joint field staff negotiated cease-fires while the buses were leaving. As other convoys throughout Bosnia were being stopped and their passengers detained or killed, every one of La Benevolencija's convoys got out unharmed.

In October of 1992, as I was trudging through preparations for my bar mitzvah and trying not to cry again in front of the girls in my class, a boy arrived in Israel with as much religious knowledge as I had. Ivan Hrkas was twelve years old and had been on one of the first Jewish community convoys out of Sarajevo. When he arrived with his parents, the whole thing still felt like an adventure. He didn't speak any Hebrew, so he would begin learning it immediately, not the divine sounds I was memorizing, but words with immediate power: *bread, bathroom, football, friend.* He didn't have a bar mitzvah and he didn't have to perform his Judaism. Being a Jew in the land of Israel was enough. Like the Israelites in my Torah portion who followed Moses into the desert, Ivan became a Jew in exile. He hadn't considered himself one before and didn't really consider himself one then, but being a Jew had saved his life, and Israel had given him a new one. More and more Bosnians arrived as the violence escalated. Ernest Grin, a little younger than Ivan and I, arrived with his parents. Ivan Ceresnjes sent his sons.

The "Jewish cease-fires" that allowed the convoys to escape were a testament to the skillful negotiations of the community leaders and the goodwill extended to Bosnia's Jews by all parties to the conflict. But the evacuations came with a price: many of the older Jews who had survived the Nazi occupation and rebuilt their community now had to watch the younger generation board buses and leave. As Ceresnjes recalled in Edward Serotta's *Survival in Sarajevo:* "We all knew the heart of our community was already gone. Everything we had built over the past forty years had come to an end."

During the war, the Jewish community and its humanitarian arm,

La Benevolencija, employed an equal number of Jews and Muslims, as well as some Serbs and Croats. There seemed to be no doubt among any Jewish community members that their services should be available to all. I asked Jakob Finci how this was possible, why the community would want to open its doors so wide. "The answer, from my point of view," he replied, "is a simple one. After more than four hundred and fifty years of living together with citizens of Sarajevo of different religious and ethnic backgrounds, we became part of Bosnian society. We are well incorporated but not assimilated in Bosnia, and during the war, under the siege and permanent attacks, we became all as an extended family."

As the conflict wore on, the Jews emerged as the closest thing Sarajevo had to a neutral party. Jakob Finci, using connections in Zagreb and Belgrade and support from the Joint, negotiated with the Serbs to keep the Jews' supply lines running in and out of the city. The community organized a postal service that got mail through the Serb lines. Often, when other aid trucks were turned away or held for days, La Benevolencija's deliveries passed right through. It was understood that if you wanted medicine and the Jewish community didn't have it, you shouldn't bother looking further. No one would have it. During the war, they filled 1.5 million medical prescriptions.

It was not just neutrality and influential friends that helped the Jews. According to a Joint field-worker during the conflict, "an awareness of the Holocaust, of what had already happened to the Jews of this region, was one of the elements that everyone had in mind." Empathy with the Jews was nearly universal. All sides wanted to be the historical brethren of that persecuted people, drawing on Holocaust imagery to win sympathy for their respective causes. Parallel to this reading of history, there may also have been a Serb fear of international intervention if Europe or the United States suspected a second attempt at genocide against European Jews in the twentieth century. Either way, the Jewish community's unique ability to import food and supplies ensured that not only their own would be fed—a priority—but their neighbors as well. By the time the siege ended, the Jewish community had served over 360 tons of food, and cooked over 110,000 hot meals.

"WHY DIDN'T I LEAVE?" ELMA KAUNITZ furrowed her brow and took a drag on her cigarette. She laughed. "One of my legs was heavier than the other. I planned to leave, but when I went to the bus, I just didn't get on. I wanted to see what would happen here. I was young and didn't have children, so I could take chances I wouldn't take now. I wasn't actually a community member before the war. I came because I wanted to help. I offered my services to the Red Cross, but there was no work available for me there, so I went to the Jewish community and offered to help with English or German translation— there were a lot of internationals in the city by this point—or anything else they needed. I needed to work, needed to do something so I wouldn't go crazy. They took me on, and later my mother came with some documents showing our Jewish origin. A lot of people came to the community like that. It was obvious because of their names that they had Jewish backgrounds, but they did not participate in community activities until the war. I think there are still a lot of Jews who identify as Jews, who feel like Jews, but are not registered members of the community."

"I remember during the war," a nineteen-year-old girl named Matea told me when I sat with her and her friends on a Sunday afternoon. "We were at the Jewish community [center] all the time. We had Jewish symbols in the house, but I was not raised with any of the Jewish tradition. I didn't know what it meant until the war, when they had the Sunday school."

The kindergarten and Sunday school, which drew children toward Judaism in numbers not seen in Sarajevo since before World War II, were started out of desperation. Sonja Elezar, daughter of a prominent Jewish family, worked as an economist and lived in an apartment building in

Grabavica, a neighborhood on the front lines between the Bosnians and the Serbs. Early in the war she lost her job and, that same day, learned that her building had been occupied by the military and she could not return. She moved in with her mother, but one month later, that house caught on fire and became uninhabitable. She moved in with her sister and was at her wits' end.

"I went to Ivan Ceresnjes and asked for something to do. He told me to organize a women's club, so I organized Boherta, which is the women's club to this day. We organized programs to help people get aid, we made cards for community members, that sort of thing. While I was coming to the community every day, I saw that there were children living in the basement. So I created the kindergarten in 1992."

The kindergarten and the Sunday school became focal points for children in the Jewish community, who put on Purim celebrations and learned about Jewish history and culture. Everyone was so desperate for distraction from the daily stress of life under siege that Jewish children began to bring their non-Jewish friends—Christian and Muslim alike— which provided opportunities for the children to learn about all of the ethnic groups in Sarajevo. Soon, interfaith education became part of the curriculum. In a city where ethnic differences had turned deadly, the children began to learn that difference could be a cause of celebration and curiosity too. It didn't have to lead to death. Under the aegis of the Jewish community, Club Young Friends members played together every Sunday while the adults looked on happily. Outside, the Serb and Bosnian armies clashed every day. Serb snipers had taken over the old Jewish cemetery and were using their position there to pick off civilians in the city below. The Bosnian soldiers attempted to oust them, and battle raged among the graves. The plots were heavily mined. To this day, there are bullet holes in even the oldest graves, dating back to the sixteenth century.

On my first visit to Sarajevo, I visited the cemetery and wandered through the rows of tombstones. In the center of the cemetery stood a memorial to the victims of the Holocaust. I crouched behind a faded old monument with some Hebrew text on it and took in the view of the city as a sniper would have seen it. I had a clear view of the empty twin sky-scrapers, former symbols of Sarajevo's diversity and prosperity, and the narrow streets of the city center. Strategically, it was an ideal spot. From here, almost no one was safe from a well-lobbed grenade or a high-caliber bullet. During my first visit I was more interested in the mementos of violence and in imagining the terror of Sarajevo's children than I was in the graves that surrounded me. I didn't take to heart the lesson that this bullet-pocked cemetery had to tell about the Jewish genius for survival. On a grave near the entrance, someone had spray-painted a swastika. My eyes fixed on it instinctively. The black lines were sloppy, clearly done in haste. Somehow, with all the surrounding bullet holes, the clumsy symbol looked pathetic rather than threatening. What could this one lonely emblem do in the face of centuries of Jewish survival in Bosnia?

My taxi driver, a Bosnian Muslim, interrupted my grim sightseeing to tell me that this was where he fought the Serbs. He lifted his sleeve to show a scar on his arm and pointed toward the edge of the cemetery. His English was not very good and I could not understand what he was trying to say. He pointed again to some of the graves, to some of the damage, and then to his arm again. "*Boom boom,*" he said and squeezed his arm over the scar. I got the point.

I went to the summer camp on Mount Igman thinking about what could help children heal from the wounds of ethnic violence and civil war, not yet seeing the connection between the history of the Jews and the gifts they gave back to the city.

On Igman, we played a lot of soccer. Knowing I was interested in the history of the war, children kept running up to me with old shell casings they'd found in the dirt. By the end of the week, I'd accumulated a small collection of all different calibers. In town they had to deal with all the troubles of postwar Sarajevo: drugs, violence, unemployment, alcoholism, an entire generation of traumatized grown-ups. On the mountain, they could forget about those things. They could try, as one child said, not to mess things up the way their parents had.

"We have lived together for hundreds of years," Dragica Levi told me when she was the secretary general of La Benevolencija in 2004. "We have not had problems with our neighbors, except during World War II. But that was something different." I asked her if the goodwill that the Jews of Sarajevo have received was because of the community's generosity during the war. She just scoffed at the suggestion. "You see, it was like this before the war too," she said. "We have always been relatively safe. We are not like other places."

I heard the same idea from Elma, who'd taken over from Dragica during the years between my visits. "Sarajevo is my home," she said. "I am more comfortable here. I wouldn't move to Israel. This city is my Jerusalem. This way of life is my way of life. If I left here, like so many who did during the war, I would miss it, and I would get nostalgic, the way all of those who left do."

During the years between my visits, I certainly grew nostalgic for Sarajevo. When I started to think about being Jewish in the world, my thoughts constantly bent toward the model the Jews of Sarajevo had provided, that saving ideal of humanitarianism they embodied. They had taken the lessons of their history—displacement, disaster, and reconstruction—and used them to give back to their city. They tied themselves to Sarajevo in spite of the danger and the hardship and the loss. Unlike the Jews of Burma, these people made themselves Bosnian in every way, from their language to their brand of cigarettes. I couldn't help but think again of that Psalm, *If I forget thee, O Jerusalem . . .* The words formed in the mouths of so many people, and so many used Jerusalem as a blank space in which to write the place they longed for most, the place they felt most at home.

* * *

WHEN I DECIDED TO TRAVEL BACK to Sarajevo in 2008, to see this community again, to learn about its brand of Jewish identity, I stayed in Dada's apartment, which hadn't changed a bit in the four years since my last visit. It was pristine and smartly decorated. During the siege, her apartment had been a gathering spot for all her neighbors, as its location at the back of the building protected it from mortar fire. Now, one of her young neighbors, a law student, still comes by to visit. He's interested in the history of the Jews in Bosnia, in ethnicity in general, partly because of his childhood during the war, and partly because he is unhappy with life in Bosnia.

"The society is limited," he told me. "It's sort of how the Jews here were depressed after World War II; they all intermarried and lost their traditions. They had a kind of renaissance during the war in the nineties because they had a purpose again. It was a grim purpose, but they did a lot. The other reason they survived, and that they did what they did to aid the city, is that they were always Bosnian first, then Jewish. They could have these layers of identity. But other groups, it's harder now, since the war, to have layers. You are what you are. People didn't care before the war, and now they do. The whole place is pretty narrow-minded, uneducated. It's what I always admired about Jewish people, their education. Most Bosnians don't value that sort of thing too much, at least not when you get outside the cities."

Here was a young Muslim man who openly admired Jewish values and Jewish adaptation. What conservative Jews see negatively as assimilation into the dominant society, Nesha saw as incorporation. The Jews were Bosnians, but they were still Jews. They still held their history and traditions in high esteem, even as they evolved. They embodied the idea of a people with a historic role to play, the idea that the Jewish people could be "a light unto the nations," as they are called in the Book of Isaiah. They took this role very seriously.

I had always thought of this famous line as a comment about Israel, hope for the potential of a Jewish state and a reminder of how far it fell short of that potential. The line seemed a bitter comment on the failure of politics and nation states to embody the best ideals of mankind, and suggested to me the dangers of tying a religion to the policies of a state. This one line seemed to me an articulate argument against Zionism. No state can serve its immediate political and security interests while also fulfilling a sacred duty.

But the Jews of Bosnia, by defying ethnic nationalism and embracing the highest of humanist ideals, had done with this divine commandment what Israel had failed to do since its inception. Of course, they could not have done it without a safe place for so many of them to flee to during the war. I can't imagine Ivan Ceresnjes or Jakob Finci or any of the leaders dashing so bravely through the perilous streets of Sarajevo to deliver aid if they also had to worry constantly for their children's safety. I knew of people in Sarajevo who were killed by mortar shells while sitting in their living rooms reading the paper.

So Israel had been a place of refuge for the Bosnians, as it was for so many Jews since its founding, but it was the Diaspora community, embattled and aging, that manifested the divinely mandated purpose of the Jewish nation. The Jews of Bosnia are not Zionists, nor are they deeply religious, but thanks to an understanding of their history they are experiencing a renaissance. Young people, with strong memories of their wartime childhoods and the sanctuary provided by the Jewish community, are excited to be Jews and are building a future for Judaism in Bosnia for themselves.

I spent a Sunday morning with some members of the community's youth group talking about being Jewish. They ranged in age from fourteen to twenty-two, and they were helping to make a movie for the Joint. They had come together to talk about "roots."

"To be a Jew is something unique here in Bosnia," said Verdan, a tall nineteen-year-old who was one of two leaders of the youth group.

"It is unique to keep the traditions alive, to be something different. If we didn't, this community wouldn't exist anymore, so it gives us a sense of . . . "

"Purpose," the other group leader, Vladamir, chimed in. He was the oldest, at twenty-two, and had lit a cigarette the moment the meeting started. About half the members of the youth group were smoking. All around us, adults were smoking too. Cigarettes were one of the central elements of Sarajevo culture. The other was coffee, which was served while we talked. The youths were happy to get up early on a Sunday to meet for the sake of the future of Judaism, but they weren't about to do it without cigarettes and coffee. Verdan, however, didn't smoke. He also wasn't too keen on making the movie if it was going to be shown on Bosnian television.

"I don't want everyone to know I'm a Jew," he said. The others scoffed at him, but he persisted. "I've had some problems, you know, with some of the more militant Islamists. Whenever something happens in Israel, there's always some anti-Semitism."

The others denied having ever experienced anything like that, but Verdan went on. "Sometimes I think it's better to be a secret Jew," he said. Everyone else laughed. Leading the Jewish youth group was one way to go about being secret, they said. He just smiled.

"So how did you find out you were Jewish?" Vladamir asked the group as if we were telling "coming-out" stories, which in a way I sup-pose we were. He looked at me to answer first.

I told them how I had been raised knowing I was a Jew but that it hadn't meant anything to me until I came to Bosnia in 2004 and saw a different kind of Judaism, one that was inclusive and welcoming, one that embodied a saving ideal and that had, in very practical ways, made society better. I felt I wanted to be part of that. I told them about the journey I was on and the other communities I had visited so far, and how I was beginning to see that we were all connected by something, some purpose for which we clung to this identity, and that I was looking for that purpose still.

The teens nodded and thought about it. They were, in fact, more predisposed to understand what I was doing than anyone else I had met so far, because they were doing roughly the same thing. Not the traveling, obviously, but figuring out who they were, and how being Jewish was a part of it. They were defining it for themselves, and building it into a much larger sense of their identity.

Zlatan, the fourteen-year-old, spoke next. "My father's a Jew and his father's a Jew, so I'm a Jew."

"My grandmother told me I was Jew," Tina said. Mattea added that she learned it during the war, when they were always at the community center. The older kids nodded with recognition. The war had drawn them all closer to Judaism and given them an idea of who they were. Just like the leadership of the community, these children found a sense of purpose in response to the unraveling of society.

Tina and Blanka, the two seventeen-year-olds, recently became the first bat mitzvot in years. Zlatan had also had his bar mitzvah that year, at age fourteen. The traditional meaning of bar/bat mitzvah is "one to whom the commandments apply," marking the age at which a person becomes responsible for adherence to Jewish law. The community wasn't married to the precise age for the ritual, which is usually thirteen (and sometimes twelve for girls). They kept the tradition alive with the communal spirit, the idea that at any age a young person can stand before the Jews and answer that vexing question that Hugo Kahn put to me—*Ayeka?* Where are you?—with the proud statement "*Hineini.* Here I am."

It wasn't just about a party, the way it tended to be in America, or even a rite of passage, as it was in a religious sense. It was about becoming a part of the Jewish people publicly, and knowingly committing to participation in the future of the Jews. For them it was about the tradition more than the religion, about establishing their place in that line and committing to carrying these traditions forward.

I began to wonder if I'd actually done that yet. If my bar mitzvah had meant almost nothing to me at the time, could it really count as my entrance into the Jewish faith? It had really been the last thing I'd done as a Jew, before this journey began. These young people showed me the distance I still had to go. I had yet to identify with any part of the vast continuum of Judaism, except perhaps with those who chose not to participate in it. I was still a tourist in my own ethnicity, a novice in my own religion. As I traveled, I was just pantomiming my way through. I'd learned some facts about Jews and Jewish communities and I'd participated in the ceremonies, but I lacked that sense of purpose that has enabled Jews to survive for millennia, from their earliest dispersion.

IN 536 B.C.E., SOLDIERS OF THE Babylonian king, Nebuchadnezzar sacked Jerusalem, destroyed Solomon's Temple, and sent the Jews into exile. During the forty-seven years the Jews were captives in the Babylonian Empire, the culture of sages and scribes found its voice. Jeremiah and Ezekial, two of the greatest prophets, emerged from the exile, and Ezra, the scribe, codified the Torah during this time. During the sojourn in Babylon, academies formed wherein intense debates and Torah commentary were hashed out. These commentaries would eventually form the Talmud, the rich layers of Torah interpretation that have guided Jewish life since they were first set down on paper. In Babylon, many Jews began to adopt the cultural norms of Babylonian society and marry Babylonian women, much to the dismay of pious Ezra. He railed against intermarriage and the evils of life in exile. When the Babylonians fell to the Persian Empire under Cyrus the Great, Ezra led forty thousand Jews back to Jerusalem to rebuild the Temple. While there, the story goes, he dissolved the marriages of Jews to non-Jews, read the Torah aloud, just as Moses read the commandments aloud, and demanded that his followers publicly assent to the commandments once more. The commandments of the Torah, rather than the physical temple, were held by Ezra to be of paramount importance, and according to him it was for transgressions against these commandments that the Jews had been cast into exile.

As Torah culture gained prominence, another enduring aspect of Jewish life emerged: the tension with assimilation. Jews had encountered a foreign culture, and many had embraced it and prospered. While Ezra lamented this development, many Jews would remain in Babylon, just as many, such as the majority of the Bosnian Jews, choose to remain apart from Israel today. By the time the Romans destroyed the Second Temple in 70 C.E., Jews had already spread throughout the empire, and they carried with them the commandments that Ezra had reaffirmed in writing.

These commandments made Judaism portable and allowed the Jews to practice it in whatever land they chose. Ironically, it was because of the destruction of the Temple that Judaism survived. Had they clung to the Temple, their ways would surely have vanished into archaeological history, but by elevating the scribes and holding to the text, they gave themselves the tools to survive in exile. Wherever the Jews were—Babylon, Rome, Burma, America, Bosnia—they could be found observing the Sabbath, interpreting the Torah, wrestling with God. The relationship with God, the laws, the covenant with God, and with each other gave them a purpose that went far beyond the dictates of sacrificial offerings on an altar. Physically being in Jerusalem wasn't necessary. The Jewish world no longer revolved around the Temple, and the Jews adapted. The Torah became their homeland, the center of the Jewish world. As it had turned the Israelites from a collection of peoples into a nation when they fled Egypt, the Torah again unified the Jews, even as it invited new tensions into their existence. The high priests no longer had a role to play, as the scholars became the most important figures in religious matters and the act of reading became the most sacred skill, the doorway to all the laws. Anyone who could read, or who could listen to a reader, had access to the divine.

"You won't find many Zionists here," Vladamir said. "There're more patriots." He was proud of the Jews' connection to Bosnia as a nation and to Jewish tradition as their heritage. He saw no contradiction between these loyalties and had no desire to immigrate to Israel. None of the children in the youth group said they wanted to go to Israel. Zlatan wanted to leave Bosnia, but for America, "the land of opportunity." The others simply said that they loved the Bosnian lifestyle and couldn't imagine living anywhere else.

I heard the same thing echoed over and over again, even from young people who'd fled to Israel during the war and returned to Bosnia. They lamented the lack of economic opportunity in Sarajevo and, sometimes, the narrow-mindedness of its people, but they preferred their way of life here, and they always felt that their home was in Bosnia. Ernest, whose parents had remained in Israel after the war ended, came back to Sarajevo even though he had trouble finding work. He didn't like the tension in Israel and didn't want to serve in the army. He didn't like the politics of the Jewish state and the divide between Muslim and Jew. He didn't care for labels at all.

Though Orthodox Judaism wouldn't recognize many younger generation Bosnians as Jews—given the rampant intermarriage and the fact that not many kept kosher or strictly observed the Sabbath—they were certainly keeping their brand of Judaism alive and finding great fulfillment in it.

"If we didn't meet, there would be no more Jewish community here," Vladamir said. "We have to keep the traditions alive here or the traditions would vanish."

He illustrated the condition that brought the Jews of Bosnia together, that had sustained Judaism through various exiles, and that had sparked Ezra to write and Jeremiah to prophesy and Moses to lead. It had even created the state of Israel.

Threat.

Threat was a constant across Jewish history, and it sparked much of their creativity and innovation. It brought together diverse strains of thought and dynamic groupings of people. Of course, threat had pushed the Jews around the world, often destroying communities that could not or would not rise to meet the challenges. For every Sarajevo there was a Rangoon; for every new community like Bentonville, Arkansas, there was a Berkley, Virginia. But there was also always a springing forth somewhere. Anywhere people took the tradition seriously and found some value in it, some purpose, they survived.

After the fall of the Soviet Union, people in Bosnia needed a new saving ideal. Communism could no longer provide it. The religious and ethnic communities filled that role for many people, setting off the violent destruction of the country but also the rebirth of Jewish communal life and ideals. People came together in order to help and to connect to nearly vanished traditions and give themselves bearings in a world that had shattered. A community of concern with a messianic purpose—to protect and heal their city—brought Jews back to traditions far older than the city they loved and ensured that they would continue to exist in it.

The Jews have moved into a new mode of being since the end of the war. Their concerns are now largely economic. Because of the war, an entire generation finds itself out of work, having lost valuable years of employment, saving, and training. Economic stagnation and corruption dominate the concerns of the young, and the community is struggling to meet their needs. It continues to run a pharmacy for those who need it, and it serves about sixty-five free meals a day to pensioners and Holocaust survivors. It runs a clinic and maintains a library, but it also has a microcredit institution to promote small businesses. It has even opened an art gallery in the old Jewish quarter, and its oldest synagogue is now a museum.

The multiethnic summer camp that I visited, Club Young Friends, has closed its doors due to financial considerations. Children now have too many competing activities demanding their attention, and the community could not provide a viable alternative to organized sports and clubs and games without more funding. The volunteer staff had aged in the decade and a half since the war and needed more help than they could afford to keep the program competitive. It is a sign of stability that the marketplace would overtake the good intentions of a few child-care professionals. But the skills that they learned and the purpose that drove them remain intact. The community still participates in interreligious and interethnic dialogue. It remains ready to fulfill its role should crisis ever again descend on Bosnia.

DURING THIS VISIT, I TOOK A day trip to the city of Mostar, where a river separates Serbs and Croats, and the ruined old bridge became a symbol for the disintegration of the country. During the war the city was a living hell, and there are still dozens of ruined buildings pocked with bullet holes. Though the old city has been repaired to lure tourists, and the bridge restored, walls outside of the old city still bear nationalist graffiti.

The small Jewish community of Mostar did what it could to help the city during the war, just as the community in Sarajevo had. In the intervening years, its numbers had shrunk dramatically as a result of the terrible economic conditions. If things were hard in Sarajevo, they were downright depressing in Mostar, but the community maintained a meeting hall, which also served as a synagogue, and a cemetery, reminders of more prosperous times. I went with two friends from Sarajevo to see the cemetery.

"It's across the street from the gas station," the president of Mostar's Jewish community told us. "They have the key to the gate."

As the sun set, we pulled up to the gas station and my friend Jaca ran inside to ask for the key. She was pregnant, though that didn't seem to endear her to them. The station employees were unfriendly, and unhelp-ful. We'd seen it for much of the day in Mostar.

"They hear my accent," she said. "They know we're from Sarajevo and don't like it. It's probably better if you ask."

So I explained in English that I was a Jew from America looking to visit the cemetery, and the mood changed immediately. It reminded me of the concentration camp guard in Germany. Just by being a Jew, I was al-lowed admittance. The gatekeepers assumed that my curiosity had some more valid purpose than my companion's.

The key appeared and was turned over to me without ceremony. We rushed across the street and I unlocked the gate. Some people at the gas station watched us with interest as we wandered through the rows of stones. The grass was trimmed and the place well cared for. There were no graffiti and no toppled graves. Someone loved this place, someone tended to it. Everyone I spoke to had great respect for the Jews of Mostar. They were an old presence in the city and, like the Jews of Sarajevo, could cross ethnic lines to be a bridge between peoples. They had no reason to fear for their safety in Mostar, at least not as Jews.

"Albert is a Jewish name?" Jaca asked, looking at a plaque commem-orating those who died in Holocaust. "We're going to name our son that."

"Yeah, it's a common Jewish name, I think."

"But non-Jews have it too," she said. Her grandmother had been Jewish, but for some reason the idea of giving her child a Jewish name concerned her.

"Does it bother you that it's a Jewish name?"

"No," she said.

"Maybe he'll be powerful like Jakob Finci," her husband joked. "The Jews are well connected in Bosnia . . . " He laughed, and we finished up quickly so we could begin the drive back to Sarajevo before it got too dark. I returned the key to the gas station, and we hit the road, passing the construction site where the Jewish community had laid the corner-stone for a new community center before running out of funding. The cornerstone sat lonely in a dirt plot. Across the street a fight had broken out at a café, and my head whipped around to catch the first blow as we sped off into the dark. Outside of Sarajevo, the violence lurked much closer to the surface.

"MOSTAR IS PRETTY," IVAN HRKAS TOLD me the next morning when we met for coffee, "but it's a very different place from here. The city is a lot more divided, and there is a lot more tension. I miss Israel."

I was amazed that he would miss Israel if he didn't like the tension in Mostar.

"Tel Aviv is just a wonderful place, far more cosmopolitan than any-where in Bosnia, but Sarajevo is my home." He teaches photography at the University in Sarajevo and is developing a series of photocollages based on the Kabbalah. He is drawn to Jewish mysticism as a creative motif, though not neccessarily to the religion or the community. I met him at a performance by a visiting Israeli dance company. He sat behind me in Sarajevo's National Theater, hooting and clapping loudly after each piece. I assumed he knew the performers, but no, he explained, he was just pas-sionate about modern dance and eager to support young Israeli artists. We all went to a bar that night, and Ivan was thrilled to speak Hebrew with the dancers, a language with which he was far more comfortable than English and which he didn't get much opportunity to speak. As we drank, he explained that he saw himself more as a universal person, not drawn to any nationalist ideology like Zionism. And he was certainly no Bosnian nationalist. "I love Israel and I love Sarajevo, each in its own way, but I don't want to limit myself with these labels—Jewish, Muslim, Bosnian, Israeli, gay, straight. I don't like labels."

Funny, I thought. I'd begun this journey trying to identify more with one specific label, and found nothing but hybrid identities and people who shunned the limitations that labels imposed.

Ivan is a product of the war in Bosnia and the Jewish community there, but also of Israel and the cafés of Tel Aviv. He speaks three languages, shares Muslim and Jewish heritage, and draws on a multitude of influences for his art. The war that displaced him when he was twelve turned him into a kind of global citizen, disconnected from any one nationality and in love with multiple places. He mirrors, in a sense, a long strain of Jewish history: those Jews who still hold the keys to the homes in Spain from which their ancestors fled during the Inquisition, those with one eye toward London and the other toward Jerusalem, while their feet remain planted wherever they were born. He lives the ideal of a spiritual homeland detached from a physical homeland, or perhaps attached to too many physical homelands.

After I left Sarajevo, Ivan and I kept in touch on Facebook, through which he seems to stay in contact with hundreds of friends all over the world and in a variety of languages. Social networking on the Internet has provided a much more accurate model of his identity than an attachment to a specific nation or religion. He'd lived with virtual social networks since fleeing Bosnia and becoming a refugee. He grew up taking on and discarding traditions, habits, and languages as a matter of survival, and online he had found the right medium for this mode of being. The fluidity of exile identity mirrored the flexibility of Internet identity and, in a sense, the long tradition of Jewish adaptation. He wasn't grounded in a geographic space or a specific tradition. He was a cultural nomad, just as Diaspora Jews always had been, and that multiplicity without physical geography had helped him, as it had helped them, to survive.

LEAVING BOSNIA, I FELT I'D FOUND what I was looking for. I'd seen a multitude of Jewish answers to Hugo Kahn's question, a variety of ways of forming identity and keeping a community alive. You could find your place in the Jewish world through religious observation, community involvement, service to your neighbors, or even online social networking. I also felt somewhat more lost. I'd seen a model of Judaism based on service and commitment regardless of religion, and I'd seen that model make the Jews more secure among a Muslim majority than they were almost anywhere else in Europe. But I'd also seen a different kind of identity, one without any borders at all, one suited to the information age, one that lost none of its potency for its lack of attachment to a place or, rather, one that felt attachment to many places and formed itself in a postgeographic way. When I ran these ideas by Ivan, he was amused but not convinced.

"I miss home," he said, meaning Israel. For all my theorizing, there was, quite simply, no place like home, no matter how fraught it was or how complex the cultural and linguistic hurdles one had to surmount to live there. Facebook was just a tool for staying in touch with the very real people in the very real places that Ivan loved, and reading too much into it, I'd missed the point entirely. Ivan could love more than one place, but he could only live in one at a time, and the one he had chosen, for now, was Bosnia. There would always be a hole in his heart in the shape of Israel, and if he moved there, there would be another hole in the shape of Bosnia. Ivan Ceresnjes, just after the siege of Sarajevo, called nostalgia the Bosnian disease, though it goes back much further than Bosnia, to the Book of Lamentations and the brokenhearted psalmist Jeremiah. I thought of the line again, *If I forget thee, O Jerusalem* . . . Everyone has a place they never want to forget.

six

Converts:
The Jewish Community of Uganda

Those who sow in tears shall reap with songs of joy!
—PSALMS 126:5

THE MUNICIPAL MARKET IN Mbale, Eastern Uganda, has all the usual hallmarks of a market in Africa: narrow rows of stalls selling dried fish and meat, cloth, trinkets, batteries, toys, CDs, home-brewed booze; and everywhere the smell of sweat. Between the stalls run rivulets of mysterious liquid. It could be runoff from the butchers; it could be battery acid. Better not to know and better yet not to step in it wearing flip-flops. I watched kids dash through it barefoot, weaving through the crowd toward the day's entertainment.

A man in a dress was singing a love song in Luganda, one of the dozen local languages. He crooned that his heart was broken, but finding new love could repair it. He flirted with the men in the audience like an aggressive hooker, and an eager crowd laughed and clapped. I knew homosexuality to be utterly and completely taboo in Uganda, but public drag shows seemed to be family entertainment. The man didn't make any concession to drag other than the dress, but he was a decent singer. The crowd noticed me, the *mzungu*—the white man—and insisted I pay a little to help the musician eat. Everyone cheered when I passed a few coins through to the front.

The aisle was narrow, and I jostled some people as I walked away, hot and needing to get out of the impossible smells assaulting my nasal pas-sages. As I squeezed away from the musical act, one of the vendors called out to me, and I turned toward him. His embroidered cap and long white robe told me he was a Muslim. Islam had been the official state religion in Uganda for some time, and still competed with Christianity in terms of missionary zeal throughout the region. This vendor didn't call out for me to buy his rice or the beans stacked in sacks around him, or to push bad copies of the latest pop music out of the Congo "at a very reasonable price." He had a simple message, unexpected, but one that I learned was typical of this particular market and no others in all of Africa.

"Shabbat Shalom!" he called with a smile. "Shabbat Shalom!"

"Shabbat Shalom," I repeated, stunned, and continued on my way toward fresh air. Samson, my guide and a member of Uganda's small Jewish community, waved at the man and wished him a peaceful Sabbath as well. Samson was tall and thin, with a wide face and quick, searching eyes. He was a member of the Bugisu tribe, which meant that he spoke at least one other language in addition to Luganda and English. "I also study Hebrew," he explained, slipping on his sunglasses and heading into the afternoon sun. I followed, squinting, because I'd forgotten my sunglasses. My friend Jon, whom I'd grown up with in Baltimore and who'd come along as a photographer, made his way out of the market behind us.

"Someone just whispered to me that you looked like a Jew," he told me.

"What gave it away?"

I was wearing one of the knitted *kippot* that the Ugandan Jews wore.

They were based on the design of Muslim skullcaps but decorated with Jewish symbols. It was the first time I'd worn a symbol of my Judaism in public, other than the tefillin in the bowling alley in Arkansas. I had wanted to see what the reaction would be. All over town that Friday afternoon, people came up to me to say Shalom. Jon was greeted as a *mzungu*, like most white visitors. Samson and I were greeted as Jews.

We headed back to the van to take the twenty-minute drive up a bumpy road to Nabugoye Hill, where the Abayudaya, the Jewish community of Eastern Uganda, were preparing for Friday night services. We had to be back early to change for the evening because the Abayudaya celebrate the Sabbath with serious commitment and we did not want to be late. As we made our way to the van, others called out to us, "Shabbat Shalom." The friendliness was slowing us down.

The Jews and their Sabbath were widely known here. I found it remarkable that such a public form of Judaism existed in Uganda, where Judaism had been illegal less than thirty years earlier. This was, after all, the land of Idi Amin and the Lord's Resistance Army, a place that had known unspeakable ethnic and political violence, and still battled crushing poverty. This was the sort of environment in which I imagined Jews would want to keep a low profile. Even in Bosnia, where the Jews had earned a lot of respect in the community, they didn't go around advertising themselves in the market, and they certainly weren't greeted by their Muslim neighbors with hearty wishes for a peaceful Sabbath every Friday night. What was going on here?

Samson was the Ugandan Jewish community's resident tour guide and taxi driver, with a reputation for overcharging foreigners, like any self-respecting taxi driver the world over. He had a generous laugh and a great deal of knowledge about Jewish history. He knew that the world was becoming curious about Uganda's black African Jews, and he took that curiosity as a good opportunity to expand his tourism business. But his commitment to the Jewish community ran much deeper than just acting as a tour guide. He served on the board of the Jewish primary school and the brand-new guesthouse run by the Abayudaya. He also helped with the services in the synagogue, translating between English and Luganda. He loved being Jewish. He had even been arrested for it when he was a teenager, during the community's fateful uprising, which he promised to tell me about another time.

WHEN WE ARRIVED AT NABUGOYE HILL, the center of Jewish life in Uganda, a gaggle of children was sweeping out the whitewashed Moses Synagogue in preparation for the services. Samson hopped into his car to drive home to clean up and change. A group of Israeli backpackers arrived to witness the evening's festivities, as did some American tourists in the country for a safari. An American actress I recognized from *Law & Order* checked in to the guesthouse. Friday night on Nabugoye Hill had found its way into a lot of itineraries. To get away from all the other visitors before the services, Jon took a nap. I strolled around the hill, admiring the mango and banana trees, studying the locked door of the Shalom Internet and Shopping Center and wondering what went on inside, as I had been assured there was no Internet connection that worked on Nabugoye Hill.

The hill itself is a lovely place. The area is rich with colors—the rusty red of the soil and the deep green of the foliage. It is also rich with different customs, shared by Christians, Muslims, Jews, and practitioners of various Bantu traditions. A dirt road cuts from the main route into Mbale, turning at a sharp angle up to the village, where it passes clusters of mud brick houses. Banana, cedar, and mango trees cast shade over the rutted lane. The Jewish community's first aid clinic is just off to the side of the road, opposite the Shalom Internet and Shopping Center. Dr. Samson Wamani, the first doctor in the Abayudaya community, runs the clinic, though he is in Mbale at the moment.

After the clinic, the road turns gently past the Moses Synagogue and rolls down the slope, where it skirts Semei Kakungulu High School and leads out of Nabugoye Hill toward the border with Kenya. Children run around barefoot and unsupervised, playing games and chasing each other. On other days the Abayudaya children would join in, but now they are dressed in their best and preparing the synagogue, and their cleaning is no less celebratory than the other children's play. The boys wear knitted *kippot* just like mine, and the girls wear long dresses. Some of the community's men always wear their *kippot*; others only put them on in the synagogue. As I stand and watch the quiet village play out its Friday dusk rituals, passersby on foot and bicycle wave to me.

"Shabbat Shalom," they say. The children run up to me and shout "*Mzungu!*," as children throughout East Africa always do. But these children add, smiling, "Shabbat Shalom!" The air smells of smoke from cooking fires. A goat tromps through the brush on the side of the hill that slopes back down to the guesthouse. I have the momentary feeling that he is wishing me a happy Shabbat too, but he goes on chewing the grass.

Everyone knows that a white man visiting Nabugoye Hill must be Jewish. The Jewish community of Nabugoye Hill has become a magnet for visitors and, with these visitors, international aid and media attention as well. The new guesthouse, where Jon and I are two of the first guests, is only one of the investments made by Jewish organizations. The house is so new that the bathroom fixtures sparkle and one hardly needs flip-flops to go to the showers.

Aaron Kintu Moses steps out into the cooling evening air. Aaron, principal of the Hadassah Primary School and acting religious leader of the Abayudya while his brother Gershom is in California studying to be a rabbi, lives behind the Shalom center with his wife and children. He is much shorter and darker skinned than Samson. He and his brothers—all community leaders in their own right—descend from a different ethnic group than Samson. Though they're all black Africans, and all connected in some way by parentage or marriage, the Jews of Uganda have an array of ethnic and linguistic backgrounds, mirroring much of the rest of world Jewry.

I first met Aaron when he came to New York on a speaking tour. I took him on his first subway ride and stood with him for half an hour on an outdoor train platform, a story he'd already told everyone in the village. "It was so co-oo-old! Ooooooo!" he'd shout in falsetto, shaking and stomping to illustrate his point.

"It is time for Shabbat," he says now with a smile, when he sees me standing outside on the hill. He looks far younger than his forty-seven years. He scratches his head underneath his gray skullcap and makes his way slowly up the hill to the synagogue, where the Abayudaya are starting to gather. Aaron's knowledge of Jewish law and customs is incomplete, I was told, but growing fast. He devours any new knowledge that comes his way, considering it deeply, integrating it with what he knows and what he believes. He is looking forward to Gershom's return and eager to study at the yeshiva they plan to establish, the first in sub-Saharan Africa. Aaron feels called to be a religious teacher. I remembered sitting on the subway, rumbling toward Grand Central Station, while he shook his head at me in disbelief.

"You should know the story of Purim!" he cried and rubbed his forehead. I had asked what he wanted me to bring to the community when I visited, and he suggested supplies for Purim. My follow-up—"what supplies are those?"—elicited his shocked declaration. Commuters glanced over at us. A dark-skinned African man in a strange yarmulke was yelling at a young Jewish guy about Purim. Only in New York, they must have thought. He suggested I come immediately to Uganda so I could learn what it meant to be Jewish. It took me a few months, but I got there, and Aaron embraced me when I arrived. I'd missed Purim by a few weeks, but Passover was coming, and I'd brought a few things, including "ten plagues" finger puppets for him to use at the primary school.

We walked the thirty yards to the synagogue together. Men and women of all ages, wearing colorful African patterns and freshly cleaned shirts and slacks, poured through the opening in the chain-link fence around the building. The men covered their shoulders in prayer shawls. The women and girls took up seats on one side of the room, the men and boys on the other. Nathan, a young man I'd met the day before, handed out prayer books to visitors as they walked in. He also handed me a laminated card. On it were the Psalms that the Abayudaya sing at services. They had translated them into the Luganda language. As I looked around at the mixture of foreign visitors and the mass of dark-skinned Africans who continued to arrive, laughing and smiling and preparing to celebrate a Jewish custom together, I knew I was in a place unique in the world.

Isaac, a nineteen-year-old DJ, who I noticed had a tattoo on his forearm that looked like a graffiti tag, was preparing to lead the prayers, while Rabbi Aaron, as they called him, welcomed everyone individually. I was struck by how excited the women were to be at services. I always imagined Judaism, especially in its more traditional forms, to be rather stifling for women, and assumed that in a patriarchal society like Uganda's, those aspects would be even more prevalent. All the leaders of the community were men, after all. But as people continued to pour into the building, the women soon outnumbered the men.

The service started with singing. JJ Keki, who is a half-brother to Aaron and Gershom, stood in front of the congregation with his guitar. If Samson's personality projected knowledge, and Aaron's piety, than the word that came to mind when first meeting JJ was joy. He was also one of the leaders and founders of the Abayudaya, and led the songs throughout the service. And the songs were like nothing I had ever heard.

The words were in Hebrew; some of them, and the prayers seemed familiar. I felt as though I'd heard them before, though I couldn't place them. Jon, who'd spent more time in synagogue as a child than I had, couldn't place them either. The melodies were new to me, a mixture of traditional Jewish singing and African rhythms. Everyone joined in, smiling, clapping, stamping, and dancing. The men in their prayer shawls told the group when to rise and when to sit. A mixture of languages fluttered around the room—Hebrew and English, but also Luganda and Lugisu and some other Bantu languages I couldn't name. Aaron walked up and down the center aisle singing and smiling at the children, who looked at him with a mixture of awe and terror. He was their principal during the week, as well as their spiritual leader, and he was smiling with such joy that it was breathtaking.

JJ nodded at me with a wink. We'd also met a few weeks earlier, when he came to America on a speaking tour, and I'd grown fond of his mischievous smile and his robust laugh. When he spoke his voice had a slight rasp, but when he sang it was sweet and smooth. He was a coffee farmer and a politician and a businessman, but his most beloved role was as a musician, and he brought to it the most simple and encompassing joy. As he played and sang, there was nothing else in this world for him but the melody and this moment and this congregation.

Looking around, the mood was infectious. After a week of the hardscrabble life on Nabugoye Hill, which is mostly populated by subsistence farmers, after a week scratching in the dirt and cooking and cleaning and tending the fire and walking miles and miles in the heat, struggling against the vast array of challenges that the land and the poverty present, the sheer delight at the arrival of the Sabbath was overwhelming. It was a feeling of total release, and I understood why the women, who do all the housework in Uganda, were so engaged in the celebration. The Sabbath was truly a blessing for them. As the sun dropped completely below the horizon, the congregation arrived at the song "Lekhah Dodi," a mystical Hebrew chant that welcomes the Sabbath as a beautiful bride, the feminine divine. This was the essential character of the Sabbath, and the reason that in traditional homes the women are the ones who light the candles on Friday nights. I saw now, in the Ugandan community, that for women the observance was not a yoke, but a blessing, a celebration of their unique role in the home, the society, and the sacred. Every one of the women singing and stomping acted fully and equally as a participant in the ritual (and, unlike in Orthodox congregations, they were allowed to make *aliyah*, to read from the Torah on Saturday mornings).

In the course of my travels, I had heard "Lekhah Dodi" sung all over the world, but this time the tune and the excitement in the air were quite different. As they celebrated the Sabbath bride, the women were quick to move and sway to the song, their voices nearly washing out the men's. Children jumped up and circled the bimah together. Men and women joined them. Aaron gestured for Jon and me to stand too, so we rose, and in front of the congregation, surrounded by children and men in prayer shawls and women in their brightly patterned dresses, we bopped and danced in circles, singing an ancient tune that Jews all over the world were singing, but doing it with a uniquely African spirit.

"Lechah dodi likrat kallah pnei Shabbat nekabelah," we sang. "Let's go, my friend, towards the bride, and receive the presence of Shabbat."

We stomped and stamped and clapped and held hands. I had never experienced a religious moment like this before. There was nothing solemn about it. Through the music and the movement of the bodies and the laughing little children in their *kippot* and their dresses, I truly felt as if I had welcomed something new into my life and bid farewell to the week that had passed. I couldn't believe it was like this every week.

The song must have been audible to everyone on the hill and I cannot imagine they didn't feel a little better having heard it, regardless of their religion. A smile crept over my face as the service went on, and I couldn't possibly make it go away. Natan, the young man who'd given me the prayer book, pointed to where we were on my laminated card (Psalm 92) and I did my best to sing along in Luganda.

"Kirungi okwebazanga Adonai! N'okuyimba okutendereza!" we

sang. "It is a good thing to give thanks unto the Lord, and to sing praises unto thy name, O Most High," I read in the English prayer book. The congregation swayed with the tune, as if it were a wind sweeping through the packed room. Some sang with their eyes closed; others looked to the ceiling or at each other. JJ grinned broadly as he moved around in front of the congregation, at home in his music, looking at one of his sons, Mac-cabee, and nodding with him as the boy's lilting voice carried the melody. It seemed everyone in the community had a gift for music.

"The Abayudaya are a community in the process of building their Jewish self-expression," Rabbi Jeffrey A. Summit had explained to me before I visited Uganda. Rabbi Summit is an ethnomusicologist at Tufts, who has spent years studying the Abayudaya's music and even produced an album of their songs for Smithsonian Folkways Recordings. "When I first started visiting them in 2000, I saw a community that was actively deciding how to affirm their traditions and reach out to the mainstream Jewish community. So on the one hand they are trying to build bridges with the rest of world Jewry, but they are also committed to preserving their African musical traditions."

The Abayudaya are one of the newest Jewish communities in Africa and certainly the most rapidly growing. They've been visited by several *bet din*, rabbinic courts, which ritually verify their conversion to Judaism. Hundreds have gone through the ceremony, which is recognized by the Conservative movement in America but not by the religious authorities in Israel, whose demands for conversion are far more strict and who are wary of black Africans, whom they suspect of using Judaism as a way to immigrate to Israel.

This community, however, has no intention of leaving. They fought too hard for the little patch of earth they now have, and they are deeply tied to being Ugandans. Their story begins under British colonial rule, and it passes through the last hundred years with moments of terror and bloodshed, dictatorship, and poverty, the clashing of modern ideas and traditional beliefs, and a lot of song. Throughout it all, there is song. It shares more deeply in the history and traditions of the red dirt hills of Eastern Uganda than of the hills surrounding Jerusalem. But such open singing and public celebration were not always the norm for this community.

IN THE EARLY TWENTIETH CENTURY, A Muganda tribal chief named Semei Kakungulu hoped to become a king. He wanted to rule the large swath of land at the base of Mount Elgon. He was a military man, and he supported the British, thinking they would give him the power for which he longed. He took on local tribal leaders and brought them under the control of the colonial power. He established Mbale Town, which would grow into the third largest city in Uganda. He was given title over the land he desired, but he was not made a king. Provincial Governor was the highest title he would ever be granted by the British.

This enraged him, and he withdrew from the life of a soldier. He refused to serve the British, who had betrayed his trust. He went to the top of a hill in his territory outside of Mbale, where he built a beautiful mansion that overlooked his land, a place where he could reflect on his life, in search of a spiritual center. For a time he aligned himself with the Malakites, a sect that mixed Christian practices with local Bantu beliefs and Christian Science.

Semei Kakungulu soon grew dissatisfied with this belief system as well. When he proposed the observance of the biblical command pertaining to circumcision on the eighth day of life, the Malikite leaders objected. Bodily mutilation went against all their religious norms and those of the local tribes. In the story, as Samson relayed it to me, the Christian missionaries and the Malakites were dismayed.

"You can't do that! You'll be a Jew!" Samson waved his hands in the air as he told the story, a big toothy grin spreading across his face. "And Kakungulu answered, 'Well then from this day onward, I am a Jew!'"

Kakungulu began to study the Bible. At first his followers practiced a mixture of Judaism, Islam, local custom, and some Christianity. They called people to prayers with the beating of drums; they took their shoes off before entering a house of worship. And they proselytized. Kakungulu gave gifts of grain and soap to followers of his new religion, the Abayudaya, which translates into English as "the community of Jews." He sent out men to establish synagogues all over his territory, and he adopted orphans to raise in the traditions of the Jews. Like Abraham on his hilltop, Kakungulu became circumcised as a grown man. He instructed his followers to do the same and to circumcise their male children on the eighth day.

In 1922 he completed writing a prayer book of songs and rituals for the Abayudaya to follow. The British, angered by both his political and religious rebellion, moved to take away some of his land. He went to Kampala to stop them and, while there, met a Jewish man from Yemen. It was his first contact with a Jew from the outside world, who explained that Jews did not follow the New Testament.

"So," Samson explained, "Kakungulu ripped the Bible in half, and from then on only followed the Torah." Samson told the tale while Jon and I stood with him at the site of Kakungulu's grand old home, meant to be his castle, high on a hill overlooking the whole valley, all the way to Mbale, where the dust and the car exhaust kicked up a haze over the small city. Behind us, Mount Elgon rose into the low clouds. The "castle" had fallen into disrepair, but some of Kakungulu's descendents still lived there, trying to maintain it, though life was hard and isolated for them. There was no running water and the nearest well was a long trek down and up again, on steep and uneven slopes. The planned seat of Kakungulu's empire now survived on support from the Abayudaya living below on Nabugoye Hill and donations from tourists. Kakungulu loved nature, and his old property feels like a slightly overgrown park, with benches and boulders to sit on while admiring the landscape. A cool wind blows through the trees, and birds call to each other in the distance. I could imagine the place as more of a cloister for religious searching than as a seat of military power. From this spot, in fact, Kakungulu began the religious study and training that brought Judaism to Uganda.

The Yemenite taught the Abayudaya Hebrew prayers and encouraged Kakungulu to establish a Jewish school on his land. But when Kakungulu died in 1928, his biggest plan hadn't yet been realized: a large synagogue on Nabugoye Hill. After his death, other Jewish visitors came to the community and taught the leaders Hebrew. The Jews, however, generally developed their individual communities without much outside help. They taught themselves the liturgy and went unrecognized by international Jewry for decades to come.

One of Kakungulu's students, Samson Mugombe, became the Abayudaya's spiritual leader, but he lacked the means or sophistication to maintain Abayudaya control over the land. The Abayudaya were peasant farmers, and their claims were no match for larger organizations, corporations, and governments that wanted to use their land. Their numbers soon dipped below three hundred, from several thousand during Kakungulu's time. The Jews lost the site of their school to the government, and soon lost control over most of the rest their land to Christian missionaries. They tried to finish the synagogue that Kakungulu had envisioned on Nabugoye Hill, but it fell into disrepair. Most of the children, educated in missionary schools, became Christians and knew even less of the Jewish religion than their parents did. When Idi Amin seized power in 1971, it seemed that would be the end of the brief flicker of Jewish life in Uganda.

Amin made Islam the official state religion and the Abayudaya were forbidden to read the Bible or practice Jewish burial. The remaining Jewish children were taunted in school for being different, for being "Christ killers," and the teachers allowed such taunts to go unchecked. The community leaders, Samson Mugombe and a man named Kek—JJ's father—continued to hold services in a cave on one of the plantations in Nangolo, where coffee and bananas grew thick on the ground. The cave had been a favorite spot of Semei Kakungulu's, and now it was a secret refuge for the Jews. Every Friday night, the children would pound on the roof of the cave like a drum to summon the Jews who wished to pray, and Kek or Samson Mugombe would lead the prayers. Aaron remembers once, when he was a small boy, playing on the top of the cave and being frightened by a large snake. He and his brothers hesitated to go up there again for a long time.

A village chief once heard Kek praying from the Bible and threatened to turn him in to the police, which would have meant torture and possibly death. He bribed his way out of danger, but the community continued to be persecuted, forcing them to withdraw even further from the public eye. More and more people converted to Islam or simply lost touch with the Abayudaya and the Jewish traditions.

As the seventies progressed, the Abayudaya's position became even more precarious. In 1976 Israel humiliated Amin by freeing the hostages of Flight 139, who were being held at Entebbe Airport. The Israeli Defense Forces raided the plane on the runway and spirited the hostages to safety, right under Amin's nose. His response was fiercely anti-Zionist and anti-Jewish. He arrested the Abayudaya's spiritual guide, Samson Mugombe, and imprisoned him as a spy because he had information in Hebrew about Jerusalem. He was held for a few days, but released when the police were convinced he was illiterate.

It was during the Amin years that Aaron and his brothers, young boys at the time, started to learn about Judaism. They traveled with their father to conduct furtive funerals whenever a community member died. Most people were buried by their homes on their own plots of land, though there is an area near the Nangolo cave synagogue where a few of the Abayudaya are buried together, making it the closest thing Uganda has to a Jewish cemetery. One of the community's earliest leaders, a man named Kabbalah David, JJ's grandfather, is buried there with his sons. Many of his grandsons converted to Islam. There had been a synagogue in Nangolo near the cave, but the grandchildren tore it down.

When Amin fell from power two days before Passover in 1979, the few remaining Abayudaya were ecstatic. The reign of terror had ended, and Judaism was legal again just in time for the Feast of Freedom, as Passover is sometimes called. The remaining Abayudaya called their community to prayers with drums once again, made matzo, and gathered for a service in what was left of the synagogue on Nabugoye Hill. But many of the elders had forgotten how to pray, and many of the younger generation had converted to other religions or simply drifted away. When one of the elders died a few months after Amin fell from power and the Jews held the first public funeral in over a decade, their Christian and Muslim neighbors taunted them, laughing at their strange customs.

Kek's middle son, a young man named Gershom, and his brothers, JJ and Aaron, along with some other young men formed the Young Jewish Club just after the fall of Amin. They studied and taught themselves Hebrew together. As the eighties went by, they were hungry and weak, and universally reviled by those around them. The Jewish communities spread around the region were aged, and as their leaders died they were fading away. In the village of Namatumba, Samson Mugombe, who was one of Kakungulu's original students, and an old rabbi named Eli, tried to rebuild their little synagogue in a mud hut. Destroyed by Idi Amin, it had been the site of the first synagogue established by Kakungulu. They rebuilt it in 1980 with a thatched roof and a hollow spot in the wall for the Torah. They wrote the Ten Commandments on the wall in chalk. Mugombe passed away in 2004, but Eli is still around and his community is growing. He himself has thirty children, from several wives.

"Polygamy was our custom, but not anymore," he said. "Now I have just one wife. It is enough for me. But it is good to have so many children. We are growing as a community and we will not be driven away."

With the community weakened, the Anglican leaders on the Hill saw a chance to take advantage of the situation, and they seized the site of the synagogue in order to expand an Anglican school. There were no Jews living on Nabugoye Hill by that time.

When the Anglican leaders were granted permission to take the land on Nabugoye Hill where the synagogue had been, a group of young Abayudaya men realized that they had to do something to save it. This land had been given to them by Semei Kankangulu; it had been willed to the Abayudaya, though Kakungulu had never given them legal title over it. They believed it was the land of their forefathers, their birthright.

So the young men simply came to the site, which was now being used as a staff house, and occupied it. They brought Hebrew books and guitars and they started to write the music I would hear years later on a Friday night in the synagogue. They prayed and chanted and defied requests to leave the hill and go back to their villages. There weren't any other Jews on Nabugoye Hill, so the young men were isolated. The village leaders brought in the police and arrested Gershom, JJ, and Aaron. Samson escaped in his underpants. The young Jewish activists were taken to the district police station, beaten, and forced to hold stress positions, squatting with their arms in front of them for hours. When they were released, they returned to the hill and went right back to the staff house.

As 1988 turned to 1989, the youths were still there on the hill. They refer back to this era as the "kibbutz time," when they lived and worked together on land they saw as sacred. This was their answer to that old question *Ayeka?*—Where are you? They had spent decades in hiding and decline, and now the young men were prepared to answer that question loudly and proudly by singing and praying and declaring openly, "*Hineini!* I am here!"

Jewish elders from the surrounding area rallied around them and began to send their daughters up to the hill to meet Jewish men for marriage. Samson met his wife, Dinah, during the occupation of the hill

when they were teenagers. In spite of the arrests, JJ urged the Abayudaya to start building their synagogue next to the occupied staff house
and they began making bricks and laying out the foundation. Though
they had only a limited knowledge of Israeli history, it seemed that they
understood one of the earliest policies of the Zionist movement: creating facts on the ground. On their own version of the Promised Land,
they staked their claim with a physical structure. The Anglican school
headmaster objected to the construction, but the young men simply lied.
They said they were going to donate the bricks to the school. The police
came back to arrest the troublemaking Jews yet again.

Gershom was said to have charged at the police chanting, "If it is
our time to die, let us die!" I had never met Gershom, but I had heard
him described as a wise man, the spiritual heart of the community, their
pride. When he returned from California later that summer, he would
be the first black rabbi in sub-Saharan Africa. He had a lovely wife and
two children. I tried to reconcile this image of the learned scholar and
leader with the stories I was hearing about a militant youth charging at
the police pounding on his chest and yelling for martyrdom. The young
men were taken to the police station and tortured again, but this time the
Abayudaya elders appealed to an attorney, a man who was not Jewish but
was a descendant of Semei Kakangulu. He went above the local authorities and proved that the Jews had a legal right to the land on the hill, that
it had been theirs all along. After a long uncertain time, the Jews finally
had the authorization to stay.

They started to raise funds more aggressively, reaching out to foreigners and developing businesses. Gershom earned extra money tutoring
village children. JJ grew coffee and bananas and mangoes and anything
he could plant. He loved farming and saw himself as a latter-day Kakungulu. Just like Kakangulu, he started planting cedar trees, not for their
valuable wood, but simply because they were beautiful. He saw steward-
ship of the earth as a Jewish value and part of his spiritual duty.

As the years passed and the community drew more and more interest from outsiders, their fortunes improved. Working with a Jewish outreach organization called Kulanu, which means "All of Us" in Hebrew, they installed the first electric water pumps on the hill. They partnered with Heifer International to get livestock for anyone—Jewish or not—who wanted to be part of the program. They opened a medical clinic and—realizing Semei Kakangulu's dream of a Jewish school—established Hadassah Primary School and Semei Kakangulu High School, the former headed by Aaron, the latter by the youngest of the brothers, Seth, who has a master's in education from the Islamic University in Mbale. Jewish volunteers were constantly visiting the community to teach Hebrew and Jewish studies and to run health and social programs.

BY THE TIME I VISITED, THE Jews on Nabugoye Hill were an ascendant community. They had become the most prosperous group in the area and they had shared their largess with their neighbors, those same neighbors who had sent them to prison years earlier. JJ even ran for local office and was elected to a term as district supervisor in Namanyoni District, where there is another synagogue and where many of the Abayudaya live.

"I went door-to-door and convinced those same people who had abused us to vote for me. And they did!" he said laughing. "You see, it doesn't take a lot to make an enemy into your friend."

JJ insisted that you could see him on the news on 9/11, a Ugandan man in a *kippah*, running from the scene of the World Trade Center attack. He was visiting New York City for the first time to speak about the Abayudaya, of whom he was the chairman in 2001. He'd gone to the World Trade Center to meet a friend and was about to step inside when the first plane hit.

"I was nearly a victim," he said. "After that, I began to wonder what I could do to help end this religious violence. People use small differences to make hatred. I am a Jew, and in Israel Jews and Muslims are killing each other . . . I began to wonder what I could do to make peace. What did I have with which to make peace?" JJ smiled again, his default expression. "Coffee. I have coffee."

It was Sunday, two days after our Shabbat celebration, and we were sitting in JJ's house, which was about a ten-minute drive from Nabugoye Hill. On top of his role in the Jewish community, JJ is the chairman of the Mirembe Kawomera Coffee Cooperative in Mbale, an interfaith coffee cooperative of over seven hundred Jewish, Christian, and Muslim coffee growers. His business card identifies him simply as Music Director, the title printed neatly beside the Star of David, the star and crescent, and the cross. His face is thin, lined slightly with age, and spotted with a patchy beard. He is the proud father of twenty-five children, fourteen of whom he adopted, though he is by no means a wealthy man. He is a coffee farmer, like his father and his father's father, like most people in the hills outside of Mbale, in the villages of Namanyoni District. Along the dusty road that leads west to Kenya and north to the Sudan, and that passes by JJ's farm, I saw countless fields of coffee plants. It seemed that everyone grew coffee.

I drink coffee every day, though I spend little time pondering its production. I couldn't live without it, I often think, though hardly in the same sense as farmers like JJ. One out of eight people in Uganda depends on coffee for his livelihood, but the price is unstable, and when the market collapsed in the 1990s, many Ugandans became discouraged and cut down their coffee trees. They were only getting about sixty cents per pound, not enough to buy mosquito nets, not enough to send their children to school, hardly enough to feed themselves. The farmers were impoverished, the people mistrustful of each other. JJ had overcome some of the religious prejudice when he won the election, but the economic woes of the area continued to press on everyone. And under such pressure, people tended to resort to old habits and old hatreds.

In 2004, with the memory of 9/11 still haunting him, JJ walked up and down the dusty, pitted roads to the homes of his neighbors. All of them needed to be getting a better price for their coffee. He knocked on their doors and told them he had a dream about cooperation, about bringing the Catholics, Anglicans, Muslims, and Jews together into one cooperative to grow coffee and, with coffee, to spread peace.

"At the time, we had some differences among the Christians, the Muslims, and the Jews," Sinina Numudosi, a young Muslim woman, now a board member of the coffee cooperative, told me. "We could not go to each other with our problems, we were not certain about trusting each other. But together we heard JJ's dream and we formed Mirembe Kawomera, which in the Luganda language means 'Delicious Peace.'"

"We really taught ourselves from scratch," Laura Wetzler, an American volunteer with Kulanu, said. "I had first encountered this community through their music, and I came as an ethnomusicologist. But I'd heard about fair trade, and JJ was certainly down with the whole organic thing. We wanted to move from charity to empowerment, so we began the long process of getting organic certification and finding a distributor."

They found a distributor in the Thanksgiving Coffee Company in Fort Bragg, California, a company committed to fair trade and organic farming. The farmers now get around two dollars per pound that they sell. As Ben Corey-Moran, Thanksgiving's sales director, explained, "We are in the business of creating a different kind of business and through that business creating a different kind of world. Imagine an economy where we talk about *interactions* rather than *transactions*."

JJ saw this kind of business as deeply tied to Jewish values and these sorts of interactions based on mutual benefit as essential for the future of the Abayudaya and the region. He took me on a tour of his coffee farm. Standing by one of his low trees, he smiled his trickster grin, excited that he had had a revelation. He was fond of revelations and aphorisms, which served him well as a politician and religious leader. They served him well as a coffee farmer too, it seemed. His latest revelation was simple enough.

"The coffee tree does not do well to be alone," he said. "It needs shade; it needs to be near other trees—bananas, cedar, avocado, mango." He pointed his long fingers at each tree as he named it. He plucked some leaves from another one of his coffee trees, his fingers delicately stroking the branch as he did so, firm and gentle at the same time, a stroke then a tug. The extra leaves rob the tree of water and need to be plucked to keep the tree healthy.

"You must always be in your garden," JJ continued. "Today one coffee berry could be ready to pick, you see—." He showed me a tree with one bright red coffee berry in a bunch of green. "Tomorrow three more. It is not yet the season. In a few months there will be so much work. The berries are not ready at the same time. They need constant attention . . . Just like people."

He paused a moment, adjusted the *kippah* on his head. "Just like people," he repeated, smiling. And then added a high-pitched "*Eh?*" in Ugandan fashion, his voice rising with exclamation, making the monosyllabic sigh sound like both a question and an agreement.

He pointed proudly at the tall cedar trees dotting his land. He had planted them himself and hoped they would survive to be a legacy for his children, all twenty-five of them. He worked hard to protect the trees because, aside from being beautiful, their wood was valuable, and many of the trees Kakangulu had planted in his time had been cut down by loggers.

"The environment is part of God's gift to us, so we must care for it. To me, responsibility for my farm is part of being a Jewish person. It is part of the covenant. You know the covenant?"

I asked him to tell me about it.

"*Eh?*" he said again, laughing. "It is just this," he said and swept his arms over the landscape. "Just this," he repeated, and left me to puzzle out his meaning. He also insisted I hear one of the songs he'd written to urge people to plant coffee and to grow it organically.

"I've traveled the world and seen nothing so good as coffee," he sang in Lugisu, one of the dozen languages spoken by cooperative members, as he played on his little guitar. "Our only solution is to grow coffee. Brothers and sisters, come, grow coffee."

"It is simple to cause peace," JJ explained. "We use what we have to make our enemies into our friends. I have coffee. You don't need PhDs. It's just us, we ourselves, who make peace."

THIS IDEA OF PEACEMAKING HAD CERTAINLY taken root in the area. The farmers saw how cooperation dramatically improved their standard of living. The coffee and the Heifer projects are just two examples. Everywhere I went with JJ, people came up to shake hands and to say Shalom. When I visited Hadassah Primary School, I asked the children to raise their hands if their family grew coffee. Nearly all the children raised their hands. I asked if any of the families were members of the co-op, but few children knew. I asked how many of the children came from the Abayudaya (I could see some boys wearing kippot), but the teacher interrupted me.

"We are all Ugandans here," he said. "I am a Muslim, some are Jews, some are Christians, but we are Ugandans first." The children all clapped for his message of unity. As Jon and I left the school, the children began to assemble for a performance of Jewish songs, led by an American volunteer. We walked slowly up the red dirt road, listening as the sounds of the song "Ose Shalom" (The One Who Makes Peace) faded into the trees.

The coffee cooperative was just one example of how the Abayudaya were putting tikkun olam into practice and sharing with their neighbors. The schools were another. By teaching Jewish values and customs, they were building a multicultural society of mutual respect and they were undoing the years of damage that state-sanctioned prejudice had inflicted on the area.

The situation is not all cheerful, and the stream of casual visitors who pass through the community for a weekend on their way to see the gorillas in the national park miss some of the conflicts that shape the community, that challenge it, and ultimately, that make it more typical of Jewish communities all over the world. There is some jealousy of JJ's success. While many farmers are still quite poor, JJ has purchased a new car. With the mounting influence of foreigners on Nabugoye Hill, some worry that the Abayudaya's religious values are becoming lax or that their brand of Judaism will be drained of that which also makes it uniquely Ugandan. And there are other villages with Jews who do not get as much aid money or attention, and who want for themselves and their communities what the Jews on the hill have. They want new synagogues and income-generating projects and foreign volunteers too.

Visiting Rabbi Eli in the dusty village of Namatumba, I saw the disparity. While the hill has an abundance of shade, and the houses are wired with electricity and, in many cases, running water, Namatumba still consists mostly of mud-brick houses with thatched roofs. It is flat and hot. As I stood near an enclosure that held their cow—a donation from Heifer International—a group of children watched from the shade of a nearby building. Chalked on the wall of the small round hut were a menorah and a Star of David. Only one boy dared step into the glaring sunlight to linger closer to Jon and me. He was all smiles, but his eyes were blank and his motions jerky. After he began poking at one of the goats with a stick, an older girl rushed from the shade and maneuvered the boy away from us into the darkness of one of the huts again.

They had two synagogues in Namatumba: the original one, the oldest still standing in Uganda, which was, like all the other buildings, a mud hut with a grass roof and a small nook to hold a Torah. When I visited, the Torah was being held on Nabugoye Hill for them while they tried to build a new synagogue, just next door. It was a big brick building with a tin roof and enough space for sixty or seventy people—though they have about a hundred and twenty Jews in the area—but they were short of funds to finish it for the time being. Rabbi Eli, looking much older than his sixty-two years, pointed proudly at the planned place, explaining what it would be like when it was done. In his visions, it was even nicer than the synagogue hours away on Nabugoye Hill.

The coffee they grow in Namatumba—Robusta—is not as marketable as the Arabica grown on JJ's farm. The community has some livestock, and they raise bees for honey. They grow some fruit too and are working to create a dried fruit cooperative, much like the coffee cooperative JJ started. They use a solar fruit dryer that Kulanu helped them purchase, but they were having trouble with some of the parts, which burned up in the merciless sun. The elders of the community urged me to lobby on their behalf, to make sure that not all the attention—and development dollars—went to Nabugoye Hill. Rabbi Eli stayed silent during that discussion. He was clearly a proud man, a longtime spiritual leader, and did not want to acknowledge that there was any tension among the people he saw as his flock. Let the younger generations squabble. He had seen the arc of Jewish life in Uganda swing up and down many times before.

It was the religious rift among the Abayudaya, however, that caught my interest. There was another member of the new generation of leaders, a cousin of Aaron and Gershom and JJ's named Enosh, who was rarely spoken of and who did not visit the hill. He led his own community, called She'erit Yisrael, which was based in the distant village of Puti. Enosh and his congregants were committed to Orthodox Judaism. They disliked that women were allowed to read from the Torah at the synagogue on the hill, and that certain members of the community, like JJ, drove on the Sabbath. They also disliked that Gershom was studying at a Conservative yeshiva and not an Orthodox yeshiva. They adhered to a strict interpretation of Jewish law, and the disagreements had led them to break away and establish their own synagogue.

"They won't talk about it," an American volunteer told me. "But there is a lot of bad blood between them now."

I visited Puti on a hot Sunday afternoon, after JJ had given me a tour of his land. A large snake slithered through the rafters of the new synagogue the She'erit Yisrael members were building. The old one stood nearby, having fallen into disrepair. The community was growing and needed the space. Next door was the ritual bath and nearby was a little school building, with the Hebrew lessons still on the blackboard. No one was around. The place was silent. She'erit Yisrael didn't get a lot of visitors, and it was the middle of the day. Everyone was working in their fields, Samson said. The heat was intense, and I couldn't imagine working in the field on a day like that, but the Sabbath was over and work had to resume. Losing a day of work was not an option for subsistence farmers, and I wouldn't find many people loitering about on Sunday. With the joy of the Sabbath also came the recognition that the other six days of the week must be fruitful. These Jews might disagree with each other on interpretations of the law, they might have "bad blood" between them, but they were just as committed to the spirit of the Sabbath and just as tied to working the land the rest of the week.

"There are about fifty Jews in this community. Many in this area converted away, but thanks to Enosh I do not think this generation will deteriorate," Samson said. "And I am sure they will remain our brothers and sisters, even if there are differences in our practice."

I wanted to tell Samson the old joke about the Jew on the desert island who'd built two synagogues, but I suspected the humor would be lost on him. I took the opportunity that the quiet village afforded to ask him some questions instead. The first one had been vexing me since I arrived in Uganda.

"Is everyone here related?"

Samson laughed and said that yes, it was a challenge to marry because everyone was a cousin or a brother or connected in some way. He drew a family tree for me in the dirt. There were just a few patriarchs—Samsom Mugombe and Kek and Eli, the rabbi at Namatumbu, and, of course, Semei Kakungulu, each of whom had many wives. Few of Kakungulu's descendants still practiced Judaism. Most of them had left the Abayudaya for Christianity and Islam, which made me want to ask the next question I had had in mind since arriving in this community of converts: Why be Jewish?

We were strolling along a path near the old cave that the community had used as a synagogue during the Amin years. The Jewish community no longer owned the land where the cave sat, and the owners sometimes got annoyed with vistors tromping through their farms. They were friendly, but they wanted a small payment, as a sign of respect and to help maintain the space. The path was on a steep hill that sloped down toward farming plots, where men and women dug in the bright sunlight, pulling cassava from the soil and plucking bananas and mangoes from the trees.

As we strolled—as if illustrating Samson's point about everyone being related—Aaron and Gershom's mother ran out to give us ripe mangoes she had just plucked from the trees. She knew of me already, of her son's trip on the subway in New York, and she smiled at the strange events that had occurred in the lives of her children. Who would have thought her poor boys growing up on these hills would find themselves in America, riding trains through the tunnels under New York City? She piled more mangoes into my arms, so I would have something to eat later. Samson and I each peeled a mango right there and began gobbling the yellow fruit. The sweet juice poured down our chins and arms.

"So," I asked again as we chewed and walked and looked over at the farmers below. "So many Abayudaya left Judaism during the Amin years . . . and now others are coming in, converting. I wonder, why be Jewish?"

"Well," Samson said, sucking at the mango's pit and tossing it into the forest, "you see, Judaism is not just a religion. It is a culture. It is an ancient culture and beloved by God, so we choose to be part of it, to practice those things to be Jewish. It is not like you, who is simply Jewish from your ancestors. Our ancestors were not Jewish. In Namatumba, they are the Busoga people, and the Bugisu and Buganda in the other areas. There are a lot of different ancestors, but we all come from one God, so we do these things to be Jewish. We have to practice and observe because if we do not, then we are not Jews."

I pressed the question. "Why do you, Samson, want to be Jewish?"

"For me, the most important thing is to get along with all your neighbors. That is the most important Jewish teaching, I think. Look at what has happened to the Jews here. We have worked hard to make peace and to help everyone to develop. These beliefs have benefited everyone."

Indeed, that spirit of cooperation had benefited most people who lived near the Abayudaya. Poverty was greater in the Abayudaya villages away from the hill, like Namatumbu, where Rabbi Eli lived, but they all had development projects in the works, such as the solar dried fruit cooperative and Heifer International initiatives. And the younger community members made the long trek up to Nabugoye to attend the Semei Kakangulu High School, the only Jewish high school in Africa. I had met the older generation of leaders in Rabbi Eli and the new generation in JJ and Aaron. I wanted to see for myself what the future held, in the teenagers. I had to go to the high school.

THE STUDENTS AT SEMEI KAKUNGULU WERE holding a dance party to welcome a new class that was joining the school. Loud afro-pop beats shook the quiet of the hill. I stepped into the dance for a minute, watching the boys in their *kippot* grind with the girls in bright patterned dresses. There were Christians and Muslims and Jews in the room, a mixture of faiths and styles and cultures. There were young people who practiced more traditional animist beliefs too. But they were all united by the great equalizer: teenage hormones. The room smelled powerfully of body odor. There was no air-conditioning. Isaac, the young man who'd led the prayers on Friday night, now played the music, headphones around his neck, bumping to the heavy beats, surrounded by eager hangers-on. Boys shouted at each other across the space, girls giggled their secrets the way girls all over the world do, and little kids, not allowed in, crammed their faces into every window and crack in the building to get a view of what the older kids were up to.

Aaron made a brief appearance, but did not approve of the music or the overtly sexual dancing and left quickly. He didn't want to be a downer, because he liked to see children of all backgrounds coming together without stigma or mistrust, but he didn't want to lend his approval either. He preferred organized dancing, like a show, where the youth could show off their traditional talents and learn about their culture. Rihanna and pelvic thrusts did not fit into his program.

I sensed I was falling into a Judeo-African remake of *Footloose*, and I slipped away to meet Seth, Aaron's youngest brother and the headmaster of the high school, in his office. It was too hot to close the office door, so we endured the loud and jarring leap from Ugandan hip-hop to Shakira's "Hips Don't Lie" as best we could.

"My brother Gershom taught here during the kibbutz time," Seth told me. "I was too young then, so I was not arrested or anything like that, but I saw the struggle, and I saw my brothers arrested, which was very embarrassing. Things are better now that we are recognized as a community and have helped to bring development. The Abayudaya attend the school for free, but the others must pay fees. The teachers are not paid enough. We have a problem with poverty. I would like for all students to attend for free, but we do not have the means. This school was built to improve literacy and to build better relations with our neighbors. In previous times, we Abayudaya were seen as Christ killers—"

I interrupted him to observe that the Abayudaya had not been Jews until the twentieth century. They couldn't be connected in any way to the Jews during the time of Christ.

"Prejudice is not rational," Seth said, laughing. "You cannot question it this way. You must only work to change minds through your actions. So we brought all the faiths together to build this school. We bought the land and the materials from non-Jews and paid a fair price, so they saw we could be trusted. Now, as you see, all the students are together, dancing together and studying together. We teach Hebrew lessons for the Jewish students, and we get about fifty non-Jewish teenagers who come to learn Hebrew, just out of interest."

There is a lot of interest in the Jews from other Ugandans. In the district of Apac, about four hours from Mbale, a community has started to reach out to the Jews on the hill, hoping to be recognized. They have a small synagogue and limited knowledge of Judaism, but, living as they do in a remote region of Uganda, the fact that they have any knowledge of Judaism at all is remarkable. About thirty kilometers beyond Apac, there is another small Jewish community. A few months after my trip, a rabbinical court from the Conservative movement of Judaism would be coming to Uganda to investigate the claims of many of these Jewish communities and offer formal conversions, as they had done a few years earlier. Hundreds of people took advantage of the opportunity the first time, though a minority objected, claiming they did not need to convert because they were already Jews. Critics argue that the Jewish knowledge of these people is too limited, that they have no genealogical connection to Judaism, and that they only want to be Jewish for the perceived material benefits, or for the possibility of emigration to Israel. That last critique stings Aaron and the other community leaders.

"We are Jews, and so we feel a connection to Israel, but Uganda is our home," he said. "We have struggled to build the community here and we do not want to leave it. We are Ugandans and we are Jews. But for us, this, Nabugoye, is like our Jerusalem. We struggled for this place, for our rights to be here."

The Israeli government will not recognize the Abayudaya as Jews anyway, in part because they are not Orthodox, in part because they cannot trace an "authentic" Jewish heritage back to biblical times, and in part because of the Israeli experience with the most famous of African Jews, the Beta Israel in Ethiopia.

THE BETA ISRAEL, AS THEY CALL themselves, are sometimes called Falasha and sometimes simply Ethiopian Jews. Their story provides a stark contrast with the story of the Abayudaya, who can trace their origins precisely within the last century, who have developed a practice of Judaism that looks much like the dominant Western form of Jewish practice, albeit with an African rhythm, and who have very little desire to leave their African home. Most of the Falasha are already gone from Ethiopia.

Falasha was a derogatory term at its inception, emerging in fifteenth-century Ethiopia under a Christian emperor who decreed that only those baptized as Christians would be able to own land. The rest would be Falasi, or landless ones, exiles. The Beta Israel saw themselves as exiles from Jerusalem, and took the name as their own because it so well encapsulated their sense of self. In Ethiopia, they were sojourners, as Abraham had been in the land of Canaan.

Their central tradition asserts that they are descendants of the ancient Hebrews, children of the union between King Solomon and the Queen of Sheba. They recount the story of Solomon's son Menelik, who settled in Ethiopia, taking the ark of the covenant with him. This story plays an important role for all Ethiopians in the idea that Ethiopia is the new Zion, which is why Emperor Haile Selassie called himself the Lion of Judah among other things. Other Beta Israel stories claim they are descendants of Hebrews who fled Egypt with Moses, or who fled Jerusalem after the destruction of the First Temple or the Second Temple. The popular claim in recent years is that they are the Tribe of Dan, one of the Ten Lost Tribes of Israel.

Since the advent of Christianity in Ethiopia, the Falasha have been compelled to live as tenant farmers and to supplement their income as craftsmen. Scholars have asserted that they were forced into crafts as a way to stigmatize them, suggesting that they are descendants of the smiths who made the nails with which Christ was crucified. Crafts were also associated with magic and transformation, which might have contributed to the belief that the Jews could transform themselves into hyenas.

Even as the Falasha were mistrusted, many Ethiopians still believed they were a holy people who had a special relationship to God. Priests and elders from other traditions often came to the Jews to ask for their prayers for rain or other blessings. Much of their existence was defined by their relationship to the dominant Christian culture. Some skeptics have even said that the Falasha emerged not through ancient immigration from Palestine but as a heretical sect of Christianity, indigenous people who adopted Judaism from Ethiopian Orthodox Christians. The Beta Israel, however, have never wavered in their belief that they are descended from the Israelites and that their origins predate Christianity.

None of these claims has been historically verified, but it is certain that, as long as they have identified themselves as a group, the Beta Israel have had their longing fixed on Jerusalem. In their prayers and songs, Jerusalem is the focus of all their yearning. For most of their history, none had ever actually seen the place, but that hardly mattered. Zion was the promise of God, the place from which they came and the place to which they dreamed of returning. When circumstances presented the opportunity for them to make their dream a reality, the Beta Israel risked everything to take it.

In May of 1991, the Israeli government, in concert with Mossad, the CIA, the White House, and a variety of nongovernmental organizations, airlifted over fourteen thousand Falasha to Israel in less than forty-eight hours, just before Addis Ababa fell to the rebel army. The Falasha left the relative safety of their villages to assemble in dangerous areas, where they waited, starving and vulnerable to attack, on the promise of a return to Zion. They deliberately put themselves in harm's way to achieve this dream. As Stephen Spector notes in his thrilling book on what became known as Operation Solomon, "The Jews left their villages because of a confluence of conviction, desire, and opportunity." Some have argued that, before moving from their villages to Addis Ababa and Gondar in order to go on to Israel, they had not been in any real danger, that this move into danger was a way of forcing the international community to let them emigrate. They had lived in Ethiopia for thousands of years, and yet, urged by their leaders, they left it all behind to go to the Promised Land. Many died on the way, and the entire airlift operation has been questioned for destroying the social fabric of the Beta Israel community.

Over the centuries, many Beta Israel converted to Christianity but continued to practice their Judaism in secret. This group, known as the Felas Mura, are controversial because they too want to make aliyah to join their extended families in Israel. They want to be Jews and have left their villages to move to the city of Gondar in order that they be given the chance to migrate to Israel also, though their fate is uncertain and subject to ever-shifting policies of the Israeli government.

Over the years since the operation, thousands of Jews have left Ethiopia for Israel, taking with them a rich and ancient culture but few of the skills necessary for an advanced and complex economy such as Israel's. Their strange customs and language have alarmed more conservative elements of Israeli society, who have struggled to recognize these black Africans as Jews. Their need for social services, retraining, and education has strained government programs, which had long dealt with new immigrants but rarely with so many pastoral people from a pretechnological society.

"There are some major challenges with integration," Shoshana Ben-Dor told me. She is the director of Israel and After-School Programs for the North American Conference on Ethiopian Jewry, which assists the Beta Israel in Ethiopia and Israel and advocates on their behalf. "Most of the community has been in Israel less than twenty years. There are enormous technological and cultural gaps. Eighty percent of them are illiterate in their own language, let alone Hebrew. But we are working to overcome these gaps. Our goal is full family reunification—anyone of Jewish descent, no matter how far back, should be able to come home."

I couldn't help but wonder how, after thousands of years, Ethiopia was not the Beta Israel's home. Their story was the manifestation of the religious Zionist idea, an idea that existed in the Falasha long before Zionism became a political movement. The natural home for all Jews was Jerusalem, their beliefs told them, and no matter how long the sojourn, home would always be in the land of Israel.

"I recognize that on the one hand it is sad to have the Jewish communities disappear from Ethiopia," Ben-Dor continued. "In Eastern Europe, you know, it was done for us—there is no one to maintain the cemeteries and synagogues—but for the communities who wanted to come to Israel, this is the fulfillment of their dreams and prayers. In their history, they never felt at home in Ethiopia."

WITH WHAT REMAINS OF JEWISH LIFE in Ethiopia struggling to survive and mostly focused on emigration, the people live physically in one place and spiritually in another. The future of Jewish life in Africa, it seems, is not to be found in its oldest Jewish community. The future is in the Abayudaya and the model of integration without assimilation that they are living. The model is made manifest in their commitment to Uganda, to their homes, to each other, and, most of all, to their neighbors. With or without Israel's recognition, they plan to increase their presence on the continent and to keep their community strong by developing religious institutions alongside economic growth. Aside from their coffee co-op and solar dried fruit program, they are studying other opportunities to bring more resources to the area, fully aware that their community can only grow if their youth feel they have a future.

"We have many concerns for the coming years," Israel Siriri told me. He is the president of the Abayudaya, an engineer by training and one of the most affluent members of the community. We sat on folding chairs on the hill just below his house, watching his children run around. A goat chewed grass in the bush and occasionally cast a wary eye in our direction.

Israel Siriri is a large man, with a bald head, broad shoulders, and muscular arms. When one of his little daughters ran by, he scooped her up effortlessly onto his lap. While he spoke, she plucked at the fabric of his brightly patterned shirt.

"There is the problem of the economy, of course," he said. "The people are still very poor. But there is also the size of the community . . . We must grow so that the young people have other Jews they can marry."

He set his daughter back on the ground and she immediately scrambled up the slope toward her house to play. He watched her go with an amused smile on his face.

"So you're worried about intermarriage?"

"Yes, that also. We don't want that here."

I was confused. What did he mean by "also"?

"We are concerned about finding other Jews for our young people to marry and also about this intermarriage."

I had to ask him what he meant by "intermarriage." I had thought intermarriage *was* Jews marrying non-Jews.

"I mean boys marrying boys and girls marrying girls."

I didn't know how to reply. Homosexuality was not only taboo in Uganda, it was illegal. The country was one of the worst places in the world to be openly gay. I had certainly not mentioned my own sexuality to any members of the community, and the topic had never come up before. I hadn't expected it to. Regaining my composure, I asked him if he thought that was a big problem here.

"Not right now, but there is always this temptation, especially with all the visitors we have. They might bring some ideas . . . " He let his voice trail off. "But our main concern, of course, is finding Jewish people for our youth to marry so that they do not leave the religion. We have one girl who married an American and moved to Pennsylvania, but we would like the people to be able to stay. These new villages who wish to convert, they give us hope that we will find more matches."

I couldn't let the topic of sexuality drop. I had to ask more about it. I had felt so welcome here on the hill, but had concealed a large part of who I was. I wanted to know why it was such a big worry.

"For our culture, it is not acceptable. We must make children. The marriage must produce a future. And of course there is the Torah, but I am not an expert."

It turned out that Israel Siriri's fear of same-sex marriage stemmed from the imminent return of Gershom from rabbinical school. Gershom would be ordained that summer at the American Jewish University's Ziegler School of Rabbinic Studies in California, where just two years earlier one of his rabbinic mentors had successfully argued that same-sex marriage was permitted under Jewish law. The Abayudaya leaders were worried that Gershom would come and push a radical program of liberalization. "We are not ready for this thinking," Israel said.

The community does have progressive ideas about women's rights and continually pushes women's empowerment in both the religious and secular spheres of life in Uganda. The coffee cooperative has an even number of men and women on its board, and women are encouraged to study the Torah and participate fully in the life of the synagogue. I saw in the Abayudaya great hope for the liberalization of this region, and I liked the idea that gay rights might ignite in Uganda from a spark that the Jewish community provided. But Israel and Aaron had no intention of allowing that to happen anytime soon.

"We would resist this idea," Aaron told me when I pressed him on the subject. "It is not something we are prepared to allow." But he added a similar caveat to Israel's. "Not yet. It is not our way."

Progress was possible, he seemed to be saying, but in their own way. Time will tell.

In July 2008 Gershom returned to be installed as the chief rabbi of Uganda, to inaugurate the first yeshiva in sub-Saharan Africa, and to take the leadership of his community once again. Officials from international Jewish organizations, journalists, backpackers, and 260 new converts to Judaism from Nigeria, Tanzania, Ghana, South Africa, and Uganda watched as Gershom accepted his role and expressed his hope that their "relations with surrounding communities would serve as a model of peace to the entire universe."

Jon and I left Uganda months before Gershom's return. I had continued to wear my *kippah* throughout the country, and as we drove farther and farther from Mbale it drew more and more stares. Aaron came with us to Kampala when we left, also wearing his *kippah*. When we stopped to buy some water in the tourist town of Jinja, near the source of the Nile River, a young Muslim man stopped us on the street.

"Salaam Aleykum," he said.

"Aleykum As-Salaam," we both responded, just as Muslims in Mbale responded with Shalom to us. The young man then spoke rapidly with Aaron, pointing at me and laughing. He shook my hand many times and waved over and over as we went back to the van.

"He thinks you are a Muslim," Aaron said. "He had never heard of an American Muslim, but he saw your skullcap and was amazed."

"He didn't know the Jewish symbols on it?" I asked.

"No, he doesn't know these symbols. I did not explain to him. It might have confused him more. I am sure he has never heard of an African Jew either." Aaron laughed as we pulled back onto the road for Kampala. I promised I would visit again.

Maybe next year, I thought. Next year in Uganda.

seven

Imperiled?
The Jewish Community of Iran

The sons of Adam are limbs of each other, having been created of one essence. When the calamity of time affects one limb the other limbs cannot remain at rest.
—SA'DI, A PERSIAN POET

AT THE JAMKARAN MOSQUE outside of the city of Qom, in the Islamic Republic of Iran, I gave thanks to God in the language of my people. I didn't think I knew any Hebrew prayers by heart until I said this one. My lips formed the words on their own. Passersby, curious worshippers sliding their shoes back on as they stepped into the cool night air, stopped and listened. They didn't recognize the language. Not many had ever heard Hebrew before, nor had they imagined they would run into an American inside their mosque, let alone a Jewish American. Foreigners were banned from entering Jamkaran Mosque—the ban being the Iranian government's response to unfavorable media coverage during the Sadr City uprising in Iraq. Jamkaran was one of President Mahmoud Ahmadinejad's most revered places, the center of his messianic theology, and a rallying point for his political base. I knew I was in a holy place that night; I just didn't imagine it would be holy for me.

"*Baruch ata Adonai Elohenu Melech ha'olam,*" I began, "*shehekianu v'kimanu v'higianu lazman hazeh.*" Blessed are You, Lord our God, Ruler of the Universe, who has given us life, preserved us, and enabled us to reach this moment.

The spring air was cooling off after a hot and dusty day. In the distance, the mountains were fading into the darkening horizon, their faint outlines barely delineating the meeting of earth and sky. Stars began to pop out. Behind me the minarets of the mosque framed the moon perfectly, and floodlights made the facade glitter in blue and green and gold, like a kaleidoscope. The site was meant to produce a feeling of awe, and it had achieved its intended effect on me. As my mind reeled toward the sublime, the smell of sweat and feet emerging from the men's section kept me fully grounded in my body. The juxtaposition of divine architecture and severe landscape with the sights and smells of a mass of humanity made my head spin.

This was the first time I'd said a Hebrew prayer on my own in public since my bar mitzvah. That the most profound spiritual moment of my Jewish journey should happen in the Islamic Republic of Iran at the Jamkaran Mosque on the eve of Israel's sixtieth anniversary came as quite a surprise to me, as did the hugs and friendly questions from the Iranian worshippers who had heard it.

"If it were not for politics, we would be brothers," an older man said, embracing me. "Jews and Muslims are from the same God," he whispered, leaning in to me. "But these politicians, they make hatred between us." Several people came up to me to express the same idea, loudly proclaiming our fellowship, quietly condemning the politics that separated us. By the time I left the grounds, tears welled in my eyes.

Perhaps two weeks of exhausting travel had caught up with me. Perhaps I sensed that for all the goodwill and hospitality of the Persian people, the situation between our countries and our faiths would only get worse. Or perhaps, in that place, on that night at that mosque, I'd had the Jewish experience I'd been looking for. I had sincerely and publicly declared myself a part of the Jewish people, voiced my belief in God, and made my statement—*Hineini*, Here I am—in the heart of the so-called Axis of Evil.

The Jamkaran Mosque is about four miles from the city of Qom, which is the center of Shia scholarship in the world. In one of the most conservative areas in Iran, Jamkaran has in recent years become an important pilgrimage site for Shiite Muslims. The devout believe that Al-Mahdi, the twelfth imam, appeared at Jamkaran to offer prayers in the tenth century, along with the prophet Al Khidr. The Mahdi is a messiah figure in Shiism, and as the popularity of messianic theology has grown, the Jamkaran mosque has become a dynamic religious site, receiving substantial support from President Ahmadinejad, who fervently subscribes to the Madhi theology. He has led numerous rallies at the mosque and donated nearly twenty million dollars to expand the complex. In his speeches, Ahmadinejad regularly calls upon the Mahdi to return and rid the world of corruption, cruelty, and violence, even as he speaks out in support of Hamas and Hezbollah, which are, regardless of how one sees them politically, violent organizations. Yet his alignment with violent movements even as he called for peace caused far less controversy in Iran than his subscription to messianic theology. It is disconcerting to have a political leader calling for the end days, though, as a Jew, I found it far more disconcerting to hear him call for the end of the Jewish state.

In Iran, I found myself wanting to talk about Israel. I had never wanted to before, but somehow the warnings I'd been given about even mentioning Israel to anyone once I got to Iran made me want to talk about it even more. Ahmadinejad, and most Iranians, publicly refer to it as Palestine or the "illegal Zionist entity." Every chance I got, I spoke of it as Israel. I had still never been there, and certainly did not consider myself a Zionist, but I wanted people to know I would not be afraid to talk about it. I had come to open a dialogue that precious few of my countrymen or coreligionists seemed willing or able to participate in, and I had also come to see a different view of Zion than I could get in America.

"Israel is not our enemy," another worshipper at Jamkaran Mosque whispered to me. He was a young man, thin and muscular, wearing a dark red T-shirt and blue jeans. He had been inside praying fervently near where I'd knelt. His forehead still bore the indentation where he had rested it on the small prayer disc on the floor. I'd seen images of young men like this on the news, devout young Muslim men deeply committed to Shiism and Islamic deliverance theology. This young man was supposed to be the thing I feared most. He had his hand on my shoulder and his other on my waist. The contact was surprisingly intimate. "We have no quarrel with anyone."

Before I could ask him any follow-up questions, I was whisked out of the mosque and toward the bus. The group I was with had a long drive to the airport.

Jamkaran was the last stop for the Fellowship of Reconciliation's seventh peace delegation to Iran. FOR is the oldest interfaith peace organization in the world, founded at the advent of World War I, and I had signed up to go on this trip to Iran as one of two Jewish delegates, the other being Rabbi Lynn Gottlieb, a colossal figure in the peace movement, a founder of the Shomer Shalom Institute for Jewish Nonviolence, and one of the first female rabbis in Jewish history. She was also a lighting rod for right-wing ire. When news of her trip to Iran hit the *Jerusalem Post*, the blogosphere did not respond kindly. She had grown used to death threats.

The other eighteen delegates were mostly older white Christian liberals, though they included a young Afro-Brazilian activist, a Navajo woman, two Buddhists, and a best-selling author. But it was the two Jews who seemed to interest the Iranians the most (perhaps with the exception of the first Native American most had ever seen). Everywhere we went people were curious and excited to meet us. It started to irritate some of the other members of the delegation, but being peace activists they did their best not to let it show. It was hard not to feel the significance of the moment. Rabbi Lynn was the first female rabbi ever to visit Iran. It was due in part to her presence, I think, that we were allowed into Jamkaran Mosque at all.

For two weeks I had been peppered with questions about Judaism, from the divine (What do Jews believe about the efficacy of prayer?) to the political (Is there hope for peace between Muslims and Jews?) to the profane (Are Jews allowed to have oral sex?). I had heard how the Jews caused the Holocaust and 9/11 and how Zionism was the source of all cruelty in the world. I also heard how anti-Semitism was a Western invention and how the Jews had lived peacefully in Persia for almost three thousand years. I had seen Iranian Jews walking openly in their yarmulkes, praying openly and enthusiastically, selling Judaica in their shop windows. I'd seen young women, caked in makeup, arm in arm with their boyfriends, defying the so-called morality police, and I'd seen artists inventing a new and provocative visual culture. I'd been drinking with a member of the Majlis—Iran's Parliament—and gotten stoned with jaded Iranian youth. I'd prayed with Shiite Muslims and Armenian Christians. I'd found myself in a so-called enemy nation and had met little but friendship and warmth, at the same time mixed with a lot of ignorance and confusion, on both my part and my hosts'. I was in a land of impossible contradictions and, that Monday night at the Jamkaran Mosque, I added my own with the Shehekianu prayer.

When our group left, worship continued, broadcast over loudspeakers, and a crowd of people followed us to the bus, asking questions, shaking hands. Police also lingered nearby, watching and listening closely. The sun had set and the mountains beyond the mosque disappeared fully into darkness. All I could see was the blue and green and gold of the massive arches and domes of the floodlit mosque. All I could hear were the cries of the devout and the happy chatter of families heading to their cars.

Never in my life would I have dreamed that I would bow my head to the floor of an Iranian mosque with hundreds of barefoot young men praying tearfully for the divine to enter their lives and proclaim my Judaism to every one of them who cared to listen. I'd been born in the middle of the hostage crisis, and had decided to explore my Jewish roots in the middle of the Bush administration's War on Terror. I came to Iran a skeptic about the Jewish state, and found myself discussing the need for its existence with Iranian officials. I came as a secular Jew, and found myself eagerly attending synagogue in Tehran. After two weeks, Iran had touched me with some of the contradictions with which its citizens live.

ARRIVING AT IMAM KHOMENI INTERNATIONAL AIRPORT two weeks earlier had not been a simple matter. Our delegation had learned that our visas had been cleared only a few hours before the flight left from New York, and once we arrived we were held at passport control for nearly three hours. Customs agents took our fingerprints, though they didn't seem to care much about matching them to our names and passport numbers. This was simply an act of reciprocity for the United States' policy of fingerprinting all foreign arrivals. The Iranian customs agents were polite and friendly, even as our group grew hot, exhausted, and grumpy. At least the waiting area had Wi-Fi.

"Anyone want to blog?" one of the younger delegates asked.

The streets of Tehran were deserted at that time of night. While the bus zipped along blaring gaudy Persian pop music, the stern gaze of Ayatollah Khomeini stared at us from signs and billboards. Next to his photo, the current ayatollah, Ali Khamanei, also watched the streets, a smirk on his face that suggested a more personable, grandfatherly supreme leader. And on almost every wall, there were murals paying tribute to Iran's martyrs from the long war with Iraq. Everywhere I looked were reminders of either Islamic revolution or the death of Islamic warriors. We hadn't passed anything calling for death to America or Israel, at least not that I could read, though I knew such murals existed. I'd seen them on the news for years. I had imagined they would be more prominent. The signs and billboards I did see referred back to the Iranians themselves, exhorting them to be the kind of Muslims the state thought they should be. The propaganda was nationalistic, but deeply personal.

As we turned near our hotel, I saw a small stencil on a wall that did send chills up my spine: the symbol of the Revolutionary Guard, an arm raising a Kalashnikov rifle in the air. It looked strikingly similar to the logo of Hezbollah. I sighed, and wondered what was awaiting me—a gay American Jew—in Iran in the next two weeks. Everything I'd been taught and everything I'd seen in the media screamed out at me not to be here, not to tell anyone who I was or, more to the point, what I was. It was five in the morning before we got to our hotel, and I fell asleep as soon as my head hit the pillow.

On Friday afternoon, after a slow first day in Iran, our entire delegation visited the Jewish community of Iran's proudest institution, the Dr. Sapir Hospital in South Tehran. South Tehran is considered the most conservative part of the city, though the Sapir Hospital complex is in what used to be a Jewish neighborhood. South Tehran is poorer and more religious than the upscale neighborhoods of North Tehran, and it was from South Tehran that Ahmadinejad drew his support when he was mayor. The hospital had started as a clinic in Jewish homes and had grown over the years into the largest charity hospital in Iran. When

75 percent of the Jewish community left after the 1979 revolution, the makeup of the neighborhood changed. The area is now entirely Muslim, and the charity hospital, true to its founding mission, serves their community diligently. The sign out front, written in Persian and Hebrew, welcomes all in need.

Iran's Jewish community has lived in the region since the fourth century B.C.E., following the destruction of the First Temple, and it is the largest Jewish community in the Middle East outside of Israel, numbering between fifteen and twenty thousand. Some of the most beautiful and important pieces of Jewish writing came from the community in exile in Babylon, including Psalm 137, *If I forget thee, O Jerusalem* . . .

Aside from their contribution to Jewish literature, ancient Judeo-Persian texts remain the earliest written examples of New Persian and are a valuable tool for linguistic scholars. As the oldest continuous Diaspora community, the Persian Jews have a unique perspective on relations with their neighbors. They have lived through the rise and fall of empires, through persecutions and redemptions, and they have maintained their way of life by staying close to the Torah and to their neighbors.

"Most of our patients are Muslims," said Dr. Ciamak Moresadegh, the president of the Jewish community, director of the hospital, and newly elected member of Parliament (the Jewish community is guaranteed a seat in Iran's parliament no matter how few Jews there are in the country). "We have maybe two percent Jewish patients, but we don't ask their religion. We treat everyone." He explained that 90 percent of the hospital's staff were Muslims, though the administration and leadership were entirely Jewish. Historically, the hospital's specialty had been obstetrics, but over the years they'd expanded to provide a wide range of services. "Plastic surgery is popular these days," he told us. "Of course, for elective surgery the wait is much longer, but it is less expensive here than at the bigger hospitals." I had already seen countless young women in Tehran with white bandages on their noses. Nose jobs were the latest fad to hit the city. It made sense for the hospital to expand its plastic surgery services. They had to meet the market's demand.

Ciamak Moresadegh is a big man, who has lost most of his hair. "I am good for drawing caricatures," he said, laughing. "You can describe me as the Persian Michael Moore." Then he lit a cigarette and blew the smoke into the air. "This is the only hospital in all the world, I think, where you can smoke." He laughed again, a deep belly laugh, and then looked to Morris Motamed, who sat at the head of the table.

Morris Motamed, always impeccably dressed, was the outgoing Jewish member of Parliament, and would be taking over leadership of the hospital from Dr. Moresadegh in about a month. He is the most well known of Iran's Jews. He'd made news in 2006 when he held a press conference that was critical of the Holocaust Denial Conference, which President Ahmadinejad had organized. A variety of anti-Semitic writers, historians, and political figures, including the notorious David Duke, were invited to speak about the "lie" of the Holocaust that diffused through so much of Jewish identity and that, they argued, the Zionists manipulated to justify their imperial ambitions in the Middle East. I couldn't help but think of the unassuming neighborhood bar I had driven past in Metarie, Louisiana, where Duke was known to hold court, just down the street from the Kosher Cajun deli. Even with a KKK leader nearby, the New Orleans Jews weren't terribly concerned with anti-Semitism. With Ahmadinejad in charge, and the Revolutionary Guard all around them, the Jewish community in Tehran didn't seem all that worried about anti-Semitism either. Our group asked these leaders about the Iranian Jewish community's response to Ahmadinejad's conference. The Jewish leaders nodded. They'd expected this question and were emphatic in their response.

"I will let Mr. Morris Motamed answer this," Dr. Moresadegh said.

"For any Jew, for *anyone*, the Holocaust is as real as the sun," he said. "I must stress this. The conference that was held was expressing personal opinions—and I objected in the press at the time—but it is important to know that it was *opinions*, not the position of the Iranian government, which only comes from the ayatollah."

"You know, this anti-Semitism," Dr. Moresadegh added, "it is a European idea, not a Persian idea. Last year President Ahmadinejad donated about thirty thousand dollars to the Jewish hospital . . . The money is not so important, but it is the symbol. Even Ahmadinejad wants the Jews in Iran to live well."

Ahmadinejad does often say that he distinguishes between Jews and Zionists, and while he hates Zionism, he has nothing but respect for Jews. He publicly embraced the anti-Zionist ultra-Orthodox rabbis from the small Neturei Karta sect of Judaism, based in Monsey, New York, when they attended his 2006 conference. Their position enraged much of the mainstream Jewish community, but their spokesman, Yisroel Dovid Weiss, defended his attendance at the conference, saying they had not come to deny the Holocaust—he had lost family in concentration camps—but to stand in unity with those who objected to the misuse of the Holocaust by the state of Israel. He told the *New York Times* that "it is a dangerous deviation to pretend that the Iranian president is anti-Jewish and anti-Semitic."

Dovid Weiss and his group are shunned by the rest of the ultra-Orthodox community as well as by mainstream Jews, so I didn't necessarily want to take their word at face value. Anti-Semitism cannot be wished away by displacing it onto criticism of Israel. Irrational hatred of Jews existed long before the state of Israel, and if militant anti-Zionists had their way and Israel ceased to exist, anti-Semitism would no doubt continue. I didn't believe that all anti-Israel sentiments were anti-Semitic, but I also believed that some of them were.

The existence of Israel in its current form cannot be separated from anti-Semitism in both Europe and the Middle East. It emerged from the genocidal climax of Europe's anti-Semitism and found itself filling the

role of the Jewish "other" on a geopolitical scale when it was created between Egypt, Jordan, Syria, and Lebanon. Like the "court Jew," who allied
himself with the ruling class in order to survive and thus gained the ire
of the ruled, Israel was allied with the United States at a time when an-
ticolonial movements were at their height in the Middle East. Zionism
was very quickly equated with colonialism, and the Jewish state was cast
as an invading foreign body. Since its founding, Israel and its support-
ers have been accused of controlling world markets and political institutions, as well as the media, to further some ill-defined secret agenda. In
short, these accusations take all the old fears of Jewish insidiousness and
place them on the state of Israel, crediting it with far greater power and
influence than it could possibly have. The demonization of Israel tended
to obstruct any real dialogue about its flaws and often dashed any hope of
rapprochement in the Middle East.

There are real issues in the debate over Israel, a state that does not
suffer a lack of very real political, religious, and moral failings, and these
issues have led to the polarization of the right and left all over the world,
with those who support Israel often supporting it blindly and those who
criticize it often cast as anti-Semites or self-hating Jews. I was certainly
on the left when I began this project, and as my sense of Jewish spirituality grew I remained skeptical of the link between the Jewish faith and the
Jewish state. I didn't like the idea of a government that claimed to have
a divine mandate. Israel and Iran, mortal enemies, both claimed inspiration from God and both claimed to fulfill a messianic role. It was the
usurpation by politics of what should have been God's role that so upset
the rabbis of Neturei Karta. It was like praying for one football team to
win over the other. Would God really take sides like that? And would
God want the teams to have F–18s and nuclear arms?

"We believe, from a religious standpoint, that the state of Israel is
illegitimate," Rabbi Weiss later explained to me. He was attending an
interfaith dinner in New York meant to open a dialogue with President

Ahmadinejad. Outside the hotel where the dinner was held, a variety of Jewish groups had gathered to protest, comparing the president of Iran to Hitler and the Islamic Republic to the Third Reich (there were also plenty of comparisons of then presidential candidate Barack Obama to Osama Bin Laden). Inside, pinned to his black coat, Rabbi Weiss wore a badge with an image of the Israeli flag crossed out. "A Jew is not a Zionist," the badge said.

"As the High Holidays approach," he told me, smiling, his warmth flying in the face of the hostility we could hear echoing from outside, "we must think about our relationship to God. This anti-Zionism is not a hobby for us. It is part of a larger religious observance, a duty to Jewish law and to justice. The Jewish people sinned and their punishment was to live in Diaspora until God redeems them. So even if the land in Palestine was empty, it would not be correct for Jews to establish a political entity there. Add to that the terrible crimes against the Palestinians, and it is just terrible what is done in the name of Judaism."

Long before I went to Iran, and before I met Rabbi Weiss, Neturei Karta had issued statements that the Middle East was not dangerous for Jews who were not Zionists, and they urged Muslims to make every effort to demonstrate that. I took that message to heart. In Tehran, our group visited the former home of Ayatollah Khomeini, the first leader of the Islamic revolution and one of the most vitriolic enemies of Israel. I made it a point to tell the soldier of the Revolutionary Guard who stood by the entrance that I was Jewish. He shrugged. He couldn't have cared less.

"Yes, I'm in the Revolutionary Guard," he said, "but I don't do much." He seemed more like a bored frat boy than a committed jihadist. We posed for a picture together. An older couple visiting the house, which had been turned into a nationalist shrine, gave us a nasty look for acting so frivolously in such a serious place. The woman, dressed in a full black chador, shook her head. Her husband rolled his eyes. The soldier resumed his stone-faced sentry duties. Chastened, we walked back to our bus, but we couldn't help returning the friendly waves from the other members of the Revolutionary Guard we passed on the street.

THE AYATOLLAH ALI KHAMENEI, WHO REPLACED Ayatollah Khomeini as Iran's supreme leader in 1989, has absolute power over the president and the Parliament, and it is his opinions far more than the president's that represent the position of Iran's government. He has issued several fatwa, or decrees, that have granted rights and protection to Iran's Jews and other religious minorities. There had long been a folk belief in Iran that Jews were unclean and that to touch one after it rained would pollute a Muslim. Ayatollah Khamenei issued a fatwa attempting to disabuse the public of this belief, even as he continued to deny the legitimacy of the Jewish state, and to sanction a brand of anti-Zionist rhetoric that relied on all the old tropes of anti-Semitism while denying that anti-Semitism played any role in it. This two-step is common in Iran, and I believe that in most cases it is sincere. Most people simply do not realize that their legitimate grievances against Israel are manipulated toward the demonization of Jews in general. They can claim in one breath to respect all nations and peoples and to love the community of Persian Jews, while simultaneously believing that all the Jews in New York were warned in advance about 9/11, that they were somehow complicit in the terror attacks and the resulting violence throughout the Middle East. People had no answer to my objections that I live in New York and was not warned in advance, that I knew of many Jews who were there that day, that many Jews had died in the attack. In general, they were open to that discussion and correction, recognizing that I lived in New York and they did not. Often, when they asked me these questions about conspiracy theories they had heard, they would begin their question, "As a Jewish person, can you tell me about . . . "

On Iranian television around the time of my visit, a new show was airing, *The Secret of Armageddon*, in which various "experts" discussed plans for Zionist world domination and a "genocide of humanity" and argued the validity of the infamous *Protocols of the Elders of Zion*, which was long ago established as a fake document manufactured to vilify Jews.

According to one of the experts on the show, Iranian university lecturer Ali-Reza Karimi, "What is known worldwide today as *The Protocols of the Elders of Zion* contains the plans and policies of the elders of this sect to conquer the world and establish a global Jewish government, which were discussed at the 1897 [Zionist] Congress in Basel, Switzerland."

The show's claims were disturbing, but no one I talked to in Iran seemed to be watching. As much as the clerics in power worried about Zionists and their plots, the average Iranian, it appeared, couldn't have cared less. People knew of a different miniseries from 2007, called *Zero Degree Turn*, about Jews who had escaped the Nazis with the help of an Iranian consul in Paris. *That* show had been extremely popular. It placed Iran on the side of the angels, and everyone knew about it. Was it possible that anti-Semitism was struggling, unsuccessfully, to take hold in Iran? Was it possible that Iranians understood full well the difference between Zionists and Jews, even as their leaders used language that blurred the line? The rhetoric on television and the curiousity and welcome I received on the streets seemed to contradict each other.

I couldn't believe, as Dr. Moresadegh claimed, that there was no anti-Semitism in Iran, but perhaps I had been conditioned to believe that the Middle East was filled with it, from suicide bombers to the killers of *Wall Street Journal* reporter Daniel Pearl. Images of Islamic prayer and Islamic militants were de rigeur in American news media. But with over a billion Muslims in the world, it did seem unlikely that the entire Middle East would harbor endemic anti-Semitism. If that were the case, there would be no Jews left. Or perhaps the influence of American Jews and the close alliance between the powerful United States and little Israel stood as the only defense against just such a holocaust. But then why was I being treated so well in Iran? Why were the Iranian Jews living so openly?

"We are a religious minority in a religious country, so there are some problems," Dr. Moresadegh said. "But they are not major and we are working together with the other minority communities to solve them." He then summed up the position of Iran's Jews succinctly: "As a general rule, our condition is a reflection of the condition of every Iranian. We may speak English, pray in Hebrew, but we dream in Persian."

DR. MORESADEGH TOOK US ON A hasty tour of the hospital, proud of their two kitchens—one for kosher food—their various labs, and the operating theater. After the tour, it was time for us to drive over to the Yusef Abad Synagogue, the largest and most ornate synagogue in Tehran, to attend services. Most of the delegation would not be staying for the entire Kabbalat Shabbat and evening prayers, but the rabbi and I were excited about seeing it. How many people would attend? Would they be cowed in terror, creeping in and out lest the authorities see them? What would the services look like in a community that had been settled in Persia since the time of the Babylonian exile? What would they sound like?

Of course, before we could get to the synagogue, we had to cross the street from where our bus had parked, and if ever a person needs faith in a protective God, a merciful God, it is when crossing the street in Tehran.

The streets are broad and the traffic moves fast and unwaveringly. Pedestrians step right out into traffic and stop between lanes, centimeters from the cars streaking by on either side of them. There was a reason for Bruce Feiler's warning about staying on the side of the street that you wake up on.

"Do not cross by yourself," my Iranian friend Suad, who had joined our delegation to provide local, nongovernmental insight, warned me on the first day. "Wait until some local people cross and cross with them."

There were no locals crossing to get to the synagogue. Just a gaggle of Americans. In twos and threes, we took deep breaths and stepped out into the unknown, trusting to the higher power that watched over pedestrians in the Islamic Republic of Iran. It had to be God, because it certainly was not traffic regulations. To reach the other side of the street was to touch the divine. After that first street crossing, I believe I understood why Iran was such a spiritual nation.

The Yusef Abad Synagogue was renovated in the sixties, and the sanctuary sparkles. Grand chandeliers hang from the ceiling, and the pillars and walls glisten with bits of mirror and glass. The Jews of Iran are a traditional Orthodox community. Men and women remain separated during prayer. I sat in the front next to Morris Motamed and Dr. Moresadegh, while Rabbi Gottlieb went to the women's side. People rushed up to greet me and shake my hand, asking where I was from. Everyone seemed to know someone in the United States, usually in Los Angeles. Within minutes of our arrival, the sanctuary was full. I noticed that Rabbi Gottlieb and the other Americans had been surrounded by curious women. One was helping a member of our delegation adjust her head scarf; another was feeling the fabric on the rabbi's gray manteau—a long tunic or overcoat required by Iranian law. Sparkling, fashion-forward head scarves and colorful manteaus were more the norm on Tehran's streets, as were bedazzled fingernails and metallic high heels, but Rabbi Gottlieb needed to make a good impression on her hosts and dressed more conservatively than most locals.

"There are usually more people here," Morris Motamed said to me, "but after Nowruz—the Persian New Year—many people have gone to have picnics and celebrate in the countryside."

The room looked full to me. There were dozens of young men in the rows behind me and dozens more off to the sides. A young man acted as hazan, standing on the bimah and leading the prayers, as the DJ Isaac had in Uganda. I imagined that most synagogues in the United States would thrill to have this many teens and twenty-somethings on any given Friday night. The room also felt a bit like a fashion show. The continuum of Tehrani couture was on display, from older men and women dressed conservatively, to young men with radically styled hair, tight shirts, and jeans with rock-star belts and young women whose head scarves barely touched their heads at all and whose Islamic dress appeared shockingly form-fitting. It looked as though all the young people were dressed to go clubbing immediately afterward.

The services were lively and, for me, totally incomprehensible. I had never been to an Orthodox service before. Every word was in Hebrew, and, while the hazan stood on the bimah chanting, people moved around, talking and gossiping, occasionally turning to their prayer books and singing along or muttering to themselves in quiet devotion. Morris Motamed, Dr. Moresadegh and I were constantly interrupted by well-wishers or petitioners. These men were the community leaders, and Friday night was a big time for them.

"I'm not so religious," Dr. Moresadegh whispered to me, "but I come here for my community. This is a time for people to see me. And that is its own kind of duty."

Though everyone's attention appeared dispersed and erratic, suddenly the whole congregation stopped chatting and turned toward the ark, which meant they faced Jerusalem. The room burst into "Lecha Dodi," the song to welcome the Sabbath. The melody was different from the one they sang in Uganda. The men's voices were deep and booming; they were not filled with joy but seemed to come from a primal place; it was impossible not to imagine a thundering God on a mountaintop. My ribs vibrated with the sound.

The service progressed, and people returned to their raucous mixture of chatter and prayer. Morris Motamed told me about his visits to

New York and California to see family and friends, and about his devotion to the Jewish faith. He pointed out to me where we were in the
siddur—the prayer book.

"You should really learn Hebrew," he said. When we arrived at the
Amidah, I was excited, given how much thought I had put into it in
Bosnia, and I eagerly took three steps forward when it began, bowed to
the sides, and then stopped. I wanted to chant along with the congregation, but there was no transliteration, and again I found myself unable
to follow the tradition. So I prayed in my own way, asking for health and
happiness, asking for peace. The men around me rocked and murmured,
and eventually I stopped thinking about anything and just watched and
listened and enjoyed the sound of collective yearning in the air and the
feeling of a place where all thought and sound was bent toward holiness.
Why was it that I felt so much more spiritually alive in these far-flung
places than I did at home? Why did the services seem so much more
meaningful to me when I had traveled halfway around the world to witness them? Was it because I had traveled halfway around the world? I
was beginning to understand the purpose of pilgrimage. By leaving the
normal space of your life, by leaving behind language and geography and
your own comfort, you open yourself to the possibilities of the sublime.
The effort you put in imbues the act with meaning. I could go to synagogue every week in New York, but the ease with which I would be able
to do it would never have given me the clarity I needed. I had to uproot
myself in order to see the meaning that spiritual practice could have in
my life at home. I had to pack my bags in order to ditch my baggage.

Or maybe this was just more pantomime, as during the Amidah in
Sarajevo. Maybe I was kidding myself, longing to feel the way these men
around me felt, a religious contact high. Wasn't Judaism a way of life that
created a divine rhythm for one's days? It wasn't a religion that lent itself
to these "born-again" moments. It was more of a commitment to a mode
of constant consciousness of the divine, and performance of those duties

that created a relationship with holiness—the laws of kashruth to make eating sacred, the tefillin to center ourselves and express devotion, the Sabbath to make even the days of the week an expression of our relationship to the act of Creation. It was a religion of constant allusion.

What I experienced standing in Yusef Abad was not some holy presence called to the room by our prayers—as if we could summon holiness so easily—but the creation of meaning. Each time the Amidah is prayed, with its three steps forward and its bobbing and bowing from side to side, it creates a consciousness of what is sacred. The genius of the prayer, of the whole service, is that each step reminds us of what is holy in ourselves and in each other. That's why there is call and response; that's why there are solitary prayers said in unison. All of it is a tool for reinforcing who we are and what we care about, like the laws of kashruth and the Sabbath, and those myriad other rules that have sometimes been described as "the yoke of the commandments."

I chose to see them, however, not as strict rules but as methods, as divinely inspired tools. The service itself was a kind of holy technology, a way of reinforcing the principles of the religion and the connections between people and principles. The men wandering about talking the whole time were just as much a part of the service as the solemn chants and songs. They were all doing the work of strengthening community, even if they thought they were just catching up on gossip.

Services continued, and Dr. Moresadegh mounted the bimah to address the congregation in Farsi and, for our benefit, English.

"I would like to welcome our visitors from the United States," he said. "We are very pleased to have them in Tehran. They have come on a mission of peace, to promote dialogue between our nations. I would now like to introduce the leader of the delegation, Rabbi Lynn Gottlieb."

All heads on the male side of the room turned to look at me, with expressions of surprise and curiosity on their faces. I sat in the front row, after all, with the community leaders. But I was so young . . . could it be? Their surprise turned to stunned silence when Rabbi Gottlieb stood from the female side of the room. A hush fell over the sanctuary for the first time that evening. Slowly, the rabbi mounted the bimah, the first female rabbi to do so in the three-thousand-year history of the Jews of Persia.

She spoke briefly about her gratitude to the community for welcoming us and our mission of peace in Iran. Dr. Moresadegh translated. The congregation nodded in agreement.

"And I hope that when I next come to your beautiful country," she said, "I will find women leaders of the community as well as men." The female side of the room cheered and clapped when her words were translated. I noticed some of the men clapping too, while others looked at her with blank stares or at each other with wary eyes. Iran has long been a patriarchal society, but the roar of applause and laughter suggested that the march toward equality for women was under way, a process that had begun long before we got there and would continue long after we left. By the time services ended, the rabbi was nearly in tears, knowing that for one brief moment she had been a part of that movement, sharing her hopes with a group of Iranian women.

When we stepped out onto the street, members of the congregation swarmed us, peppering us with questions about where we were going to have dinner, where we would visit in Iran, what we thought of their country. One young man asked, with great concern, what we could do to save the embattled Jewish community of Suriname. Dr. Moresadegh had to drag me from the crowd by my arm. A small group of us went back to his house for Shabbat dinner.

"You drive on Shabbat?" I asked him.

"Of course," he said simply as we wove through Saturday night traffic in Tehran. Young men and women were out at cafés and cruising the wide boulevards. Cars filled with young men pulled up next to cars filled with young women. A ritual of honks and waves led to the exchange of phone numbers. With just about all public contact between males and females banned before marriage, young people found ways to create their own private spaces, turning apartments into discos and traffic into a dating scene.

BACK AT DR. MORESADEGH'S HOUSE, A feast was laid out. I couldn't begin to name all the dishes, but the air was thick with the smell of spices and currants and butter and pastries. As soon as we arrived, the doctor's father-in-law cornered Rabbi Gottlieb, urging her to lead us in the blessings and prayers, prodding her to perform, and smiling with amazement and pride that he had a rabbi in front of him and that that rabbi was an American woman. He simply could not believe it. A female rabbi? After the blessings over the wine and the bread, and some Sabbath songs that he cheerfully insisted the rabbi lead, we broke up into private conversations while we ate. But the rabbi could not so easily get away from the doctor's devout father-in-law. He had so many more questions and wanted to ask them in so many more ways. Did she read Torah? Did she study Talmud? Was she really a rabbi? She answered with grace and patience. Another of the delegates played backgammon with his youngest son, and I sat on the couch next to Dr. Moresadegh. He'd changed out of his dark suit into a massive pair of drawstring blue jeans and a T-shirt.

"It is the Sabbath," he laughed. "I should be comfortable. Have a drink of wine." Alcohol, though illegal in Iran, is allowed for religious minorities. He was only allowed to drink when he had company, he lamented as he poured me a glass of wine, not because of the Islamic government but because of a force far more powerful. "My wife," he said, laughing again and patting me on the back. "She's a feminist. She runs this house and runs me. I don't tell her what to do. She tells me!" He raised his glass to her and smiled as she sipped her own wine and returned to the conversation she'd been having with the two other Americans in her home.

We spent the next few hours eating and drinking and talking. Dr. Moresadegh defended Iran's nuclear program to me privately, and even their right to nuclear weapons if they wanted them—"Which we don't!" he insisted. He talked about his emotional affinity with Israel, though his desire to see justice for the Palestinians kept him from really identifying with the place in any meaningful way. Then he leaned toward me conspiratorially, clutching his glass of wine in his large palm. "You know," he said, "the world has a lot to learn from us Jews in Iran . . . We know how to get along with our neighbors. We've been doing it here for three thousand years."

It was after two in the morning when we made our way, bleary-eyed, into taxis and back to our hotel. The evening had unfolded in such an unexpected way my mind could hardly keep up, and the exhaustion and the wine weren't helping me process it all.

The Persian Jews' communal concern, their openheartedness, their mixture of piety and tradition with modernity, their wealth and poverty, along with their political acumen, reminded me a great deal of the Jewish community in America, with all its diversity and contradictions. Both were intensely organized; both had complex political structures and fluid relationships with the national power structures, which at any given moment might or might not have their best interests at heart. The difference was that these Jews in Iran had built their community over thousands of years, survived persecutions beyond anything even my grandparents' generation of American Jews had endured, and had a deeper understanding of interfaith dialogue than just about any people I had ever met. They knew what it was to be different, to be a minority, and to cherish that status while defending their way of life. They would not be used by Western Jews who wanted to believe they were persecuted, and they would not be used by the government of Iran, which struggled to learn the difference between tolerance and respect. There was much work ahead for them, but they proceeded with confidence and cautious optimism.

As the taxi sped through the empty streets of Tehran, I could only imagine the private parties going on behind every lighted window and drawn curtain. Dr. Moresadegh's words bounced around in my head: "the world has a lot to learn from us Jews in Iran . . ."

During my time in the Islamic Republic, I continued to make it a point to tell everyone I met that I was Jewish and American. I did keep my sexuality generally quiet, as homosexual acts are a serious crime in Iran and I didn't want to invite any suspicion toward the Iranians who talked to me or invited me to their homes. But as far as being Jewish, I told strangers on the street; I told soldiers and members of the Revolutionary Guard, I told government officials and cabdrivers and clerics. I found myself proudly owning my Jewish identity as I had never done before. I wanted to reach across to these people, not just to gauge their reactions but to see for myself what it felt like to be identified first and foremost by my religion. Everyone I told said the same thing in response: "Welcome to our country! Thank you for coming to see for yourself that we are brothers." And often they added, looking over their shoulders first: "If it weren't for politics, we would be brothers."

THAT WEEKEND WE FLEW TO SHIRAZ on an old Russian plane. I couldn't help but think of the sanctions against Iran that had for years prevented new airplane parts from being imported. I found myself saying a little prayer during takeoff, just before I closed my eyes for a nap. Before I knew it, the plane had landed.

Shiraz is home to Iran's second largest Jewish community, as well as the burial site for several revered Sufi poets. The supreme leader was in town that week, so the city was awash in honorific posters. In the five-minute drive from our hotel to the tomb of the poet Hafez, I counted ninety-nine posters or billboards bearing Khamenei's smiling face. The streets were impeccably clean. An army of garbage collectors and street sweepers had been mobilized for his visit. Colorful banners and garlands decorated storefronts and awnings. The stalls in the markets were bursting with color—the deep red of dried plums and the ruby glisten from baskets of currants. Flower beds bloomed in median strips and parks, and fruit trees peeked over neighborhood walls. Shiraz is known for its flowers and gardens, its songbirds, its poets, and its wine—though, given the ban on alcohol, I doubted we would experience that last pleasure. But the others were on full display.

On our first day, the spring weather was perfect, and a good mood filled the air. I wanted to hear music in the streets, but under Islamic law in Iran, that sort of entertainment is more confined to the home lest it offend the modesty of the pious, and the pious call the morality police to enforce their sensibilities. What music I heard was subdued. But there was no shortage of public joy in Shiraz. Outside the tomb of the poet Hafez, men held boxes of cards, and each card held a verse. For a small price, a colorful bird on one man's shoulder would pluck your fortune from the box, and the words of Hafez would provide some insight into your soul. My fortune, a Persian friend traveling with us explained after she read it aloud, promised me that my kindness would be rewarded with great success. The other Iranians standing around us were jealous.

"That was a really good one," she said, laughing. "And we're all terrible for being jealous of it." She repeated herself in Persian and everyone else laughed too. Shiraz is a city that loves poetry.

THE HEAD OF THE JEWISH COMMUNITY of Shiraz squeezed us in for a meeting at its "community and welfare center," as the sign out front called it. It was down a narrow street off of the congested main roads, and the neighborhood was very quiet.

In the building's courtyard, a giant poster of Ayatollah Khomeini's face leaned on a wall with a quotation written above it in Persian and, strangely, English. "Iran is a country shared by all races, and monotheism is a religion shared by all. We are one nation." The Iranian Jews took great pains to reinforce their Iranian identity, which seemed to me a sure sign of some kind of insecurity. There are about five thousand Jews in Shiraz and around twenty synagogues. The president of the Shiraz Jewish community had a meeting later that afternoon with the supreme leader himself. With their signs in Persian and English, I wondered who, exactly, they were trying to convince.

A group of community leaders came to the meeting, including the leader of the women's group. She was eager to ask Rabbi Gottlieb her opinion about a woman's right to divorce. Every time she asked a question, the five older men in the room argued among themselves before allowing the rabbi to answer. When she gave her answers, which came from a fairly feminist perspective, the room burst out into a discussion, and our translator couldn't keep up. Eventually, the president responded.

"Of course, we are a traditional community. We do not have movements like the Conservative and Reform, like you do in America. I have been to America and seen the Reform synagogues. The men and women were mixed during prayer, and this should not be. In the Jewish religion, they should be separated . . . As for marriage, whatever is in the Torah, we do."

"There is a very traditional interpretation here," the young woman added. "Under Iranian law, the religious minorities have jurisdiction over themselves for civil matters like divorce. That is why I ask your opinion as a rabbi."

"We believe that the women have a right to initiate divorce," the rabbi answered calmly. The room broke out into debate again.

The president responded, "We are traditional, as I said. Whatever is in the Torah, that is what we do. There are eight things that must be established for a divorce."

"But there are different ways to interpret the Torah," the rabbi said. "For example, different commentaries say that it is a commandment to live in Israel, while others say it is not."

"We follow the Torah," he answered again. "We are the most religious community in all of Iran." He was proud of this fact and expanded on his thought. "The Muslims of Iran have their city of Qom. The Jews have Shiraz. It is our Jerusalem."

On the subject of Israel, he spoke more candidly than the leaders in Tehran. "Of course we would like the state of Israel, but not the government that's there now." Then he moved to change the subject. "I have a question for you," he said. "In America, how is the relationship between Jews and Muslims?"

Our discussion went on for another half hour. The president of the Shiraz community continued to boast about the religiosity of his city. "Look in our synagogues in the morning, you will see all the young people coming to pray." He talked about the ways in which he thought U.S. foreign policy was the cause of all the violence between Muslims and Jews, and he urged us to see his synagogue. We walked next door to the small building, which was lovingly maintained. Indeed, there were a half a dozen young men finishing their morning prayers, fervently bowing and bending in their *tallit* and tefillin.

Thinking of the young men of the Jewish community, I asked the president what would happen if Israel or the United States attacked Iran, what the young men of the Jewish community would do.

"They would fight for their country," he said. "Just as they did during the Iran-Iraq War."

In Tehran I had asked the same question of Dr. Homayoun Mohaber, one of Sapir Hospital's board members. He was also a general in the Iranian army, who served during the war against Saddam Hussein. He too had asserted the young Jews' readiness to fight for Iran. "Though I am the only Jewish general," he added, "we have captains and other officers serving from our community."

Later that night I walked into a shop just before closing. Outside, merchants had laid their wares on mats in the street, selling everything from shoes to electronics to DVDs. Inside the shop the shelves were tidy and the clothes neatly folded. I noticed that the man working behind the counter wore a Star of David around his neck. He saw me looking at it and quickly hid it under his shirt. Then he denied it was a Jewish symbol. But then he whispered to me that he missed the days of the shah and that "these Muslims, they will shoot you." He made a motion for me to keep my lips sealed and winked at me. I couldn't inquire further, but he suggested that not everything was as cheery as the Jewish community leaders said. Later that night I saw the man walking happily on the street, talking to friends and laughing as he made his way home. Whatever anxieties he'd expressed to me didn't seem to put a damper on his evening.

For the rest of my time in Iran, I sought out young Jews and asked them what they would do in the event of an attack on Iran. One young man, who did not feel deeply connected to the Jewish community—he called himself a "secular humanist" and did not like the conservative religiosity of Iran's Jews—told me simply, "If Israel bombed us, I feel more responsible for my country." He told me that all the young Jews he knew felt this way.

If I needed to be certain, he told me, I should go to the intersection of Mirdamad and Valiasr Streets to look at the mural there. It was yet another mural dedicated to the martyrs of the Iran-Iraq War, but this one celebrated the Jews and Christians who died fighting for their country.

"You know," his Muslim friend added, "the Jews are the oldest Iranians. They've been here longer than anyone."

One young Jewish man told me he did not want to fight if it came to it because he did not think of himself as a soldier. He wished they had more freedoms in Iran, but, he explained, the problem was not being Jewish, it was the lack of freedom that all young people felt. It was an Iranian problem, and one, he insisted, they could solve themselves without outside interference. Over and over I heard the same thing, from Jews and Muslims: We do not want outside interference. This is our country. They were acutely aware of the rising threat of a bombing campaign against Iran and, with the memory of the bombings of the Iran-Iraq War etched in the psyches of everyone over twenty years old, they feared the idea of another conflict. They were all optimistic about the candidacy of Barack Obama for president of the United States, hoping he would change the policy that had kept them isolated for thirty years. But, they reminded me, in spite of their optimism, they were ready if war came.

JUST OFF IMAM SQUARE IN THE majestic city of Esfahan, Rabbi Gottlieb and I stumbled upon an unexpected sight: Judaica for sale in the window of a little shop, and outside, a middle-aged man in a yarmulke straightening his wares. Elezar, the shopkeeper, was a proud member of Esfahan's Jewish community. He greeted us with a smiling Shalom!, and in we went to his store. His sixteen-year-old son smiled proudly when asked about his bar mitzvah, but otherwise showed more interest in fixing the television than in talking to Jewish visitors. As we stood in the shop, friends and other merchants popped in to say hello. Elezar had recently been traveling. He had just returned from a trip to Israel.

"Would you ever move to Israel?" we asked him.

"Me?" he scratched his head and laughed. "No. I like it there; it's okay. But this is my home, here in Iran. This is where I am comfortable. You have heard the old saying about this city? 'Esfehan is half the world.'"

"In Farsi, the saying rhymes," Su'ad, who was translating for us, explained.

According to Morris Motamed, Jews have been able to travel freely between Iran and Israel for the past seven years, and many Jews we spoke to had been or were planning to go for a visit. They are publicly opposed to Zionism, but they openly admit to feeling a spiritual connection with Israel. I was surprised by such openness. Most Iranians were not simply forbidden to travel to Israel; visiting the Zionist state could land them in prison for treason, which was punishable by death. For Jews, this travel was a special privilege, generally understood if not widely advertised. I had been led to believe that no one would discuss it with me, either publicly or privately, but I found many people willing to speak on the record.

The Jews, like all Iranians, cannot aggressively criticize the Islamic government lest they run afoul of the state security apparatus. Dissenters are imprisoned, and reports of torture leak out from the notorious Evin prison. But change was in the air in Iran nonetheless. Walking the streets I saw young couples holding hands (technically illegal), I saw fashion statements that pushed the limits of "Islamic dress," and I heard discussions that veered very close to open defiance of the regime. Over and over I saw the paradoxes of Iran playing out: a country with no free press but with open and spirited debate; a country where such debate could land a person in jail.

I was reminded of how Vaclav Havel described certain artists' resistance to the soviet occupation. The artists simply behaved as if they lived in a free country. They carved out free space for themselves. I noticed artists doing the same in Iran. They created modes of free expression through metaphor and allusion. The youth created secular and permissive spaces in their cars and their apartments as they needed it. To some extent, political activists and feminists did the same thing. And of course, at much less risk, the Jews carved out Jewish space in society and lived fairly freely on their own terms.

For a relatively small community in Iran, which has a population of seventy million people, the Jews are not shy about making their presence known. The more observant Jews wear their yarmulkes in the streets. In addition to their outspoken member of Parliament, the community publishes a glossy magazine four times a year, and has more than thirty active synagogues throughout the country, as well as two kosher restaurants, a kosher caterer, six Jewish schools, five kosher butchers, a library, and a hospital. They have broken ground on a massive sport and recreation complex. Though, given Iran's economic problems, the future maintenance of all those institutions is uncertain.

ON OUR LAST MORNING IN TEHRAN, the rabbi and I woke up early to visit another Tehran synagogue where a small group of men were finishing morning prayers and to see a Jewish school. The editor of the Jewish magazine, *Binah*, volunteered to be our tour guide. He too wanted to impress upon us the ease of Jewish life in Iran.

"They respect the Jewish people here," he told Rabbi Gottlieb and me as we drove to the school, past the kosher restaurant. "This a religious country, so they want to encourage religion. It is harder for more secular people than it is for religious people, no matter their religion . . . but you know," he added, "we cannot separate our Persianness from our Jewishness; we are one body. If anything, tell your country, please do not bomb us. You *will* jeopardize our safety and our very existence. We are happy here. What problems we have, we can solve for ourselves. Do not let your country use us Iranian Jews as an excuse for war."

I asked him why everyone was so eager to tell us how okay they were as Jews.

"We have access to the Internet and to satellite television. We know how Iran is perceived in the West," he said. "I think we all want to tell you that it is simply not true, what you see on the news. We are not persecuted. We are not looking to escape. When these Zionist groups offer us money to move to Israel, it is an insult. We have been here for thousands of years."

Of course, some people had taken the money and moved to Israel. An evangelical Christian group from America paid thousands of dollars for about forty people to make aliyah, and then used their emigration to manufacture news stories about the rescue of persecuted Jews. Everyone in the Jewish community in Tehran just shook their heads and rolled their eyes. Of course, in the stunted Iranian economy, I wondered how long people could hold out. Many of the Jews in Iran were quite poor. Our tour guide for the morning just shrugged, not wanting to make any public conjecture on the subject.

At the Moshe Ben Amram Primary School, a portrait of Moses and Aaron looks across a classroom at the portraits of Ayatollah Khomeini and his successor as supreme leader, Ayatollah Khamenei. Though I was told that it is not a requirement that the images of the supreme leaders be hung in public buildings, it almost certainly is a de facto regulation. You cannot enter a public space in Iran without seeing the two ayatollahs looking down at you.

A class of boys, wearing their yarmulkes, studied beneath the images, flashing glowing smiles and showing off their knowledge of Hebrew. The school has about seventy students. The principal, as the law requires, is a Muslim. The students study Hebrew and Jewish religion and culture. On Fridays they hold special lessons on Judaism for Jewish students from the government schools, which are closed on Fridays. However, government schools are open on Saturdays, which makes it nearly impossible for Jewish students to be strictly observant and also to attend school dutifully. The community and the government are still working out this problem.

Rabbi Gottlieb spoke briefly to the class, the students showed off their ability to count to ten in Hebrew, and then we left. As our guide raced through the chaotic Tehran streets to drop us off at our hotel, the police pulled us over. To deal with the traffic in Tehran, drivers needed special permits to be on certain roads at certain times. He didn't have such a permit and would have to pay a fine. He threw the ticket into his glove compartment, where I saw several others just like it.

"I never pay these fines," he said. "You know, I'm a lawyer. I will go argue them soon."

* * *

LATER THAT DAY, I WATCHED AS Rabbi Gottlieb stood on one foot in a government ministry in Tehran. Her cascades of dark gray hair were tucked under a black head scarf and hidden beneath her manteau. The gathered clerics, government officials, reporters, and peace activists looked on with muted smiles as she achieved yet another first for a female American rabbi in Iran: she taught the entire Torah.

As the opening speaker for an event billed as the First Dialogue between the Center for Interreligious Dialogue of Iran and American Jews, she told the famous story of Hillel, the third-century Jewish sage.

"Someone once came to Rabbi Hillel," she said, her voice swaying and rising as if she spoke from the bimah rather than the conference table, "and he challenged the rabbi to teach the entire Torah while standing on one foot. So Hillel stood on one foot and said: 'Do not do to other people what you would not want them to do to you. That is the whole Torah; the rest is commentary. Now go and study.' "

Nods passed through the room, along with chuckles from those who spoke English. The rabbi acknowledged Morris Motamed, the elder statesman of Iran's Jewish community, and spoke about the Islamic and Jewish traditions of peacemaking. She ended with a prayer in Hebrew and sat back down in front of a large banner that read: "One God and the Common Religious Beliefs between Islam and Judaism."

I was surprised to find myself representing Jewish America to a group of Iranian officials. I could only imagine what the mainstream Jewish establishment back in the United States would think. No one had ever heard of me, yet here I was, and according to that banner, I was a stand-in for American Jews. I was glad to let the rabbi do the talking.

The host of the conference, Dr. Rasoul Rasoulipour, thanked Rabbi Gottlieb for her speech. Dr. Rasoulipour was the director of the Center for Interfaith Dialogue, which is a division of the Culture and Islamic Relations Organization, which is in turn connected to the office of the supreme leader. He spoke English with a hint of an Oxonian accent from his days getting a PhD. In spite having also studied at Notre Dame, Dr. Rasoulipour struggled to understand American English, and beseeched his guests to speak slowly when they addressed questions to him.

"I'm sure you'll see differences between the propaganda and what you see here in Iran," he said. "As I saw differences between what I saw in our media and what I saw in the U.S."

He had invited us to Iran in the interest of fostering dialogue among the Abrahamic faiths. He'd sponsored our visas, arranged our itinerary, and his office had taken responsibility for us while we were there. He was thrilled to have American Jews visiting Iran. He had been so excited that he arranged for the conference and ordered the banner long before the group arrived. He claimed that it did not bother him that there were only two Jews.

"I'm so happy to have some Jewish people in Iran, and I hope that your coming to my country will help to create a good future between our countries and our traditions," he said, his face beaming.

Morris Motamed added his remarks to the conference as well. "Interfaith dialogue has been going on in this country for at least twenty-seven hundred years. The Jews had dialogue with the Zoroastrians and when Islam came we had dialogue with the Muslims . . . There is no problem between the followers of Moses the prophet and Mohammed the prophet."

After the conference, which took up only a few hours on a steaming Tehrani afternoon, Dr. Mohammad Elmi, a black-turbaned cleric and vice president of the Culture and Islamic Relations Organization, approached Rabbi Gottlieb directly. They spoke about a shared desire to bring more Jewish people to Iran for dialogue in the hope that with mutual understanding peace could be assured.

"We have twenty-seven tombs of Jewish prophets in Iran," Dr. Elmi explained. "If you return, you will have to visit them. Many Iranian Jews make pilgrimage to the tombs of Daniel and Queen Esther." Then the turbaned cleric shook his head and expressed to the rabbi his very pragmatic reason for desiring peace between Iran and world Jewry: "You don't know how I wish to go to the Holy Land on a pilgrimage."

There it was again, that longing directed toward Israel. As a religious man, Dr. Elmi would of course want to go there, but the intimate way he told the rabbi about his desire suggested that it was only natural for her to understand. In spite of the tense relations between our countries, and the conservative nature of Iran regarding women, this government official assumed that the rabbi, as a Jew, also felt called to "the Holy Land." The connection between Jews and Jerusalem was a given for him, even as he and his government refused to recognize Jewish sovereignty over the land of Israel. For Dr. Elmi, it was a sacred meeting place for Muslim, Christian, and Jew. His vision was appealing, but I wondered, in that case, why should it matter who controlled it? The stock answer from Iranian officials was that Zionism was a colonial enterprise, and they objected to the injustice faced by the Palestinians. They made no mention of the fact that Jews were barred from visiting their holy sites in Jerusalem when the Old City was controlled by Jordan. They certainly made no mention of any injustices faced by members of their own population. They framed their opposition to Zionism as a human rights objection, even as they scoffed at human rights criticisms leveled at Iran.

Politics was the crux of it all, the center of the conflict. Human rights and spiritual longing were all well and good, but the conflict was played out in real political terms, with political actors. Hezbollah and Hamas were real. They had vowed to destroy Israel and worked constantly to kill civilians. The Israeli Defense Forces were real. Their military actions left vast numbers of civilians dead and enraged the rest of the Middle East. And these organizations had competing political goals. Spirituality and justice were often the language they used, but when everything was boiled down their actions were an extension of politics. What is politics but the struggle for control of the state? Jewish control meant Zionism, and Islamic control meant the Islamic revolution, which they worked to export through Hezbollah and Hamas. They were two states determined to mix politics with their respective theologies, and as I left Iran I couldn't imagine how that would ever lead to peace. But I could imagine who would pay the price. As so many young men at Jamkaran had said to me, "Without politics, we would all be brothers."

eight

Revolutionaries:
The Jewish Community of Cuba

We regard Isarel's chosenness solely as history's means to accomplish
the divine chosenness of mankind.
—HERMANN COHEN

A S THE SUN BEGAN to set on a Friday in Havana, I had to take my leave of the professor's apartment and go, as usual, to synagogue. I felt no desire to leave. Outside, the sticky heat reflecting off the pavement was unrelenting. June in Havana. Who visits the Caribbean in the middle of summer? We sat across from each other in rocking chairs in the professor's study, drinking cold water, listening to the hum of the air conditioner.

The room smelled like old books. It held hundreds of them. The tropical climate had been brutal to their pages; most were yellowed and warped. I saw novels, books on history, politics, and mathematics, scientific and philosophical tracts. There were books in at least three different languages on the professor's shelves. He read English, German, and of course Spanish. He had probably studied Russian as well, though I didn't notice any books with Cyrillic characters. Nor did I notice any Hebrew.

Jose Altschuler, professor of electrical engineering at the University of Havana, former president of the Cuban National Space Commission, vice president of the Cuban Academy of Sciences, author, historian, and avid collector of klezmer records, was a committed Communist and did not feel deeply tied to the Jewish community of Cuba. He remained proud of his Jewish heritage, though, and of his parents' struggles on the island.

"I am proud to be a Jew," he said, listing notable Jewish scientists. "But I am prouder still to be a Communist in Cuba. I think we have done many great things here. There have been mistakes, of course, regrettable and terrible mistakes, but they were done with the right intentions, I think. I regret these mistakes we made—the real mistakes, not the mistakes *they* say we made."

By "they," he meant the capitalists, the U.S. government, and the Cuban exiles in Miami, many of whom he referred to by name, followed by the epithet "that son of a bitch." Jose looks like a kindly grandfather, with bushy white hair and eyebrows and a jolly paunch in his belly, but he talks like a revolutionary.

"I did what I could to help the revolution. I am a Communist, and an engineer. I worked in the refrigeration business and used the proceeds to help support the underground Communist party. I was never arrested, thankfully, but there were some close calls. When the revolution succeeded, of course I was happy. Not because I follow the party blindly—I'm proud that I have never been a yes-man—but because I am, and I remain, deeply committed to social justice and equality. That is what I work for, and that, I think, is the contribution of the revolution. I helped develop Cuba's radio transmission capacity so that we would be able to use it both for commercial and diplomatic purposes, but also to broadcast our own message to the world and not to be at the mercy of foreign communication technologies. I worked very hard to develop the scientific community in Cuba."

High on the seventh floor of his art deco apartment building, we took in a view of the sunset over the Malecon, Havana's sea wall and promenade. A wide road separated the neighborhood from the walkway, and cars would occasionally speed by, but thanks to the high price of gas there wasn't much traffic down below. Couples walked arm in arm between the road and the ocean, and touts sold cigars to tourists. The early evening was the best time for the Malecon. As the air cooled, everyone came outside to see and be seen, to listen to music, drink, and dance. Though there wasn't much noise from the cars, we began to hear the sounds of the people coming out to stand by the edge of the island.

We watched the sky turn pink and red and looked at the flapping flags that blocked the view of the United States Interests Section, which provided consular services to Cuba in lieu of diplomatic representation. The United States and Cuba have not had diplomatic ties since 1960, when Fidel Castro allied his country with the Soviet Union and President Eisenhower broke off official relations.

"Some years ago," Jose smiled, "the capitalists put these displays up; these electronic billboards on their building to spread anti-Cuban propaganda." He pointed toward the flapping flags and I could see fragments of red text moving behind them, though I couldn't make out what the text said. "So the government responded by putting up these flags that you see. They just blocked off the view." He laughed. "People have access to all kinds of information here in Cuba; they don't need this United States propaganda display. I tell you, your government has always wanted to intervene in our affairs. This is nothing new."

He popped out of his chair with the agility of a much younger man, and rummaged through his books, pulling out a yellowed volume and flipping open to a page. Che Guevara's stern face stared down over my shoulder from a portrait Jose had hung on the only wall not lined with sagging bookshelves. I thought of the portraits of Moses and Aaron in synagogues around the world, and of the portraits of the ayatollahs in Iran. Those were in public spaces, though. Jose had chosen to venerate Che in his home.

"This is from Thomas Jefferson writing to President Monroe," he said. "I candidly confess that I have ever looked on Cuba as the most interesting addition which could ever be made to our system of states." He tapped the page with his index finger and smiled again, raising his thick white eyebrows at me. "It was always so. The United States has always wanted to annex this little island, then as now."

"Why do you think that is?"

"Because of the strategic location, perhaps. But also because this a remarkable place. The Cubans are a remarkable people. What other country could survive the loss of eighty percent of its economy overnight? We did. We have survived this cruel embargo too. We have a strong sense of purpose here, and that cannot be broken."

He was talking about what is known as the "special period" in Cuban history, after the fall of the Soviet Union, on whose patronage Cuba's economy relied. When the USSR disappeared, Cuba became suddenly and deeply impoverished. Changes had to be made. The island had to open up to tourism, which is now its main source of income, and certain elements of capitalism had to be allowed, like small privately owned restaurants and guesthouses. It was the only way to keep people from starving. People made "steaks" out of grapefruit peels and went days without power, and gasoline was in short supply. During this time, on average, Cubans lost 20 percent of their body weight.

"Like most of the Cuban Jews, my family came in the twentieth century," Jose told me. Unlike the Jews in Burma or Bosnia, most of the Cuban Jews do not have a long history on the Island. "My parents came from Europe, separately. They met here in Cuba. Many Jewish immigrants came to Cuba from Europe, hoping to then go on to the United States. Not my parents. My mother came from Poland because she feared the anti-Semites and wanted to go somewhere she could study. She came to Havana in 1924. My father came in '23 looking for a better future. He had heard there were good opportunities, but he was bad at business. They moved around the island for a while, but after the stock market crashed in 1929, they came back to Havana for good. We were poor people, working class people. I remember when I was the first in my class, the father of one of the wealthy students wondered how I, the son of working-class people, could do so well in school. His son answered him, 'Well, Altschuler is poor, so the only thing he can do is study!' This boy was from one of the prominent Jewish families. They're all gone now. After the revolution, most left when the small businesses were nationalized. They were capitalists and did not see their future here anymore. Now, of course, young people leave because of the economy. Things are hard here, you have no idea. Just to get by is very hard." He sighed. "That's just the way it is.

"As for being a Jew, I do not believe in God or in the rituals and I do not go to synagogue because I do not want to be a hypocrite. I am many things at my age, but I am not a hypocrite, spiritually or politically."

His statement reminded me of my father, who had long ago walked away from organized religion. He too was a man of science, though I'm sure he wouldn't like being compared to an elderly Cuban Communist. Religion—or the lack thereof—makes strange bedfellows.

The professor and I had been speaking for over an hour, and I had to rush from his apartment to arrive on time at the main synagogue, about six blocks away. His words, "That's just the way it is," echoed in my head as I took the stairs. The creaky old elevator frightened me. Like almost everything in Havana it looked run-down: the paint was peeling, the colors faded, and the door only sometimes worked.

Out on the street, a group of children were playing baseball. I heard a rumba beat rising from a passage between two tall buildings, but rushed on. Jose was the first Jew I had met on the island, and his commitment to the principles of Fidel's revolution was clear. He had a strong sense of historical purpose, which tied him to Cuba and to its hardships. I wondered what I would find in the Jewish community proper, where religious and cultural commitments played a larger role in people's lives. Jose was Jewish by heritage and Communist by choice, but what of the Jews who had an active connection to Judaism? Where would they stand in relation to the revolution? To Cuban society? To Israel? Cuba had cut off official ties with Israel decades ago and had long sided with the Palestinians, even though Fidel admired Israel's early triumphs as a socialist country with a sense of historic mission.

IN RESPONSE TO THE CORRUPT PRESIDENT Fulgencio Batista's coup in 1952, Fidel Castro, a young lawyer, began organizing a campaign to topple him. Batista, who was closely allied with both the United States and organized crime, retaliated with a wave of brutal repression and torture. On July 26, 1953, Fidel led a disastrous attack on the Moncada Barracks, during which sixty-four rebels were captured, tortured, and killed. Fidel himself was arrested but, strangely, allowed access to the media. He gave a historic speech, in which he proclaimed, "history will absolve me."

After international pressure led to his release, he spent several years in Mexico, where he met a young Argentinean named Ernesto Guevara, whom everyone called, simply, Che. In 1959 they returned to Cuba together and led an assault on the government. By the end of that year, they had overthrown Batista and, against all odds, seized control of the country. They set about purging the old elites from the government, quashing dissent, and establishing a Communist government. Eventually, against the advice of Che and several others, Fidel tied Cuba's development to the Soviet Union, which enabled them to survive the U.S. embargo and strengthen their military. The tiny Caribbean nation became a front line in the Cold War, and the Cubans in Miami worked closely with the U.S. government in an effort to return capitalism to Cuba, isolate the revolutionary government, and assassinate Fidel. In response to these plots, repression and paranoia on the island increased, leading in turn to even stronger criticism from the exiles. Cuba grew more and more isolated from the rest of the hemisphere.

The Cuban economy froze in time. There was little new construction. Old Havana's historic buildings began to deteriorate. The posh neighborhood of Vedado, filled with art deco, neoclassical, and modernist architecture, fell into disrepair. Old American cars—big Cadillacs and Fords—stayed on the streets. People couldn't replace them, just as they couldn't replace the old buildings, and so they too became part of the Havana time machine, frozen in the moment when the island's isolation began. Just down the street from Jose's apartment, a building that looked like the top of the Empire State Building sliced off and set down in the Caribbean was falling into a stunning state of decay. Men played dominoes on the median strip in the middle of the wide boulevard, and women stood in the dark doorways of the brightly colored neoclassical mansions that used to house Havana's elite. Now each home held several generations of a family packed into its once stately rooms, their multitudes of laundry drying between the columns on the porch. I passed a mural painted on a wall of a strange figure with an eye-shaped head, wielding a sword and holding the Cuban flag. Above its head were the letters CDR. Committee for the Defense of the Revolution. It's a neighborhood block association that serves the usual functions of neighborhood administration—arranging festivals, spreading information, organizing rallies—and also a decidedly less benign function: maintaining files on every resident of the block and reporting any "counterrevolutionary activity." I snapped a photo of its logo, which was oddly cartoonish, and kept walking.

When I got to the synagogue, David Prinstein's impeccable 1956 Chevy was parked outside. I'd seen the classic cars rumbling all over Havana's streets, but this was the first one I'd seen in good condition. The Prinstein family were active in the Jewish revival in Cuba, and I'd been told about David's car before I arrived. It lived up to the hype. Its fins and whitewall tires shimmered in the sunlight, spotless, as if the car had never left the showroom. The whites and greens were vivid and there was not a scratch on it. People were gathering in front of the synagogue to talk and smoke before services, and no one paid much attention to me. They had grown used to tourists in recent years. The Patronato Synagogue—named for the wealthy Cuban patrons who built it in the midfifties—was a mandatory stop on Jewish tourist itineraries and Jewish aid missions to the island, which had become more and more frequent over the years.

"Cuba Si, Yanqi No!" a voice called out to me. I turned to see a middle aged man with the telltale red face of a visitor who had gotten a bit more sun than he was used to back home. The man was Robert Fisher, a Canadian Jew who had been visiting and supporting the Jewish community of Cuba for over twenty years.

"You should have seen this place when I first came. It was terrible. The building was falling apart; people were starving. Now, things are better, but don't let the fresh paint fool you. Everyone is very poor, even the well-off ones are poor." As if to prove his point a wrinkled old man in a yarmulke wandered over to us and introduced himself as Shlomo, the shammes. Traditionally, the shammes is the caretaker of the synagogue, but I couldn't picture this guy looking after the massive building, with its facade of glass, elaborately decorated entranceway, and grand blue arch. I did recognize Shlomo, though. His real name was Salomon Leyderman, and he had a way of popping up in every article written about the Jewish community of Cuba. I'd even seen his picture in the *New York Times* a few years ago. He smiled and shook my hand firmly.

"You from Brooklyn," he exclaimed with a Spanish accent imitating a Brooklyn accent. "You a mob lawyer?" He laughed and patted me on the back. Then he whispered in my ear, "You have a few pesos for the shammes?" I slipped him a convertible peso, which was worth about a dollar, and he smiled. "A big shot, my friend." He laughed and wandered into the synagogue.

"He does that to everyone," Robert told me. "He's actually not so poor. He's just cheap. He won't spend any money. He comes here for meals on Friday night and goes the rest of the week to Adath Israel, the Orthodox synagogue in Old Havana, for his other meals. He has a sickness, I think, with this cheapness. But he's a very good man, generally. Crazy, but a good man." Robert shook his head, and we went up the steps to the synagogue.

The Patronato is not the only synagogue left in Havana—there are three—but it is the grandest, and it serves as the center of Jewish life on the island. It fell into disrepair after the revolution, when much of the community, including all its wealthy patrons, left. Under soviet influence, religious affiliation in general was outlawed for decades, and participation in Jewish life was left to a few devout older people. Younger Jews did not want to associate too openly with the synagogue for fear that it would affect their chances of attending a good university or getting a good job. For a long time, an entire generation of Jews was considered lost. But, as Cuba opened up after the fall of the Soviet Union, it opened to religious expression as well. The grand ideal of international Communism had suffered a fatal blow, and people needed new saving ideals. Just as they did in Bosnia, people turned to faith, and Jews started coming back to the Jewish community, looking for material and spiritual support.

Thanks to aggressive fund-raising by the American Jewish Joint Distribution Committee and several prominent American Jews, including Steven Spielberg, the synagogue was renovated in 2000. Bronze sculptures representing the Ten Lost Tribes decorate the facade, and a giant blue arch sweeps over the building. The Patronato stands as a bright example of modernism and modernization in Havana's rich architectural palette. The building is air-conditioned, and the second floor boasts a computer center and pharmacy. The library in the basement is wired for the Internet. The sanctuary has a working PA system and plush seats. It was hard to imagine that only ten years before my visit, the place had been falling apart, with a leaky ceiling and moldy seat cushions. Looking around the current sanctuary, I would never imagine that the community struggled for money. The decor could hold its own with just about any synagogue on the Upper West Side.

A husband-and-wife team from Argentina, Fernando and Patrica Lapiduz, who were paid by the Joint Distribution Committee, led the service. Fernando acted as the cantor. Patricia led the Hebrew school and was responsible for the children. Her son ran around the sanctuary with the other children, shouting and causing the kind of havoc that only six-year-olds can. I was struck by the diversity of the children—black, white, and brown. I'd never seen such a racial mix in a synagogue before. Patricia did her best to contain the children, but their shouts and laughs were a happy soundtrack running through the entire service.

Fernando and Patricia were the latest in a line of rabbinic students and mentors the Joint Distribution Committee had sent to Cuba to bolster the Jewish community. As in Sarajevo, in Cuba the JDC was simply called El Joint, and its aid was responsible for many of the benefits enjoyed by Cuba's Jews. Community members received financial assistance, free and plentiful prescriptions from the pharmacy, and a beef ration from the government. Beef was a rarity in Cuba, and, even though few members of the Jewish community actually kept kosher, everyone received the beef ration. Jews also enjoyed the right to emigrate to Israel. Emigration from Cuba had long been seen as anathema to the revolution, and, with the exception of two famous government-authorized exoduses, leaving the island was against the law. Those who did escape were called *gusanos*—worms. But not the Jews. Jews who moved to Israel were not seen as abandoning the revolution but as returning to their national homeland. In recent years, due to the dire economic situation, many young Cuban Jews have availed themselves of this privilege, often as a prelude to moving to the United States. One Cuban Jew who had made aliyah to Israel, a young doctor named Deborah, was at the synagogue in the row in front of me. She had returned to visit, but had no intention of staying for good. She was currently working in Equatorial Guinea, in an Israeli-run hospital.

"I moved to Israel a year and a half ago, and I love it," she told me. "In 1992 there was an opening of the country, a religious opening, and I came to join the community. This was around the age of my bat mitz-vah, and so I wanted to have that and to get involved. I started to learn Hebrew from the Joint, and I started to teach it too. So it was good; I was teaching the little children and learning at the same time. I always knew that I was Jewish. I lived with my mother and grandmother and they were Jewish. We always celebrated Passover at home. But when I came to the community—that is, when I began to get really involved, to do so many things—it was a very special time for me. I came back for my sister-in-law's bat mitzvah. Even though she is fifteen, she is having her bat mitzvah. It is important to have this time, to have these memories."

Deborah's sister-in-law, Anabel, all dressed up and looking nervous, sat in the front row with her parents. A collection of teenagers filled the rows around her for support. One boy wore a Che Guevara T-shirt. Even in synagogue, Che's stern face stared at me. When services began, the boy prayed loudly and enthusiastically. Everyone did. The room may have looked like a typical American synagogue, but the high-spirited prayers and songs marked it as something unique.

Along with Fernando Lapiduz and his wife, David and Marlene Prinstein sat on the bimah, as well as a young man named Daniel, who worked in the Jewish community library and had only recently learned to read Hebrew. He led most of the prayers, confidently though with oc-casional stumbles over a word. David Prinstein, one of the few younger men who had stayed involved in the Jewish community during the years when religious participation was not considered safe, had been the one who brought Daniel into the synagogue to become an active participant. He looked on proudly while Daniel read and chanted in front of the con-gregation. David's zeal over the years had also led his wife to convert to Judaism. Now she was one of the more active women at the Patronato. As the service progressed, Robert, who was sitting next to me, noticed that I wasn't following along very well.

"You should really learn Hebrew," he urged me, as someone always did during services. He read along and sang loudly, and he kept look-ing over at me with a wink or a nod, as if to say, "See how good this can be?"

We rose and sang "Lecha Dodi"; we sat and listened to psalms. We rose and prayed the Amidah; we sat and listened to Fernando formally introduce Anabel to the congregation as a bat mitzvah. Daniel and the Prinsteins took turns bringing the service to a close, while Fernando and his wife guided them. Then the children all gathered in front, their energy finally harnessed, and they sang some songs together. Everyone cheered for them and they all got candy, compliments of Robert. As ev-eryone laughed and cheered for the children, I noticed that the sanctuary had filled up with nearly three times the number of people who had been there at the start. They had come for the chicken dinner, also provided by El Joint.

"You will come to dinner?" Daniel urged me when services ended. His face was youthful and warm, and his head was covered with dark curly hair. He had an easy way with all the teenagers around him, and he clearly enjoyed his burgeoning role as a leader of the community. Adela Dworin, the community president, was recovering from eye surgery and, in her absence, Daniel, only twenty-eight years old, was in charge. He called out instructions to people who were headed to the banquet room ahead. "So, you're coming?" he asked again.

I couldn't picture him in a bad mood, and I hated to let him down, but I didn't want to take their food. All over the world, food prices were skyrocketing, and I felt as if I would be taking advantage of their hospitality if I ate with them when I was perfectly capable of going out and paying for dinner. In spite of the prosperity that the air conditioning and the plush seats suggested, the people were generally poor, as Robert reminded me again, standing suddenly at my side.

On top of my reluctance to take their food, I felt a bit like an intruder in the middle of the festive crowd. They didn't know me yet, and I felt strange inserting myself into their banquet, so I went downstairs for the blessings and to see the festivities, but I continued to decline the meal. Children ran in every direction; adults chatted and shared gossip. Shlomo wandered around the room, hitting up some Israeli tourists for a few dollars, and then settled in for his meal. When I said I wouldn't be staying, Daniel looked surprised, and his expression turned from a wide smile to a look of genuine concern. He put his hand on my shoulder. Cubans, I had noticed, were not shy about physical contact.

"Why not? Please. You are invited," he said and squeezed gently. Several others echoed his entreaties, but I saw that Robert would not be staying for the meal either, and I didn't want to be the only foreigner eating their food. So I apologized, which immediately confirmed my outsider status. I'd been given every opportunity to join in, and Daniel seemed disappointed that I wouldn't stay. I arranged to meet him later in the week to explore the Old City, and took my leave into the all-night party of Havana's streets.

Music leaked out of alleyways and nightclubs. Loud conversations burst from restaurants. There was rumba in an old garage in Vedado, bolero from the courtyard of the Union of Writers and Artists, salsa on an embankment near the Hotel Nacional. On a side street, a young boy sat on his porch with a guitar while an older man, taking long pulls from a bottle, showed him how to play. The whole scene reminded me of New Orleans. I watched for a while, more comfortable now that the air had finally cooled off. I thought about the Sabbath that had just arrived, and the unique privilege of celebrating it with a resurgent Jewish community, and the faux pas I had committed by taking my leave of the meal. I decided I would stay next week, once they got to know me better. I hadn't been comfortable with the feeling I had of being the rich American in the room. The meal had reminded me of what an outsider I was, how I was not a part of this community. They wanted to make me feel welcome, but there was a gulf of experience between us. Everyone was struggling. Everyone was poor. But because of that struggle, people came together. The free meal, the beef ration, the computer center—these were nice perks for being part of the Jewish community, and they did perhaps draw people to it, as the war in Bosnia had drawn people to that community, or the hurricane in New Orleans had brought Jews together there. It wasn't such a big revelation. People joined a community for the benefits, either spiritual or material. Was that the case here: the covenant as the price of admission to the chicken dinner? Or were we all looking for the same thing, that deeper connection to other people, our fellow Jews, and, through that feeling of community, a closeness to the divine?

Intermarriage was nearly 100 percent in this community. Deborah's father was not Jewish. Anabel's mother was not Jewish. Marlene Prinstein, who helped lead the services, had converted to Judaism a few years ago. There is demographic magic in this community. They say they number about fifteen hundred people. No matter how many leave the island, they continue to claim there are fifteen hundred Jews in Cuba. The number is certainly exaggerated, but even as they lose people, they gain people. Fernando told the *Wall Street Journal* that in 2007, his first year working with the community in Cuba, he led seventy-one conversions to Judaism.

Daniel had come to the community to play volleyball and ended up a leader of the youth group and the religious services. Anabel came with her family and found a group of friends. On Sunday, representatives from the Jewish community of Mexico would be giving out money to community members, based on need. Everyone would get something. This was truly a privilege in a country where a good salary was twenty dollars a month and the cost of everything was going up. People had all kinds of incentives to join the Jewish community, to show that they were Jewish or to convert. But why did so many not just join, but join and get involved?

I HAD HEARD THAT THE ANSWERS to most questions about life in Havana could be answered on the Malecon. If you wanted to get a sense of the political climate, or to find the gay scene, or to buy anything at all, head to the Malecon. The sea wall and promenade are sometimes known as Havana's front porch, and they extend along the northwest coast for almost four miles, from Vedado, past the infamous Hotel Nacional, site of the largest single gathering of gangsters in history, all the way along the edge of Havana to Habana Vieja—Old Havana—the original port established in the early sixteenth century.

The wall itself varies in height from about the knees up to the shoulders at some points, though during the furious winter months waves crash over even the higher parts, filling low-lying areas of the coastal strip with water. I was there in summer, and the sea was calm, not so much as a splash over the lip. Boys leaped from the wall to swim, and old men sat on its edge fishing. The smell of saltwater perfumed the air, and on a clear day it felt as if you could see all the way to Key West. Sections of the Malecon have been lovingly restored by UNESCO, and the colorful facades of skyscrapers and historic buildings are awe-inspiring. In other areas, the buildings sag, and the wall itself bears cracks and crevasses from the battering of the sea. I could sit on top of it for hours and watch the classic cars rumble past the classic buildings. I could watch the tourists on the hill up above sipping cocktails under a flapping Cuban flag at the Hotel Nacional. I could listen to all the laughter and the lovers' quarrels that went on around me. I could see the city without moving an inch from my perch on that wall.

Malecon has come to stand not only for the wall itself and the prom-enade that runs alongside it, but the wide road along the coast and all the buildings on the opposite side as well. Every major thoroughfare in the city runs into the Malecon. But, even more than a geographic indica-tor, it is a state of mind. It is a reflection of the city's consciousness. It is bawdy and fun and sometimes paranoid and sometimes empty and always sun-drenched. It's nostalgic too. Exiles living in Miami sometimes refer to their address as 90th and Malecon—an indication of longing to bridge the ninety miles that separate that seaside promenade from Florida. The yearning for that wall reminded me of that longing for Jerusalem that Jews had held on to over the centuries of exile. The psalmist's line again ran paraphrased through my head: *If I forget thee, O Malecon . . .*

El Malecon had already become my favorite place in Havana, but I hadn't yet seen it at night. So I walked over in the dark. Hustlers—called *jinteros*—cruised up and down the Malecon looking to sell cigars or rum or sex to tourists. The culture of *jinterismo* dismayed many Cubans. It was a by-product of the "special period" and it represented the worst vices of capitalism and materialism. Jose had lamented to me about the energy and creativity the *jinteros* used in their cons. "Imagine if they put that energy to good use, for the betterment of society?"

This *jinterismo* mentality, spreading since the fall of the Soviet Union and the retirement of Fidel Castro, didn't place much value on collective effort, on personal sacrifice. Jose saw it as a manifestation of the worst aspects of Americanization. Everyone liked DVD players and cell phones, which had only recently become legal in Cuba, but what of the materialism they symbolized? All over Havana, people were uncertain about this new society that was growing and the rapid changes that were taking place since Fidel ceded power to his brother, Raul. Private electronics—not just cell phones and DVD players but computers, air conditioners, MP3 players—they were all legal now to those who could afford them.

Though everyone denied that different classes existed in Cuba, I saw some people with new clothes and fancy cell phones, which indicated access to tourist dollars. And I saw people without. I noticed that black and white mixed freely, but though there didn't seem to be much racism on the personal level, I noticed that most of the menial jobs were held by darker-skinned Cubans, while all the more administrative jobs were held by lighter-skinned ones. I would never understand the workings of class or race in Cuba in a week, but watching on the Malecon, it was clear that race did play a role in life on the island. The central goals of the revolution, putting aside the political repression and the economic failures, had been a more just and equitable world. The older generation saw that slipping away. Even some of the younger generation could see it slipping away.

"All the time, growing up in the nineties, I was trying not to see the world outside of the community," Deborah told me. "The Jewish community was like an island in our minds. My life in Cuba was very atypical because of the Jewish community. I had a very special life socially and a very special role. My life was not the typical Cuban life. I was happy to be part of something."

The Jewish community had given Deborah a purpose greater than survival. In a sense, this is what the revolution was intended to do, but, with people starving and a class of hustlers and elites emerging, unabashed self-interest was once again rearing its head. Judaism in Cuba, while certainly not strictly religious, had a messianic purpose that echoed Fidel's revolution: service, commitment, communal striving.

On the Malecon, I saw people coming together and enjoying themselves, but everyone I spoke to, knowing I was American, seemed to see dollar signs in my eyes. I never felt unsafe—violent crime is very rare in Cuba—but I didn't feel comfortable. Everyone wanted something from me. Hustlers of every gender tried to get my attention, verbally and physically. There was never any hostility in it, but it was more forward than I was used to.

"Cigars? Dancing? What do you want?" I was asked over and over again. Hands on my shoulder, my back, my thighs. Others just ignored me, more intent on their friends and the dramas playing out in the private lives on the very public promenade. Everyone was drinking. I had no one to drink with. I felt like an outsider. I was.

After an hour of people-watching and waving off hustlers, I stopped by a restaurant near the apartment I was staying in. Thanks to the general friendliness of Havana's citizens, within minutes I found myself talking to a gregarious woman in her forties.

"You are from America?" she asked.

"Yes, I am."

"Well, I am a *Communist*," she said defiantly, looking for my response. When I didn't run away screaming, she must have decided I was an okay representative of the imperialist nation to the north, and she moved over to my table. Her name was Celia Hart, a passionate Trotskyite and supporter of the revolution. She spoke grandly of Fidel as a hero and leader. Even if he was no longer active as the head of state, he would always be the leader of the revolution.

I later learned that her family had played a major role in the history of the revolution. Her mother, Haydée Santamaría, was one of two women involved in Fidel's failed attack on the Moncada Barracks in 1953. As a result, Celia's uncle was tortured to death and his eyes presented to Haydée on a plate. After the success of the revolution, Haydée went on to establish the Casa De Las Américas, which remains an important cultural institution throughout Latin America. Sadly, she killed herself in

1980. Celia's father had been the minister of education and the minister of culture under Fidel.

Celia and I talked about the coming elections in the United States, about the growing "people's revolution" throughout Latin America, and about Fidel's resignation. She did not believe Cuba would return to capitalism, because most people still held on to their sense of purpose, regardless of the setbacks and difficulties. She spoke with messianic fervor about Cuba's "living revolution" and its power to inspire the world.

"You know Jose Altschuler?" she asked when I told her what I was doing in Cuba, about my interest in the Jewish community. "I was a student of his. I studied physics, but now I am a journalist. I should tell you, for your research, that the Jewish people have a long history in Cuba, and a long history of being committed revolutionaries, like Jose. There was never anti-Semitism here. We are all Cubans. We have enemies, a lot in Miami who want to undermine us. But they will not succeed. Fidel and Che, they will always inspire us."

Eventually, she went back to talking to her group of friends, and I made my way to the apartment to get some sleep. I thought about her passion for the survival of the revolution, and I was in awe of how it had lasted so long, how, in spite of the U.S. embargo, countless plots against it, economic and natural disasters, it carried on. My walk home took me past the Patronato and I couldn't help but make the comparison to the Jewish people, tiny next to those who wished to destroy them but filled with the same passion for survival, the same belief that their message, their purpose on earth, mattered. In fact, Fidel had told the Jewish community as much just a few years earlier when he visited the Patronato during Hanukkah in 1998.

DR. JOSE MILLER, THE RECENTLY DECEASED president of the Jewish community, spent years cultivating a relationship with Fidel Castro. He had become president of the Jewish community, as he told an interviewer in 2000, "because there was no one else," but during his tenure, he did his best to build relationships with international Jewish organizations and with the power structures in Cuba. Fidel Castro valued the opinion of the tiny Jewish community, so much so that, in spite of their small numbers, he involved them in major decisions about the social life of Cuba. Dr. Miller and Adela Dworin, the current president of the community, were invited to sit on a committee to decide whether December 25th would be an official holiday in Cuba. "How could I object to a holiday that celebrates the birth of a nice Jewish boy?" Dr. Miller was said to have joked.

In the early days of the revolution, Fidel was sad to see so many Jews leave the island, given what they could have contributed to his plans, but they never had the stigma attached to them that other emigrants had. Some even said that Fidel had Jewish ancestors, and Fidel never denied it. As a boy, his classmates had even called him *judio*—Jew—because he had not been baptized by age seven. "Jew" was apparently the common nickname for unbaptized children. Maybe this early taunting had fostered some sympathy for the Jewish people in Fidel's heart. Jews had always been respected in revolutionary Cuba.

Adela Dworin invited Fidel to visit the Patronato shortly after the pope's visit to Cuba in 1998. When Fidel spoke to the congregation, he did so in his usual style—long and extemporaneous. He spoke admiringly about Jewish history and their battles for freedom against much more powerful forces, just as he saw the Cuban struggle. He made several explicit comparisons between the Jewish people and the Communist Party.

"In 2000-some years, you have preserved your culture, identity, religion, tradition," he told the rapt audience. "I'm trying to remember if any other culture has accomplished this."

While I stood out front in the dark, imagining this speech, a dog who seemed to live in the synagogue slipped out under the gate and padded past me. The street had gone quiet and I wasn't sure how late it was. Shockingly, I couldn't even hear music on the streets anymore. I made my way back to bed.

THE NEXT DAY, I RETURNED TO the synagogue to watch Anabel become a bat mitzvah and then, after services, to see the youth group perform Israeli dances. Dozens of young people participated. They wore traditional Israeli outfits in reds and blues with billowing pants and vests, and their moves were confident and energetic. I couldn't imagine this many teens jumping into folk dancing on a Saturday where I grew up.

"They practice a lot," Daniel told me. He now led the youth group and had a lot of activities planned for the summer—trips to the Hemingway House, visits to some of the islands off the coast, beach trips. "I give them activities to do so that maybe some of the younger ones will want to get more involved in the Jewish aspects of the community too."

Daniel and I were the same age and had both recently returned to Jewish life. He first came to the community in 2005 for the activities and the social life, just like the young kids dancing around us. "David Prinstein brought me," he said. "He urged me to start studying, to get more involved. A year ago I began to learn Hebrew, and only two months ago I started reading from the Torah. You know, I can't remember the last Saturday that I didn't come to synagogue." Daniel had been officially converted a year earlier, along with several other members of the community, when a rabbinical court from the Conservative movement in America came and performed the rituals. He even had the traditional mock circumcision, the thought of which made me cringe, but which was an important milestone in Daniel's life. "Growing up I knew I was Jewish, but I lived with my mother, who is not Jewish, so I didn't participate in things. I went to the Sunday school only two times in the nineties. I didn't have an interest. But now, I'm using that experience to try to figure out how to get teens more involved. Any ideas?"

I couldn't suggest anything he hadn't already been working on. He played games; he showed PowerPoint presentations about his two trips to Israel; he took them on field trips. Judging by the crowds of young people at services on Friday night and then again on Saturday morning, he seemed to be doing a fine job. But he wanted to get them more involved. He wanted the community to have a great future in Cuba.

His cousins would be moving to Israel in just a few weeks, and the thought of losing more people pained him.

"We have so many visitors who come here to learn about us and to give us aid, it is wonderful. But it is still sad to see our people go, even though I myself love Israel so much. When I saw the way the desert blossomed, I was very moved. I want to encourage every Jew to visit at some point."

"Would you ever move there?"

"I don't know. I love Israel, but Cuba is my home. I love it here. It's not easy because of the economy, but it is where I am most comfortable. It's a special place. There is nowhere in the world like Cuba. Or like Israel. They are similar in that way."

THAT MONDAY, DANIEL TOOK ME ON a tour of Old Havana. We visited Adath Israel, the synagogue that had once been in the center of the Jewish quarter. Some of the poorest Jews still lived nearby and attended services at Adath Israel, which is technically an Orthodox synagogue. Once in a while, emissaries from the Chabad movement came to Cuba to try to support Orthodox practices and to give the community instruction in Jewish law. When we arrived, volunteers had just finished serving lunch to about forty people, mostly older Jews. And there was my old friend Shlomo, who wasted no time popping over to chat with me, to laugh, and to hit me up for some money.

"Watch out," he warned Daniel. "This guy is a lawyer for the mob."

I didn't know why he liked this joke so much, but we smiled, and Daniel showed me around the sanctuary. Adath Israel was built in 1959, and, though it hasn't received the same level of attention as the Patronato, it still boasts some unique features, like the beautiful modernist windows that cast green-tinted sunlight through the room. It also contains the only *mikvah*, or ritual bath, in Cuba. The bath is now used by the community for conversions. Before its restoration in 2005, converts would bathe themselves in the ocean, while the rabbis looked on. I couldn't help but feel a little sadness that that uniquely Caribbean practice had disappeared. As Ruth Behar noted in her book on Cuba's Jewish community, *An Island Called Home*, "now the converts will forget the sea when they become Jews."

I asked Daniel jokingly if he had forgotten the sea when he converted, and he chuckled. "How can we forget the sea in Cuba? It's everywhere."

Daniel and I strolled through the neighborhood so he could point out where the old Jewish hotel had been, where the kosher butcher was (it wasn't open that day), and where the new menorah had been installed as a monument to the area's Jewish past. We had a quick lunch of Cuban sandwiches. I'd been craving one but didn't want to eat one in front of Daniel, since pork is an essential element of the sandwich. He laughed when I told him how relieved I was when he ordered one first.

"You can't live here and avoid pork. You can try, but the beef ration would never be enough, and chicken is getting more and more expensive."

He had to get back to the community to work, so he left me back in Vedado, and I went once more to stroll along the Malecon and perhaps sip a mojito.

THE NEXT DAY, THE MEXICANS CAME. The big room in the basement of the Patronato was buzzing. Twice as many Jews as I had seen at services were seated in folding chairs, chatting and laughing. Dr. Rosa Behar, who ran the pharmacy, greeted me warmly.

"You will come by Tuesday to see the pharmacy?" she asked. I told her I'd be thrilled to see it. The Jewish pharmacy was upstairs at the Patronato and run by Dr. Behar and her daughter, who was also a doctor. Medical care in Cuba was generally excellent and always free, but they lacked supplies. Still, because of the stream of foreign visitors and Jewish charity missions that come through, the Jewish pharmacy was normally well stocked. It was open to all, though they didn't like to let too many non-Jews know about it, for fear of being overrun. Asthma medicine and diabetes testers were in short supply in Cuba.

"But we wouldn't turn anyone away," Dr. Behar explained. "We serve everyone, as a mitzvah."

The doctor, like everyone else at the synagogue that morning, had come to get the money from the Mexicans. Even Jose Altschuler, committed Communist and ambivalent Jew, came to get the money.

"I feel bad about it," he said. "If there were some other way, I would not take this money, but what can I do? One has to survive, and I have a family: my wife and son and his wife and their daughter. The situation is regrettable." Jose didn't like the idea that he was taking advantage of the special privileges afforded to Jews. "I share my beef ration with a friend who is not a Jew," he told me.

I sat with the representatives of the Jewish community of Mexico, along with Daniel, as one by one people came into the conference room. They made small talk and then presented photo IDs. Their names were checked and cross-checked and then they were given cash. No one seemed embarrassed by the handout, though no one took it without first chatting, as if they had come just to talk and happened also to be receiving this gift.

"Adela and the other community leaders determine how much people get, based on their situation and the number of people they have in their families," Daniel explained. "They will do this at each synagogue this week."

As I left, I ran into Shlomo again. He hadn't gotten his money yet, because he was scheduled to pick it up from Adath Israel on Wednesday. He lived in Old Havana, he explained.

"Why did you come today then?" I asked. He just shrugged. He seemed a little down, and not in a talkative mood. I left him alone, and he didn't seem to mind. At eighty-two he was the oldest Jew still living in Cuba, and I wondered what he thought about this once prosperous community getting handouts from the Jewish community of Mexico. He had seen Jewish fortunes rise and fall on the island, as he had seen the rise of Communism and now its shift to something else. He filled his days going from synagogue to synagogue, joking with foreign visitors and hitting them up for money. I left him sitting outside the synagogue, lost in his own thoughts and squinting into a very bright afternoon sun.

"TO BE JEWISH," THE CUBAN NOVELIST Jaime Sarusky told me, "is to have thousands of years of history behind your back. As a writer, that's what interests me. I was never so engaged with the religion, or really, with the community. In fact, I rebelled against any sort of institutional religion from a very young age." We were sitting in his book-lined study in a Vedado apartment building that had been used by Fidel's rebels as a staging point just before they laid siege to the capitol building. He was proud of the building's interesting heritage the way any novelist would be proud of a building that told a story. Sarusky, well into his seventies, is one of the most noted writers in Cuba, having won all of its major literary awards, and he continues to publish.

He was orphaned young and shuttled between families, so he never felt a strong sense of connection to one Jewish community or another. As a young man, he went to Paris and became involved in the socialist movement, leading anti-Batista protests from afar. When the revolution succeeded in 1959, he went against the flow of the many Jews who were leaving the island and returned to Havana. He worked as an editor and journalist, a critic and a novelist. He had a fascination with the mixture of races and cultures in Cuba and wrote about all the curious immigrant communities he could find there—Findlanders, Haitians, Japanese, and Jews.

"To me, these communities represent not only Cuba, but a very human drama. The tension between conflicting identities. I hear about this revival of the Jewish community—which I believe is due in large part to the collapse of the Soviet Union, which drove many people toward other belief systems. I wonder how the young Jewish people now feel about this history, about their Jewish identities . . . I mean, you have older people who remember what it was like in the old days with the yiddish radio and the kosher restaurants. There were over fifteen thousand Jews in Cuba and lively Ashkenazi and Sephardic cultures. But how did these young people grow up?"

"I think they grew up under this idea of revolutionary Cuba as the messianic state, with a duty to spread its message to the world," I told him, eager to try out my latest theory on an intellectual. "And this idea prepared them, perhaps, to shift to the idea of Judaism, which is, at its very core, a messianic religion."

He seemed to ponder this idea and then smiled. "Interesting," he said. "You should write about this."

It turns out that one Cuban intellectual already had. Maritza Corrales isn't Jewish, but she has become the most noted historian of the Jewish community in Cuba, though her primary interest, she said, was in the Jewish community "in the BC era . . . before Castro."

"You know, the Jews you are interviewing now were not really the Jews of the Jewish community," she told me. "None of them had a link to the past Jewish community. They didn't have a Jewish connection before . . . The families were really assimilated. They only came back to the community in recent times. After the former socialist bloc crumbled, people needed something to hang on to, and they came to the community to try to find another meaning. You know, you dedicate your life to something, and one day you open your eyes and it is gone. So the people you are talking to came back because they wanted something to unite them. Also, for the material benefits. But mostly they wanted a new meaning in their lives. It happens in all the religions—Catholic, Protestant churches, Islam. It's not that Judaism is unique. They have a lot of privileges—like the aliyah—but they are Cubans, so they have the same patterns of behavior. That is why the intermarriage does not affect them the same way as it does the Jews in America. It is something unique in Cuba. We are like a stew: everything you put in adds a flavor. Cubans have never been xenophobes or anti-Semites. It is like Cuban music: everything that comes in can be absorbed and used. That is why the title of my book on Cuban Jews is *The Chosen Island*, not *The Chosen People*. We Cubans feel, like the Jews, that we have been chosen . . . We think we have the truth . . . That's our messianic goal, this revolution. We believe that."

DR. ROSA BEHAR HAD A DIFFERENT perspective when I met her later that week at the pharmacy. There was a line of about twenty people waiting outside for their prescriptions. Her daughter and another volunteer helped give away the medicines while we talked. She's a short, stocky woman with close-cropped copper hair and a face that has been lined by the Caribbean sun. She has an efficient way of speaking that is warm but quiet. After dozens of rapid, intimate, explosive conversations with Cubans who seemed to have boundless energy and endless opinions on all subjects, talking to the compact Dr. Behar was soothing. I could only imagine her bedside manner and the calm, deliberate care she gave her patients.

She believed in service and was proud of what the Jewish community did to help everyone, but she didn't see their role as the same as the Communist revolution's.

"For me, being Jewish is a special feeling of solidarity and that the family is very important. Being in the Jewish family means that you will try to be the best human being, you will try to help everyone and to study. You value these things as a Jewish person. I was always a part of the Jewish community and I loved this special feeling. I had wanted to go to Israel, but my husband—he is not Jewish—he wanted to stay here. I had two children, and so we stayed. You know, it was a very good life. We had several synagogues and did everything we wanted. We never had problems as Jews. In spite of the hardships, I stay here. When my family fled the Nazis in the Second World War, this is where we came. This is my country. I am a Jewish Cuban woman." She smiled proudly and returned to her list of medicines and prescriptions, marking off who had come and what they had come for.

Dr. Behar spoke with jovial acceptance about her family's decision to stay in Cuba, not to make aliyah to Israel. But she did mention that many of the young people came to the Jewish community now because of the opportunity it presented for emigration to Israel. They didn't want to leave because of politics, she said. "They worry about the economy here. They do not see a future, perhaps."

But moving to Israel has its costs too, as Deborah explained to me, back in the community dining room downstairs at the Patronato. Her phone buzzed with incoming text-messages while we talked.

"I miss my friends and family now that I left Cuba," Deborah said. "And I miss the Jewish life."

"You miss the Jewish life, though you live in Israel?" I asked.

"Of course I have a Jewish life in Israel, but the Jewish life in Israel is different. There's no extra *effort* to having a Jewish life in Israel. You go and buy food and it will always be kosher food. You go to the festivities in the street and there is always something . . . I had to do so much work for festivities here. It's just so easy to be Jewish in Israel, sometimes I miss that extra effort it takes to feel Jewish in Cuba."

She made me think about the effort it took to be Jewish in America. It was easy enough to identify as Jewish. And there was a rich à la carte menu of spiritual and social experiences one could have as a Jew, at least in New York City. Yet I felt much more spiritually alive in these struggling communities where the options were limited. Was I overwhelmed by the choice in New York? Was the spiritual marketplace too busy for me to find my place in it? I still hadn't found a community in my hometown that gave me the same feeling that Deborah talked about, that purpose.

My second Friday night in Cuba, I went to services at Centro Sefardi, just a few blocks from the Patronato. Its main sanctuary is no longer in use, and the building's basement is shared between the synagogue and a gymnasium. I watched a bunch of men lifting weights while I waited for services to start. In the next room the older Jews who attend services there chatted and helped get ready for the dinner afterward. The services themselves were sparsely attended—only about twenty people—and I could barely hear the two women who led the prayers over the sound of the air conditioner. I didn't see the same liveliness at Centro Sefardi that I saw at the Patronato. It was clear that this place did not get the same attention or support that the Patronato received, but those who came were passionate about their synagogue.

"This is our Sephardic synagogue," Simon told me. Simon was from the earlier generation of Jews who remembered what it was like before the revolution, when Centro Sefardi would be packed with people. He'd seen a lifetime of changes on his little island, and had the gray hairs to prove it but none of the weariness. He stayed active and committed to the Jewish community and to his family. He was also the president of the B'nai B'rith lodge, another international organization that provided assistance to the Jewish community and ran educational programs. He liked to attend events at the Patronato, and his grandchildren went there for the Israeli dancing and the

Sunday school, but he was loyal to his traditions and would continue to pray at Centro Sefardi. "It is important to keep coming, so that we have a minyan," he explained.

Including me, there were eleven men in the room, most of them older. In a traditional service, there would need to be ten men for prayers. So without my visit, if Simon didn't attend, a minyan would be hard to come by. I wondered how long they could keep the place running, when all the attention—and all the young people—went down the street to the big, well-funded synagogue.

After services, I went to the dinner at the Patronato, so that I could say good-bye to Daniel and Deborah and the other people I'd met. When I got there, a voice carried across the room to me.

"Cuba Si, Yanqi No!" I saw Robert, the Canadian I'd met a week earlier, smiling brightly. He was leaving the next day and had come to give out some necessities, as had been his custom for the last twenty years. He gave out underwear and razor blades and socks to the people around him. They smiled and accepted gratefully.

"It's so hard to get these basic things here," he told me, "that I have to give them out. I think it probably hurts some people's pride, but they know me, they know I do this because they are my friends. I'm a pharmacist, though I also have real estate investments, which have served me well, so I am glad to do this work, but I'm not a rich man. You can't see this community and not want to help. Even the ones who have money can't afford all the necessities."

I asked him what he saw for the future of the community, since he'd known them for the last two decades.

"The young people all want out," he said. "They want to make aliyah, and not to go to Israel. What do they want in Israel? They want to go to the *other* Promised Land, the United States." I wondered how Israel might feel about being used by Jews as a gateway to the United States. "That's where everyone has family," he continued. "Everyone knows someone. If the economy here opens up, then—" Before he could finish, he was interrupted by Shlomo, who'd come to get his donation from Robert.

"Hey, my friend!" he greeted me and asked how I had enjoyed seeing Adath Israel in Old Havana. He just wanted to chat about what I'd done and what I'd seen around the city. "Hotel Nacional? El Floridita? Centro Sefardi?"

In our brief conversation, he didn't ask me for money, and I felt as if I'd finally arrived. I'd been accepted as a friend by Cuba's oldest Jew.

THE NEXT DAY, MY LAST IN Cuba, I took a trip to Guanabacoa, a small city outside of Havana that is known as the center of Afro-Cuban religions on the island. It is also the home of Cuba's oldest Jewish cemetery. I drove out with a professor of economics from the Universtiy of Havana, whose sister works with a lot of Jewish groups that visit the island. She was busy that day and her brother needed the money I'd be paying. He was a committed Marxist and had written scathing critiques of neoliberalism, published two books, and taught some of the best and brightest minds in Cuba. But on that day he acted as my taxi driver. It was certainly a strange economy.

"It does keep the work of an economist interesting," he replied.

When we got to Guanabacoa, we pulled to the side of the road to ask a white-robed *babaloa*—a Santeria priest—for directions. Her colorful beads glistened in the sunlight against her impossibly white shirt and headdress, and she pointed us up the road, to where the city rose on a hill. A group of women stood outside two low buildings with pastel trim in blues and pinks, watching us closely as we drove off. I looked in the rearview mirror and saw them crossing the dirt road to talk to the priest, pointing at our car.

Toward the top of the hill were the locked gates of the cemetery, which had been founded in 1906 by the United Hebrew Congregation.

We wandered around calling out for someone to open it, but the area was empty. A few palm trees dotted the hill, and a bus stop across the street leaned perilously to the side. We heard a car backfire in the distance, and a dog in the empty guardhouse barked at us but didn't appear interested in pursuing the matter. Finally, a woman came trudging up the hill from her house, surprised to have visitors.

"Usually, it is only tour groups who come," she said, unlocking the gate. "And they don't come on Saturdays. You know, Jewish people don't visit graves on their Sabbath," she explained, before asking if I was a Jew. That question again.

"Yes, he is," the professor explained. "This is the only day we could come." It seemed I couldn't escape Cuba without committing a religious faux pas. I still had a lot to learn, but given that I'd eaten pork I figured I might as well keep going. I was making my own kind of Judaism, and somehow the visit to the cemetery in Cuba seemed valid, even if it did violate a rule of the Sabbath. I went inside and wandered among the graves.

I had this vast old cemetery all to myself. I looked at the names on the graves, which were mostly European. There was a Sephardic cemetery down the road where the Turkish and Spanish Jews were buried. Some of the graves were clean and well kept—Dr. Miller's, for example—while others had collapsed into disrepair. One or two, it was clear, had been robbed, but most were in decent shape, thanks again to international Jewish fund-raising efforts. Even Steven Spielberg had visited this cemetery. Looking at the generations of Jews who had passed away in Cuba and the vast stretches of empty plots toward the edge, I couldn't help but feel a pang of sadness. I imagined the optimism with which they had founded this large cemetery, consecrating it, expecting it to grow for many more generations.

But now the community is a tenth of what it was, and no matter how much intermarriage draws people in, they will never fill this cemetery. I hadn't before considered the building of a cemetery as a sign of optimism, but why shouldn't it be? These founders were truly optimistic that they would grow old and die here and that their children would tend their graves. And yet so many of the graves now lay neglected. Tourists visited the site, but what of all the grandchildren? Do the Jews who left for Miami and New York and Israel after the revolution long to return to say the kaddish over their grandparents' shrines? Will Cuba open up enough so they can?

I didn't think about God much at that moment, but I had the urge to say a prayer. I was sweating ferociously and shade was scarce. I couldn't spend too long. The glaring reflection off the marble graves could inflict a severe sunburn. Standing next to what I decided was one of the most decrepit graves, I did what I had not done at the concentration camp in Germany. I said the kaddish, at least the first few lines that I knew, and then hopped back into the professor's car to take the drive back to Havana.

nine

Zion

If you will it, it is no dream.
—THEODOR HERZL

WITHIN SIGHT OF THE Promised Land, God forbade Moses to enter, and it seemed as if the nice young Jewish girl at passport control had the same idea in mind for me. She took a long look at my face and then back at my passport. A loud group of college kids in matching Birthright Israel T-shirts had assembled behind me in line. Several families found themselves interspersed between the students, desperately scanning for a different line to join. We'd flown twelve hours from New York. I was dazed with jet lag. The border patrol agent looked up again and asked me why I wanted to come to Israel.

"To visit," I answered vaguely. Border crossings always made me nervous and I tried to say as little as possible when confronted with them. I'd developed this habit over many years of going places one government or another didn't want me going, and I had yet to be turned back. But in this situation, more than any I'd experienced before, what could I say? How could I sum up my past year of searching, wandering really, between lost, found, struggling, and burgeoning communities? Did she really want to know about my ambivalent relationship to Zionism, my struggle to reconcile the historical and spiritual longing of the Jewish people with the sad facts of political hegemony over contested land, or my desire to visit the West Bank to see the dark side of Jewish national aspirations? She couldn't possibly want or need to know those things. Her face stayed blank. One eyebrow raised.

"And you also visited Iran?" she said, looking at the page that held my visa to the Islamic Republic.

"Yes, I did," I told her. "For research. On the Jews there," I added. I thought showing some kind of Jewish solidarity might help my chances. She sent me to a waiting room with a security guard in front of it. I hadn't yet set foot in the Jewish homeland, the Zionist state, Ertez Yisrael, and I was already tied up in the security apparatus. The drums of war were beating loudly between Israel and Iran, so I could understand their anxiety. Someone had even told me that there was a clock on the wall of a military planning office in Jerusalem, counting down to an Israeli Air Force attack on Iran's nuclear facilities. I had expected to be delayed, but needless to say the real prospect of being denied entry weighed on me. I thought about claiming my "right of return" if they tried to turn me back. The law said that any Jew who wanted to could move to Israel and become an Israeli citizen immediately. The state was meant to be a haven for Jews, after all.

When I entered Iran, my group was held for about three hours at passport control. I wondered if the Israelis would break that record. I hoped not, as it was Friday afternoon and I had people waiting for me on the other side of baggage claim. It was about an hour's drive to Jerusalem, where Jan and Amos lived, and we wanted to have a Shabbat dinner together. Amos was a sabra—born and raised in Israel; his wife, Jan, an

American who hadn't planned to live in Israel until they fell in love. Both of them did humanitarian work and spent much of the year traveling. I had been to Bosnia with Jan twice but had never met Amos. I hated to keep them waiting. They weren't religious, and didn't mind driving after sunset, but I hadn't come all this way just to violate the Sabbath immediately upon arrival.

I waited what felt like ages. The holding room began to fill up. A Palestinian family arrived followed by two European men. A lone punk girl sat across from me, looking sullen behind her piercings. Another Palestinian family came in, and a few Palestinian men. I couldn't be sure, but I thought I was the only Jewish person being held. Finally, a large security man in a simple button-down shirt and slacks pointed me toward a doorway, and I was led into a small office. A young bureaucrat sat at his computer and immediately began asking me questions. Why did I want to come Israel? Who was I staying with? Where did I intend to go? Did I intend to go to Ramallah? The West Bank? Gaza? What was I doing in Iran? Why did I want to come to Israel? Why again? I repeated myself several times. He was never unfriendly, but he was unrelenting in his questions.

Since the death of the American activist Rachel Corrie, the Israeli government had become paranoid about American leftists entering the country, slipping over into the West Bank, and getting involved in pro-Palestinian protests. Rachel did just that in January of 2003, during the Second Intafada, the Palestinian uprising against Israel. She attended two days of training in nonviolent resistance from the International Solidarity Movement, which was founded in 2001 to encourage activists from all over the world to protest the Israeli occupation of the West Bank and Gaza. On March 16, Corrie was killed by an Israeli bulldozer while trying to prevent the demolition of a Palestinian family's home. She had been turned into a martyr by the left, and no one wanted another one. I raised suspicions. I was a guy traveling alone to Israel with vague goals and a recent trip to Iran in my passport. Everything I said in my interview was entered into the computer. My picture was taken.

"You won't be doing any political activity, will you?" the young bureaucrat asked. When I told him no, he asked to call the people I was staying with. After a brief conversation, he started asking me about my past work, my book on refugee children, and again, where I planned to go and what I planned to do in Israel. I had not been questioned like this anywhere else in my travels—neither in military-ruled Myanmar nor Communist Cuba. I told him about my research with Jewish communities around the world, about my quest for connection and spiritual identity. I had never been so forthcoming with a government official before, but the thought of being cut off, of being turned back from my first trip to the Jewish state at the end of such a long year, frightened me. Everything had been leading to this.

My answers seemed to satisfy him. Jewish quests for meaning were an acceptable, and rather common, reason to enter the state of Israel. Solidarity with the Palestinians was, apparently, not. He wished me a wonderful time and a happy Shabbat and sent me on my way. I had, at last, arrived in Israel.

There had been a shortage of rain, but I couldn't tell. I was amazed by the stretches of green, entire forests that sprouted out of the desert. Just as Daniel in Havana had described it: in Israel, the desert bloomed. All my fears about the state security apparatus, all my ambivalence about Jewish nationalism and questions about the value of Zionism, vanished. I was simply in awe of what had been accomplished in this place in only sixty years. The desert bloomed.

The Jewish National Fund—a land purchase and management organization started during the time of the British Mandate in Palestine—had been planting trees since the state was founded. As I stared out of the car window, the landscape whipped past, rich in yellows and greens and whites. I saw massive apartment buildings, and elegant homes shaded by lush trees. In the distance, the minarets of mosques poked above Arab villages. And then I saw the fence.

I hadn't thought I would see it so soon after arriving in Israel, but there it was. The Security Barrier is a means of separation between Palestinians and Israelis erected by Israel. The first section was completed in 2003. It consists of fencing and barbed wire and antivehicle measures, guard towers and sections of solid concrete twice as high as the Berlin Wall. Many Israelis argue that the construction of the barrier has dramatically reduced terrorist attacks. Palestinians argue that the barrier is inhumane, cutting off farmers from the land, unlawfully seizing territory, and trapping West Bank residents inside a massive prison.

My friends in the front seat hadn't yet acknowledged it. I asked if that was what I was seeing.

"No, that's not it," Amos said.

"I think it is," Jan said.

Amos, who had lived in Jerusalem most of his life, looked again. "Ah, yes," he said. "That is part of the fence. That's the Green Line over there."

The Green Line is the 1949 armistice line established between Israel and its neighbors after the 1948 Arab-Israeli War. When Israel seized the West Bank and the Gaza Strip on the other side of the line during the war in 1967, international law concluded that they had occupied that territory, while they claimed that they were "administering" it for security reasons. Almost immediately, settlers began to move into the territory. Some were told it was necessary for the security of the state to have a civilian presence in the West Bank. Others were given financial incentives. Still others moved to fulfill a messianic vision of the Greater Israel—a Jewish state that extends all the way to the Jordan River. Regardless of why they moved there, the fact of their presence in settlements has complicated the Palestinian-Israeli peace process tremendously, and has been used as an excuse to alter the shape of the barrier to include certain Jewish settlements, cutting swathes of the Palestinian-controlled West Bank off from each other. Winding roads filled with checkpoints have become the only way for Palestinians to get around, while Israelis rely on an elaborate system of express roads and tunnels.

Like many moderate Israelis, my hosts tried not to look too much at this barrier because of all the painful emotions it stirred. One cannot deny that it has caused the Palestinians to suffer, but it is also hard to argue that it has not played a role in reducing the number of terrorist attacks. Or has it given more cause for Palestinian resentment? Has it created more potential terrorists by increasing poverty and anger? And if it has made Israel safer, at what cost? Not an hour in the country, and my head was spinning. Because of our late arrival back in Jerusalem, we had a quiet Shabbat dinner at one of the nearby restaurants that was open, and I slept soundly afterward. Once the sun sets on Friday night, Jerusalem is unimaginably quiet. Few cars roam the streets. Televisions are turned off, or at least down. Families gather in their homes or take walks together. The day of rest is official, and those who do not observe it generally try to respect those who do.

I spent that Saturday visiting friends with Amos and Jan, and the next day I took a walk to Jerusalem's Old City in. Before 1967 it had been part of Jordan, along with the rest of East Jerusalem, and no Jews had access to the holy sites—the City of David, the Mount of Olives and its cemetery (which was badly damaged during Jordanian rule), and what some call the holiest site in Judaism, the Western Wall, also known as the Wailing Wall, or the Kotel.

When Israelis suddenly gained control of East Jerusalem in the 1967 war, ecstasy erupted throughout the Jewish population. They had not had access to the wall for nineteen years. Amos told me how he rushed back to Jerusalem three days later to drive his aging mother to visit the site that she had not believed she would ever see again. Amos, who runs nonsectarian aid for the American Jewish Joint Distribution Committee, is not a religious man, but on that day he was moved to tears seeing the Kotel for the first time with his mother. The Western Wall holds a special place in the imagination of the Jewish people. It is believed to be the original outer wall of the Second Temple, connecting it with the early days of Judaism and placing it on the site where ancient Jews believed God resided: *His* Temple. Some myths say that the presence of God has always remained in the Western Wall, which explains why so many people weep when they see it, why some place wishes or prayers on slips of paper in its cracks, and why Jews all over the world pray toward it.

The whole idea makes some people uncomfortable. For one thing, the emotion stirred by the wall can border on idolatry. Another problem theologically is the idea that God is somehow more in this place than in any other. Is not God in all things and everywhere at all times? And then there are the political problems. Above the wall is the Temple Mount, which is the site of Al-Aqsa Mosque, one of the holiest sites in Islam, the place from which, it is said, the prophet Mohammed ascended to heaven. As late as 2000, the Palestinian Authority–appointed mufti of Jerusalem asserted that the Western Wall was part of the Al-Aqsa compound and not at all connected to Judaism.

"The Jews began praying at this wall only in the nineteenth century, when they began to develop [national] aspirations . . . ," he said. When Israeli prime minister Ariel Sharon, along with a group of right-wing lawmakers, ascended the Temple Mount in 2000 to assert the right of all Israelis to visit the compound, it was widely seen as an act of provocation, and it set off a renewed conflict between Palestinians and Israelis: the Second Intafada. Palestinians considered the Second Intafada to be part of their national liberation campaign, while Israelis considered it a return to terrorism. The violence of the Second Intafada pushed the idea for the Security Barrier into reality.

I wandered through the Old City for a while, admiring the little

Arab shops that sold mass-produced tourist tchotchkes, yarmulkes embroidered with the logos of American sport teams, and a wide variety
of tasteless T-shirts. Young soldiers from the IDF patrolled the narrow
lanes. The night I arrived, two policemen had been shot by a Palestinian
gunman, and the IDF was pushing back.

I rounded a corner and walked up some steps. The sun glistened
off the white Jerusalem stone and I cursed myself a little for not bringing sunglasses. I was standing at a security booth. Beyond the booth,
the steps descended to the plaza in front of the Western Wall. I passed
through the metal detector, put on the *kippah* that I'd gotten in Uganda,
and soon found myself at the vortex of Western monotheism's longing,
and the frequent object of its most violent expression.

On first sight, I wasn't impressed.

The plaza stretched out in front of me to the wall. It is divided into
two sections: the upper being more of a staging area for photos and group
gatherings and the lower being the area for prayer and reflection, with
one side for men and another, smaller side for women. An Israeli flag
flew on the upper area. A doorway on the men's side of the lower area led
into a subterranean synagogue filled with Orthodox worshippers. Tour
groups from all over the world rushed around taking pictures, singing
songs, listening to tour guides talking and pointing. The golden cap of
the Dome of the Rock peaked over the top of the wall, and on the other
end, the Al-Aqsa Mosque stood sentinel. The wall itself was topped with
fencing on one end to protect worshippers below against objects hurled
from above. Bits of green shot through the cracks in the old stone. I went
down to the lower area to have a look around.

"You Jewish?" an old Orthodox Jew asked me. Again the question.

"Yes," I said.

"Come here." He motioned and led me into the little underground
synagogue. "You married?" he asked while we walked. I told him I
wasn't.

"Ah, you should meet a nice Jewish girl," he said. "You should get married." Then, just as Mendel did at the bowling alley in Arkansas, he led me through the ritual of tefillin. And at the end he added a blessing for me to marry and have lots of children. The whole thing felt rushed and a bit formulaic; I didn't feel the same stirring of spirit as I did in the bowling alley. And then the man rattled off his request.

He ran an orphanage, he claimed, and needed to feed "all these children." He showed me a tattered photo of a lot of children in a classroom. He asked if I had some money to spare, as a donation to support the education of these children. I'd spent enough time riding the New York City subway to know when I was being given a line. I couldn't believe that this religious man would use the Kotel, and whatever spiritual stirrings I might be having, to hit me up for money. I excused myself and wandered back outside. All around me Orthodox Jews were reading and praying, their heads and legs bobbing. Standing outside in the sunlight again, I watched as the man who'd blessed me went off to look for more tourists.

I watched a little longer, but soon found myself wrapped up in a conversation with two men from Los Angeles. They were originally from Iran, they said. Their families left when they were children in 1979, when the shah was overthrown. They were excited to hear I'd been to Iran recently, and enjoyed reminiscing about the beauty of Shiraz, city of poets, where their families had lived.

"Would you go back to visit?" I asked.

"No, not with the government that's there now," they both agreed.

"Because it's dangerous for Jews?"

"No," they scoffed. "It's not dangerous, at least not for Jews."

"It's the politics," the older-looking one said. "Our families left because of those politics, and I don't have any interest in seeing what they've done to our country now."

"What brings you to Israel?" I asked them.

"Are you kidding?" the other one said. "We are Persian Jews, you know? You've been to Shiraz. It is the most religious place in Iran. Jerusalem is a spiritual home."

"So you're on a pilgrimage?"

"No." They laughed. "A medical conference. We're doctors. But we always come to visit the Kotel when we are here."

"Would you ever move to Israel?"

"No, I wouldn't," the older one said. "Los Angeles is my home now."

"Would you ever move back to Iran? If the government changed, would you move back?"

He just shrugged, and he and his friend went to say some prayers and be on their way. I stood in the sun a while longer and, not feeling anything more than tired of the heat, went up to the wall to touch it. Still, nothing stirred in me. I had felt more of a swelling of Jewish pride looking at the trees surrounding Jerusalem than I did at the Kotel. I'd felt more spiritual satisfaction at Jamkaran Mosque in Iran and at the bowling alley in Arkansas. I had someone take my picture in front of the wall, because I felt as if I had to, and went back into the Old City to wander through the rows of stalls and look at chess sets and SuperJew T-shirts.

Two days later, I took a bus south to Beersheba, the largest city in the Negev Desert, to meet some Cubans, Ethiopians, and Iranians who'd made aliyah. I was curious about their experience, having met their counterparts in their home countries. I was also eager to get out of Jerusalem for a day. The atmosphere could be stifling, with so much history.

I once read that Judaism did not preserve ancient monuments but rather created ancient moments. I felt as though I'd seen that played out from the very beginning of this journey. Chanting the Kol Nidre with Sammy in Rangoon had brought me to medieval Europe. Singing "Lecha Dodi" with the Abayudaya in Uganda made me feel as if I were among the ancient pastoralists in the desert, rejoicing for the day of rest. Everywhere I prayed, I'd felt as though the ritual itself formed some type of connection across space and time.

But now that I was in the place to which so many directed their prayers, I found it disappointing. It was a modern state, functional and not as dangerous as the media made it seem. The armed guards at every restaurant, the IDF soldiers all over the place were strange, but I'd grown used to armed men during my time working in refugee camps. After a day, they blend into the background, just as the Security Barrier blended in for Amos and Jan. But on a deeper level, all the excavations in Jerusalem, all the unearthed and reclaimed ancient monuments and the efforts to discover and reclaim more ancient monuments, left me cold. Like the Jews in Burma longing for England, I think the longing for an ideal place called Jerusalem is far more attractive than the current reality of it. New cars, old stones, and current politics dominated my perceptions. I couldn't imagine how visiting Jerusalem, drinking lattes, and taking pictures was fulfilling a commandment from God. So I got on a bus to the desert.

Beersheba is not an attractive city, and after Jerusalem the effect was jarring. Jerusalem evolved over millennia, its layout owing more to spiritual and communal longing than urban planning, but certain rules maintained the aesthetic integrity of the city. Beersheba, on the other hand, hadn't even been a city until the late nineteenth century, when the Ottomans established a police station to control the local Bedouin population. After Israeli independence, many Jews who had been expelled from Arab countries settled in the city. And more immigrants arrived in the 1980s and '90s, when thousands of Ethiopian and Russian refugees settled there. Because of the city's rapid growth, the government played a strong role in the construction of housing, and many of the apartment buildings reminded me of the Communist architecture I'd seen in Berlin when I lived there in the nineties.

The buildings of Ben Gurion University, where the bus dropped me off, looked like a science fiction fortress, but the feeling on campus was decidedly different. The tension that permeated the air in Jerusalem was absent. I saw Arab women walking arm in arm or carrying books, and groups of students lounging on lawns. I had an odd feeling of déjà vu, until I realized the cause: the students looked just like students at Columbia University, where I had been an undergrad. They were normal young people, for sure, and they were mostly Jews. I was suddenly overcome with the feeling that I was part of the majority culture. I was completely mainstream. No one even looked at me. I looked just like them, a Jew among Jews.

I spent nearly an hour lounging under a tree, waiting for the young Ethiopian woman I had arranged to meet and watching groups of service puppies-in-training run around tripping over their own paws.

A small, dark-skinned woman with long curly hair walked over to me and smiled. Yordanos was nineteen and one of only a handful of Ethiopian students at Ben Gurion University. She didn't have long to talk because she was organizing a concert and discussion about racism that night. As I looked around, she was the only dark-skinned person I could see. Even though I spoke no Hebrew and was not an Israeli, on first glance one might have thought I was more of a local than she.

"My family came late from Ethiopia," she said, "in 1995, not on those first airlifts. My father was a community leader and stayed to help other people get out before we left. But things were dangerous for us in Addis Ababa when we left. We were persecuted for being Jews, and we were impoverished. I was just six years old when we left, but I remember crying because I was leaving my friends behind, but I was happy too. We had heard about Jerusalem forever and it was our destiny to go there. A lot of Ethiopians were disappointed when they got to Israel because it was very different from the Promised Land they believed in. My family was not religious, so for us, it was not such a shock. I became religious living here, though. I went and lived on a religious kibbutz, and Judaism plays a large role in my life now. In that way I'm not typical of most young Ethiopians, whose parents are very religious and who are themselves secular."

I asked her why she had become religious in Israel.

"Because this is our land," she said simply. "This is the place that was given to us by God and it is our duty to live here. Do you not think so?" She smiled when she asked that. Then she told me she was very interested to hear about the life of Jews around the world who did not want to move to Israel, who were happy outside of Israel.

"What was that word again?" she asked. Her English was not perfect, so I repeated the word I'd used.

"*Diaspora*," I said.

"I have never heard of it like that before, that the *galut* could be a good thing." She used the word *galut*, which is the word Zionists have long used for the condition of Diaspora. It implies weakness, disgrace, and exile. It suggests that all those living apart from Israel are incomplete and degraded.

"Really? Don't you think it's helpful to have Jewish people all over the world?" I asked. "If we were all in Israel, wouldn't it make anti-Semitism worse, because no one would know any Jewish people? And wouldn't we be targets? And also, wouldn't it be impossible to distinguish between Israel and Judaism, making the state and the religion one and the same? I'm not sure I'm comfortable with a religion having tanks."

She thought for a moment and then laughed.

"I have never ever heard this before," she said. "I think all the Jewish people should live in Israel."

She was friendly and amused by my notion that the Diaspora could be a good thing, but she was deeply committed to Jewish spiritual and political autonomy. She loved Ethiopia and Ethiopian culture, she said, and one of the reasons she was involved in the antiracism concert that night was because of her appreciation for her native culture. She had even gone back to visit Ethiopia a year before. She enjoyed it. But she felt that Israel was her home, as it should be for all Jews.

"Could it have something to do with the fact that you were raised here?" I asked. "I mean, most of your conscious life has been in Israel, right?"

"Yes, that's true, I suppose," she said. "I am comfortable here, though the Ashkenazi culture can be cold sometimes. But we are trying to express our Ethiopian culture and make a space for it in Israel, and there is a movement now to preserve our way of life, even while we integrate more deeply into Israel."

She reminded me of the old shopkeeper in Esfahan, who liked Israel but felt more comfortable in Iran, despite the difficulties. Esfahan was his Jerusalem, he'd said. Was it just a coincidence, a trick of fate, that the actual Jerusalem was the spiritual Jerusalem for Yordanos? She didn't like the suggestion.

"There is only one Jerusalem," she said. "It is a real place, not just the place you—what did you say?"

"Direct your longing."

"Yes. It is not about your longing. It is about God. God gave us Jerusalem and so we are here. Zionism could not have been in Uganda, because Uganda is not the Holy Land."

I asked her what she thought of the ultra-Orthodox notion, held by people like Dovid Weiss of Neturei Karta, that it was heresy for the state of Israel to be established by anything other than divine authority. Did it not mean that the political and military maneuverings of Israel were attempts to supplant the will of God?

"Look at the Torah," she said. "Armies often do the will of God."

"Is the occupation of the West Bank part of that? Do you believe in a Greater Israel?"

"You mean Judea and Samaria?" she said, using the preferred Zionist term for the region taken after the 1967 war. "I believe the Palestinians should have their own state," she said vaguely. She told me that Jews and Arabs got along in many places in Israel, and in Haifa they shared the city peacefully. Honestly, she said, she didn't think about the conflict too much, and though she recognized the suffering of the Palestinians, she had her own battles to fight within Israel, against racism and monoculturalism and poverty.

Israel had all the complexities of any modern society, along with all the tensions of a nation of immigrants, and the added legacy of the Holocaust and anti-Semitism, and the problems of war and terrorism. She couldn't possibly take on all the problems. No one person could. She just held on to her religious faith, studied, and worked to change what corner of the world she could, to make her homeland feel more like home.

I MET UP LATER WITH A friend, Orly, a Persian Jew who had left Iran when she was one year old. Now she lectures at the university about the Jews of Iran and has even given talks on Iran to the Israeli Air Force. She was taking me to meet her aunt and uncle, who had come from Iran in 1963, and her grandmother, who left Iran in 1989, and she had offered to be my translator for the day.

When we arrived at their house, they'd made a feast for lunch that reminded me of dinner with Dr. Moresadegh in Tehran. There was chicken in a thick brown sauce, and rice with currants, and balls of rice filled with meat and spices and nuts, and seconds were more than a suggestion. They insisted I take a third helping too. In line with both Persian and Jewish custom, I was stuffed.

When the meal was done, Orly's aunt and grandmother offered to tell their story. Her aunt had left Iran so long ago, she said, that she didn't know what to say. She still had some family in Iran. The previous summer, a group of these relatives had come to Israel to attend a cousin's wedding. They seemed to be doing well, she said.

Orly's grandmother had more to say. She'd left in 1989 because her husband was very sick. If he died in Iran, she would have ended up des-titute because of discriminatory inheritance laws. All of her children had already gone to Israel, so she was alone in Esfahan and exhausted by the hardships of the Iran-Iraq War, which had ravaged Iranian society. She'd owned a fabric store and a house "in a nice location." She wept when she described how she had to sell her home and business quickly and for almost nothing when her passport and exit papers were finally approved.

"At the last moment," she said, "my husband decided he didn't want to go. He didn't feel well. And he didn't want to leave everything he knew. But I told him that the transit papers were for two, I could not leave with-out him. We ended up staying for eight days in Tehran at his brother's house. I was frightened we would no longer be able to leave. He was very ill on the day of the next flight, but we made it. I knew no one in Jerusa-lem, but there was a man from the Jewish Agency"—Israel's primary im-migration organization—"and he helped us find my family. They didn't know we were coming. I remember that first Sabbath together with my daughters. It was such a happy time."

"What do you think of living in Israel?"

"I am just happy to be with my family. Esfahan is a beautiful city, but I am where I want to be."

There are roughly 150,000 Persian Israelis, and it is a community filled with nostalgia, Orly explained. For a long time she didn't like her Persian identity, but, because she spoke Persian and Arabic, she was as-signed to Intelligence when she did her mandatory military service.

"I met a lot of other Persians then, and I fell in love with the culture. Now, I celebrate the holidays, like Nowruz, and listen to the music. I can quote Bialek, but I can also quote Hafez. These are the two identities I have."

After lunch, she and I went to an apartment block in a part of town where a lot of Russian immigrants had settled. There were signs in Russian, and people on the street didn't speak Hebrew, so we got a little lost. Eventually, we found our way to my next appointment.

Moshe and Rachel Stohler, originally from Cuba, came to Israel in 1995 in hopes of reuniting with their two children, who had made aliyah a few years earlier, and with their grandchildren. But things had not turned out the way they planned. Their children now lived scattered around the globe, and, though they are happy with their lives in Israel and do not regret leaving Cuba, it is certainly not living up to their expectations. Or rather, their family isn't. Their family is in its own miniature Diaspora, Rachel sighed. Her children were successful, but togetherness eluded them. About Israel itself, they had no specific complaints.

"We stayed thirty-five years after the revolution," Rachel said, laughing. "But we left the first chance we had. It was very hard in Cuba."

"During the special period?" I asked.

"Well, yes, that is when we left. But even before then," Rachel said. "In the seventies and eighties too. I worked at Adath Israel for twelve years, so I saw the community in decline. It was very sad. We thought the community was dying. There were never enough people for a minyan. The young people stayed away because they were afraid. During the special period, people would come to get help with everything—donations, food, clothes. At Passover, we gave out matzo, and people came for everything but the matzo. We had to tell them the matzos were mandatory. They had to take the matzo to get the other assistance."

We talked for a long time, or rather, Rachel and Moshe talked to each other about Cuba, reminiscing about their daughter at the Jewish school, talking about the Jews in the Cuban government who didn't care what happened in the Jewish community, remembering the beauty of Havana. Orly, acting as my translator, struggled to understand their heavily accented Hebrew peppered with Spanish.

"Since we came to Israel, we are less religious," Moshe told me. "Here, all you have to do is live, and it is Jewish."

"In Cuba, I went to synagogue every day," Rachel added, laughing. "I worked there, after all."

What Orly's grandmother and the Cubans showed me was the more quotidian side of Zionism. Many immigrants to Israel didn't come because they were Zionists or because they were called to the Holy Land by a religious sensibility. They came to escape hardship, or they came to be with their families. They came to have a better life. They shared more with the practical people who moved to Bentonville for work than the idealists who settled in New Orleans for *tikkun olam*. Yordanos had adopted the Zionist ideology, but that in itself was a kind of assimilation mixed with religiosity.

Theodor Herzl, the founding father of Zionism, once wrote, "In the Land of Israel too, we will remain what we are now, just as we will never cease to love, with regret and longing, the countries of our birth, from which we were expelled." The Stohlers and Orly's family, and even Yardonos, had certainly lived out that statement.

I RETURNED TO JERUSALEM, WHERE, THE next day, I met a young Bosnian Jew, Alex, a friend of Ivan Hrkas's from Sarajevo, who had also come to Israel during the siege. He was a DJ, a bartender, and a nihilist. Our conversation over beers was brief, intense, and showed no inkling of nostalgia.

"I studied Jewish studies in the university, you know, and there is some interesting philosophy, but it's really all bullshit, man." I sipped my beer and let him continue. "It's just a way of dividing people from each other. Bosnia, Israel, it's all the same. Everyone is corrupt, everyone abuses the system. Music brings people together. All this religion and politics, it divides people. I mean, this place is crazy. During my army time I had to do guard duty in Hebron, setting up checkpoints to keep the settlers safe. Like two hundred Jewish settlers in a city of two hundred thousand Palestinians. I hated it. It kills you. You have to treat these people terribly, and you're doing it for religious fanatics. The whole system is insane here. Totally fucked. And nobody sees it. People just don't look. And then the Palestinians too. They have it bad, sure, but come on! It's nothing like we went through in Bosnia. *That* was a war. This? This Israel-Palestine thing? Compared to the war in Bosnia it's like a vacation. People just need to get over themselves."

"If it's so screwed up here, would you go back to Bosnia?"

"No way," he said. "It's even worse there. After the war, all these thugs just took over. The place is run by lunatics. There's nothing there. Ivan went back, you know? I think that makes him sad. There's nothing for him there."

Over and over again, Alex used the word *nothing*. He was also fond of *bullshit*. When I marveled at his total lack of faith in society, nation, and religion, he laughed.

"I believe in people," he said. "But a lot of young people here are just like me, you know. We do this army service and it makes us crazy. We see these politicians and they are corrupt, and we see the situation with the economy falling apart, and we see the situation with the Palestinians stagnating. A lot of young people want to leave. They want to make aliyah to America, where they don't have to worry about this bullshit here. But America's the same. For me, I'd be happy just to spin music, get people dancing, spread love all around."

I decided to change the subject, to get him to talk about when he came to Israel. He echoed what Ivan had told me about it feeling like an adventure when he left Sarajevo, and the struggle to learn Hebrew and fit in in a new country. "I don't know what else to tell you," he said. "I'm a Bosnian who lives in Israel, or an Israeli Bosnian or something. Labels just don't interest me."

I left his apartment feeling a bit weary of labels myself. I had met Israeli backpackers all over the world who had just finished their military service and were feeling cynical about the state of Israel. I had met some who were cynical about Judaism too or who didn't know anything about it or didn't care. But I hadn't met any who had such a far-reaching cynicism as Alex's. I could see the cause for some of his bitterness. You could walk the streets of Jerusalem, and certainly there were Arabs everywhere, and of course the conflict was in the news, but few Israelis I met thought about what went on in places like Hebron or Bethlehem. The situation anguished them in a way it could never affect me, and ignoring it was one answer to that pain. Alex's cynicism was another. Activism was a third route.

Peace Now, a left-wing group founded in the seventies on a platform of Palestinian human rights and an exchange of land for peace, had realized that most Israelis had no conception of Palestinian life in the West Bank. Israelis had separate roads to bypass Palestinian towns and checkpoints. They had the Security Barrier, which even blocked the view of Palestinian territory from some vantage points. In response to this, Peace Now organized tours for Israelis to see the occupation of the West Bank from the Palestinian point of view, to let them see, firsthand, the growth of the Jewish settlements and the threat they posed to both the two-state solution and to basic human rights. With Alex's comments about Hebron echoing in my head, I decided to go on one of these "settlement tours" on a Friday morning.

I found my way to a parking lot to meet up with the activists from Peace Now. They had planned a walking tour of Hebron for over two hundred people. The goal of these tours, Peace Now officials said, was first and foremost to educate Israelis about the reality of the occupation. I had another reason for going. I was eager to see Hebron, which contains the Cave of the Patriarchs.

According to the book of Genesis, this site was the first land purchase Abraham made in the land of Canaan, and therefore represents one of the pivotal moments in Jewish history. Like the Temple Mount in Jerusalem, it is also sacred to Muslims, and therefore contested. It is believed that Abraham and his wife, Sarah, are buried there, as well as Isaac and Rebekah, Jacob and Leah, and even Adam and Eve.

The friendship and goodwill that Abraham gained by dealing fairly with the Canaanites in the biblical story has not survived through history, and Hebron has been the site of several brutal crimes. In 1929 a group of Arab rioters killed sixty-seven Jews in a spasm of violence. Hundreds more were saved by hiding with friendly Arab neighbors. After 1948, Hebron fell under the control of Jordan, and the Jews were expelled from the city, unable to access the cave or their former homes. After 1967, they returned to settle in the city with government support, in spite of rising tensions. Over the years, more Jews came and violence flashed. Palestinians attacked Jews, Jews attacked Palestinians. The atmosphere grew increasingly aggressive.

In 1994 a Jewish physician and right-wing fanatic named Baruch Goldstein entered the mosque at the Cave of the Patriarchs and opened fire on the Muslim worshippers, killing twenty-nine of them before he was overpowered. The resulting violence between the larger Palestinian population and the group of roughly six hundred Jewish settlers led to the city's being made into a militarized zone.

As we drove, one of the leaders of Peace Now, Hagit, talked to us over the PA system. She described the system of roads that had been built to allow the Israelis to avoid Palestinian towns, why the concrete walls were in place along the roadside (to prevent sniper fire), and how the building of the Security Barrier was cutting off more and more Palestinians from their land and from each other. She explained the Israeli government's policy of transportational continuity instead of territorial continuity—even if the land was not connected, you could drive from one part to the other—and she pointed out illegal outposts on distant hilltops. Settlers established these outposts—usually a collection of trailers—to claim more land in the West Bank, creating "facts on the ground" that would give Israel greater backing in declaring its right to more territory, or even derail any attempts to turn over the territory to the Palestinians. It was reminiscent of the Abayudaya claiming their hilltop in Uganda, except that in Uganda they used their settlement to create goodwill with their neighbors, and they certainly didn't have the military and police forces at their beck and call. Even though many of these outposts were illegal, they were, in many cases, supplied with power and water by the government, and young Israeli soldiers were assigned to protect them. The situation seemed absurd, especially as the settlers were sometimes responsible for violence not only against Palestinian civilians but also against Israeli soldiers.

There are over one hundred military checkpoints in Hebron itself, the Peace Now guide explained. When left-wing groups send tours to see for themselves, they are often harassed and sometimes attacked by the settlers, but she assured us that precautions had been taken. Peace Now had secured all the necessary permits and authorizations from the government; we had undercover police on the buses and a police escort. So it came as quite a surprise when we were stopped near Kiryat Arba, the largest Jewish settlement just outside Hebron. Several police and military units blocked our path. We were told that the city had been closed off as a military zone because another tour group had been attacked in Hebron earlier in the day. As the organizers stood and argued with the officers, a group of settlers from Hebron zoomed up in their car, led by a man named Itamar Ben-Gvir, a passionate torchbearer for the late radical Meir Kahane, whom I'd learned about from Yossi in that Arkansas bowling alley. Itamar was notorious for his activism against Palestinians and against the Israeli left. He had been arrested numerous times, though never tried in court for his activities. And here he was, surrounded by followers, screaming at us.

I had to ask a young reporter for the *Jerusalem Post* what he was shouting.

"You know, a lot of craziness," he said. "He's saying that we're bad

Jews and we should go join Hezbollah, and we're traitors, and criminals, and Nazis . . . that sort of thing. Oh, and that it doesn't matter, because we only have one child, when they—the settlers—have dozens, so we'll lose anyway."

"Nice."

"He's a sweetheart."

Itamar's face was red as he shouted at us. His rage seemed incongruous with his paunchy belly and bright turquoise shirt. Behind him, a young boy of maybe fourteen or fifteen leaned on their car. He wore a rainbow-colored *kippah,* and his blond sideburns twisted and curled down his cheeks. His icy blue eyes glared at us with absolute hate. I thought of the children I'd met in Bosnia and Kosovo who were eagerly awaiting conflict with the ethnic groups they saw as their enemies; it was so easy to choose hate.

Itamar and his followers continued to shout and cause a scene, though no punches were thrown. The police formed a line between the settlers and the tour group, and, after about an hour of arguing that went nowhere, the buses were turned back. A small group of us tried to walk into Hebron, but the police told us that we would be arrested if we went any farther. The sun beat down brutally on all of us, amplified by the pavement. Shade was scarce and we'd been standing outside for hours now. Two hundred and fifty citizens had been prevented from entering Hebron by a dozen angry settlers and the threats their ideology presented.

Itamar would come up again during my visit. On the day I left, Barack Obama, still a presidential candidate at the time, visited the Western Wall, and as he left, the news reported, Itamar shouted at his entrourage, "Israel is not for sale!"

Having failed to enter Hebron, and worn out by the brutality of some of my coreligionists, I needed to find something to restore my spirits. I wanted that feeling I'd had on first arriving and seeing the trees. I wanted to be proud of this Jewish state. It had given shelter to so many Jews who needed it over the past sixty years, and it did serve as a bastion of liberalism in a deeply conservative region. Homosexuals could live openly and freely in Israel; dissent was tolerated and vibrant. And diversity was the norm, as I'd learned talking to Israelis from five different countries in two days. There was a lot positive to look at, but to me it was overshadowed by these lunatics who screamed and ranted and encouraged violence, all in the name of Israel. I was saddened to think that, aside from being the name of the Jewish state, Israel was the name of all the Jewish people. Why had they chosen this name for their state? Thanks to that choice, we were all deeply tied to this country, no matter how we felt about its policies, which too often kowtowed to right-wing leaders like Itamar Ben-G'vir or those who sympathized with him. We were all tied in some way to whatever violence this place would endure—or inflict—in the future.

BACK IN JERUSALEM, I DECIDED TO go to the Western Wall again. It was Friday evening, and I hoped to see it more lively than I had on a Sunday afternoon. And arriving with Jan and Amos about an hour before sundown changed my entire view of Israel.

The plaza was filled with people. There were thousands of Orthodox Jews with their little children, all dressed in their black suits and robes and hats. There were Americans and Brazilians and Africans and Argentines and Brits. The cacophony of songs and prayers and accents shook my rib cage. And there were the kids from Birthright Israel that I'd seen getting off the plane. The Birthright program gives young Jews between eighteen and twenty-six years old a free trip to Israel. The goal is to stir in them a strong feeling of Jewish identity and a connection to Israel. I listened in on a group from England and Canada as the Chabad rabbi explained what they were seeing.

"This is the largest synagogue in the world," he said, smiling. He looked like a fifteenth-century Polish peasant, but he spoke like an MTV VJ. "And we're gonna rock it here tonight. We're gonna pray and dance and sing. If you don't know the words, they are there in your book in Hebrew and English and Hebrew transliteration, so just follow along or hum or whistle. Get your body into it. We are all friends here, and we're going to welcome this wonderful blessing of Shabbat together. So let's kick it off!"

The group started singing, and in no time they were on their feet dancing in circles. Another group of young men, who looked as if they were from Latin America, came running arm in arm down the ramp to the Kotel singing "Jerusalem of Gold," an old hit that had become something of a spiritual cri de coeur for Zionists worldwide. The singing and dancing, the sheer joy radiating from the crowd, started to get inside me. I had never stood with this many Jewish people before, never even seen this many in one place.

Next to me, two soldiers in uniform, their guns hanging at their sides, prayed. Their bodies rocked and swayed as they read from their prayer books. I was struck, as I was struck in Uganda, by the deep sincerity of the prayer all around me. I saw no one just going through the motions. Those who prayed, prayed intensely. Some were in groups, some were alone. Others, like me, simply watched.

"You Jewish?" the younger of the two soldiers asked me when our eyes met. I smiled and nodded and he gestured with a smirk (was he flirting?) toward an extra prayer book on the small wooden table in front of him. The plaza was littered with small wooden tables for resting prayer books. The soldier pointed at the prayer book again in case I didn't understand him. I shook my head politely. I wouldn't be able to read it anyway. He shrugged and returned to his prayers.

That question again—*Are you Jewish?*—but this time it was different. It was not to see if I belonged, but to see if I wanted to join him. The white fringes of tzitzis hung from his waist, dancing with the butt of his machine gun. Two Israeli soldiers' bodies had just been returned from Lebanon that week in exchange for the release of some Hezbollah militants, including a child-murderer named Samir Kuntar. The nation was traumatized, and as I looked at this young soldier, who couldn't have been older than eighteen, I couldn't help thinking about how he, clearly religious, must compartmentalize his mind into duty, prayer, and all the other fragments necessary to keep one's sanity in a country so filled with tensions.

The atmosphere was having its effect on me. I felt close to tears, overwhelmed by the beauty of the song and the collective expressions of longing that broke against the wall and rippled through the crowd. The moment couldn't last, but it felt wonderful. The fading light glinted off the golden roof of the Dome of the Rock above the wall, and the voices of the different prayer groups started to echo each other, different melodies for the same songs. I found Amos and Jan again, who had stopped to watch the scene from the upper part of the plaza, where men and women could be together. We didn't say much. We made our way again from the Old City back toward their apartment for dinner. As we walked, Amos made fun of the Orthodox Jews racing toward the Kotel in cabs.

"You're late," he called out in English, tapping his watch. "Shabbos has begun!" He laughed and we laughed with him. Each time one of the cabs passed us, he did the same bit. The contradictions of the pious amused Amos and had all three of us cackling as we walked away from the Old City.

I wasn't sure what the feelings I'd had at the Kotel meant. Sudden spiritual ecstasy was not an enduring thing, and could be manufactured by extreme circumstances. My day, begun outside of Hebron and ending at the Western Wall, certainly counted as extreme, but the feeling had more depth to it. All those Jewish people from all over the world hadn't come together for the wall, really, but for each other. It was the collective expression of yearning that made the place powerful, not the stones.

That is the gift of this place, I thought. Not that it is in itself holy—it is, after all, just the remnants of an outer wall—but that it provides the opportunity for us to create holiness. It provides a place to come together. Perhaps that was true of Israel too. The state is just a state, with all its contradictions and violence and policy positions, but because it is a Jewish state it provides an opportunity to express Jewish values. It is not of value in and of itself the way the right-wing claims. I didn't believe that God acted like a real estate broker, giving us this land by divine right, or that there was an innate virtue in living here, as if the ground itself was holy without us. The virtue is in what we do with the land, what we take from it and what we give back.

On Sunday I decided to go to Yad Vashem, the Holocaust memorial that is a mandatory stop for any head of state, tour group, or first-time visitor to Israel. One cannot deny the impact of the Holocaust on Israel. The state itself was born from the ashes of Europe's Jews, and there are survivors everywhere. To understand this country, I had to see how it presented this piece of its history, which changed the nature of Zionism forever. As much as I'd avoided it since that cold day in Germany, I had to face the Holocaust.

Yad Vashem is a forty-five-acre complex in Jerusalem at the base of Mount Herzl and it consists of a large Holocaust History Museum, a Children's Memorial, a garden of trees planted for the Righteous Among the Nations—gentiles who rescued Jews from the Nazis—monuments, research centers, and a synagogue. It commands views of much of Jerusalem, and, surrounded by trees and parkland, it exudes calm and lends itself to contemplation.

When I arrived, a group of soldiers, all looking impossibly young, were beginning their mandatory tour of the complex, which was part of their training. There were also two separate Birthright Israel groups, all also impossibly young, being led into the compound by their earnest guides. The Yad Vashem tour was also, obviously, a mandatory part of their free trip to Israel.

Neither the Birthright groups nor the soldiers shared one particular ideology. Both include broad cross sections of Jewish ideas and identities, secular and religious, and are a reflection of their respective countries more than a complete image of the Jewish people. If I had learned anything in this past year, it was that there was no monolithic Jewish identity, no *one* Jewish people. There are countless kinds of Jews and kinds of Jewishness.

Avraham Infeld, originally from South Africa and now a popular speaker to Birthright groups in Israel, believes that the Jewish people are like a stool with five legs: the Hebrew language, the land of Israel, Jewish values, the Jewish religion, the Jewish community. His labels were far too general to mean anything to me. Which Jewish community did he mean? Where does Jewish food fit in? Yiddish theater? Ladino poetry?

I preferred to think of the Jewish people as an ecosystem. There were unlimited elements in this system: religion, ethics, culture, language, history, geography, Israel, and all their infinite variations. We were richer and stronger for our diversity. There were queer Orthodox Jews and secular socialist Zionists and kabbalists and cynical nihilists and on and on. Perhaps that's why Jews have survived so many attempts to destroy them. Whatever you think we are, we are also its opposite.

So, if you are trying to create a nationalist army or engender support for a Jewish state, how do you make this messy conglomeration of identities and ideas, this fecund rain forest of people, into one entity? How do you help them find that sense of Jewish purpose they can internalize? Moses did it with the Torah. Contemporary leaders have them visit Yad Vashem and face the specter of Jewish extermination, because the Nazis didn't care about nuance or ecosystems or five-legged stools. Every one of us would have been killed if they'd had the chance, and we can indeed never let them try again.

I wandered first to the Children's Memorial, which is built in a cavern in the side of the mountain. The space is dark and somber. Yahrzeit candles, the traditional Jewish memorial for the dead, are reflected through mirrors, creating an illusion of infinite flames that looked like stars. A voice read the names and ages of children murdered by the Nazis. As I listened, I started to feel the effect. How could I not? Every name was like a world extinguished. There were 1.5 million Jewish children killed in the Holocaust, and each one made me shudder. I stood a long time in that space and felt, I guess, the opposite of what I'd felt at the Western Wall: Spiritual emptiness. Despair. What were all these questions of identity and nationality with which I was grappling when facing a gas chamber?

I wandered the rest of the complex—the museum, the synagogue, the rows of trees for the Righteous Among the Nations—but I didn't see much more that day. I tried to listen in on one of the Birthright guided tours, but I couldn't focus. My rage just grew and multiplied. I read some of the cards on the walls of the museum. There were some that mentioned the murdered gypsies, Communists, homosexuals, and disabled people. I knew the story of the Holocaust, of course, but somehow seeing it memorialized in the land of Israel provoked a visceral feeling in me far more powerful than what I'd felt at the camp in Germany. Yad Vashem was having its effect on me.

I'd put on my *kippah* from Uganda when I entered the Children's Memorial, and I didn't take it off for the rest of my visit to Yad Vashem. And when it came time to leave, I kept it on. This certainly didn't make me stand out in Israel, but for me, it was a statement. I wanted to show as publicly as I could that I was a Jew, and that we were still here, and that the Nazis had failed and would always fail. I wore that *kippah* to say, simply, "*Fuck you*. We are still alive."

I took a long walk through the city. I spent hours going up and down streets I didn't know, getting myself totally lost. In the newspapers there were photos of the celebration in Lebanon when Samir Kuntar returned home, just as the young Israeli soldiers were being buried. It seemed the whole Middle East was celebrating the death of these two young Jewish boys and the release of a murderer who called himself a freedom fighter. I felt sick. Israel's grief was their neighbors' joy. In response to the horror of the Holocaust, Europe assuaged its guilt by recognizing independence for Israel, which immediately declared itself a haven for all Jews in the world who needed it. And, in response, several Arab countries attacked. Everywhere else I had been in the Diaspora, the grief of one's neighbor—regardless of their religion— was a cause for everyone's grief, and their joy a cause for everyone's joy. That dynamic was not at work here. What was different? Was it because here in Israel Jews had power? Or was it because Jews had misused their power? Or was it just inchoate anti-Semitism? Or was it the inevitable condition of a place to which so much divine yearning had been directed, a religious corollary to Africa's resource curse. The land didn't have gold or oil or diamonds. It had a contested sacred narrative. And that was far worse.

Hundreds of thousands of Palestinians lost their homes when Israel declared independence in 1948, an event the Palestinians still call the Nakba—the Catastrophe. Some were told to leave by the invading Arab armies; some were forced from their homes by the Israeli army. There was enough guilt to go around. One traumatized people quickly traumatized another. Just like the Jews who fled the Spanish Inquisition, some Palestinians still carry the keys to the homes from which they were expelled.

It is indisputable that after the Holocaust Jews needed a place to go. No one else would take them. The violence that ignited upon Israel's founding suggested that Palestine would not be the easiest place to establish this haven, however. Ever since, Israel has struggled with external and internal threats, with terrorism, with scorn and hostility from its neighbors and divisions within itself.

The fear of another Holocaust has driven much of Israel's policy since the beginning, a reality that many governments in the Middle East have failed to consider or comprehend. One-third of the world's Jewish population was murdered in the twentieth century. That shaped a great deal of the Jewish mentality, and because of that, it remains essential that the Jewish people have a place of refuge, a place that will take them when no one else will. If Jews could be killed as Jews, then they must be able to fight as Jews.

I wandered Jerusalem, certain for the first time that a Jewish state simply must exist. I didn't know what form it should take, and I certainly wasn't content with the Jewish state as it currently existed, but I knew, absolutely, that it was necessary and that it was right, not because it was divinely mandated, but because history demanded it.

I had set out to define myself as a global Jew, but to be a Jew without borders was to be a Jew without Israel's borders. And without Israel, where would we find haven if we needed it? So many people, like Orly's family or Yordanos, had, in recent times, needed this place to take them. I had intended to discover a world of Jews who did not need Israel and, in so discovering, to get beyond Israel. I felt I had accomplished that, in some respects. I now had no need to define Jews *by* Israel, but I understood the need Jews had *for* Israel.

I went out for drinks that night with a friend who had just moved to Israel. She was American and was fulfilling her lifelong dream of making aliyah. We strolled through downtown Jerusalem. Ben Yehuda Street was like a carnival, with barhoppers and street performers and people shopping and the general raucousness of a living city. There was no visible trauma here. This was a place filled with life. Only a few years earlier, this area would have been almost empty because of the threat of suicide bombers. Wasn't this the triumph of the Jewish people? A perfectly normal night on a downtown street, with perfectly normal young people getting perfectly, blissfully drunk?

A group of Orthodox boys were huddled together placing bets on who could eat the most crackers. A group of Birthright kids were running from shop to shop pointing out witty T-shirts. There was a group of grubby hippy-looking guys sitting in a drum circle, wearing yarmulkes and doing a little reggae riff on "Ose Shalom." This was normal. This was the Jewish state. My spirits restored, I went home that night feeling good. I felt no ambivalence about Israel. It was a necessity and it was healthy and normal and good. A person could live here, could ignore the tensions and the contradictions. A Jewish person could make a life here, if he wanted, and enjoy the quiet of the Sabbath and the freedoms of a modern metropolis and, thanks to that same security apparatus that had almost denied me entry into Israel, even a modicum of safety. I went to sleep that night thinking the phrase *Never again*, and thinking about the drum circle and "Ose Shalom" and about the last time I had heard it on Nabugoye Hill. In Israel, you didn't need to struggle to define your Jewish life or to carve out a space for Judaism in your life. It was all around you, on the streets and in the air. I was glad for it, and charmed by it, and totally under its spell.

THE NEXT DAY, FORTY-EIGHT HOURS BEFORE I was to leave Israel, I went to meet George, a Palestinian, who had promised to show me around the West Bank. I brought Jan with me, and two other Americans who were eager to see what George had to show us. Amos, Jan's husband, reluctantly dropped us off at the barrier gate that led into Bethlehem. He urged us to be safe and wished us well.

Passing through the gate was itself a daunting experience. There are long dark passageways and you are sealed in on all sides. It feels a bit like airport passport control and a lot like a prison. Jan's long blond hair and billowing white shirt seemed to glow in the dark, and I used them to help navigate through without tripping over her. The wall and the guard tower rose off to our right. After a brief zigzag, we found ourselves on the other side, in front of a line of taxis waiting to take people to the various tourist sites around the city. The wall was covered in graffiti: Stop this Racist Wall, Ich Bin Ein Berliner, Is this your dream? And simply, hauntingly: Ghetto.

Here we were, in the city of Bethlehem.

On the Israeli side of the wall, things were neat and orderly. Roads were straight and well maintained. On the Palestinian side, the pavement was broken, buildings were ruined, garbage went uncollected. Poverty was clearly rampant. George picked us up and drove us through town, pointing out the Church of the Nativity, the Tomb of Rachel, and other sights of interest. And he drove us around the barrier.

"You called it a Security Barrier," he said to me. "But that is not what we call it. We call it the Apartheid Wall. That is what it is." He showed us where the wall came right up to the edge of houses, choking out the sunlight. It was impossible to avoid it. Everywhere you looked the wall peered down at you. This was a prison. No other word could be used. Bethlehem was a prison. It was a prison built by the Jewish state. I was in for a long day, and there was no turning back from what I was to see.

George took us past his office to tell us about the work his organization does in nonviolence training and promoting interfaith peace work. He was a thickly built man with a shaved head and big hands. He had a friendly smile and a very warm laugh that could at times be tinged with deep and angry sarcasm. He was involved with the International Solidarity Movement and with many other nonviolent resistance groups. He worked with Israelis and foreigners and other Palestinians, but his work was not aimed primarily at peace between Israel and Palestine. His goal was the liberation of the Palestinians and the end of Zionism. He did not believe in violence—at one point he described the ideology of Hamas as a social disease—but he also did not believe in the Jewish state, at least not the one that existed where Palestinian families used to live. He did, however, believe in nonviolence, even as he was deeply angry at the injustice he saw around him and the injustices to which he was subjected on a daily basis.

"I have been doing this work for eighteen years," he said, "and I have never touched a gun. All lives are sacred. But this does not mean I do not resist the occupation. To visit my father in the hospital," he explained, rubbing the back of his head, "which means crossing through the Apartheid wall, I needed to get a special travel permit . . . I was denied it until I hired a lawyer. I needed a lawyer to visit my father in the hospital? Is this right? Tell me. Is this right? This wall is stealing our land and crushing us so that Zionists 'can feel safe.' But it is not for safety. It is to take our land and imprison us.

When we talked to him about the Holocaust, his answer was simple.

"Of course it is terrible," he said. "But why should the Palestinians suffer because of it? They had nothing to do with it, but as a result, they lost their homes, hundreds of thousands displaced, and now we live under this occupation. Because of what the Germans did? That makes no sense to me."

When one of my companions, a young American named Josh, tried to explain about the Israel he knew, a place of tolerance and opportunity and a refuge for people who desperately needed one, George answered, "What good does that do me? The Israel I know is soldiers and settlers. I live under occupation."

Perhaps it was too much to ask the oppressed to see the point of view of their oppressor, and George certainly was amazing for his struggle against violence and for interfaith cooperation, which was sometimes an unpopular position to take in the West Bank. He was Christian and worked with people from all religious backgrounds who were "committed to justice for the Palestinian people." He arranged dialogues with Israelis and did regular tours of the West Bank. I thought of Ina in New Orleans and her "devastation tours." George had the same idea. He planned to show us one of the refugee camps and then drive us up to see Nablus, the largest city in the West Bank and a stronghold of extremism. Nablus was the West Bank city hardest hit by Israeli military action, which was certainly part of the reason he wanted us to see it. Hamas was still active in Nablus, and still clashed with Fatah—the dominant West Bank political party—but George smiled at our worries.

"You will see," he said. "You will be very welcome. No one will cause you any trouble. Outside, they want you to think we are all terrorists, but this is just not so. You will see the truth."

We set out on our tour anxious about what we would be shown, but ready to see what George felt we must. Just as Yad Vashem had its nationalistic purpose, so too did this tour of the West Bank, and it was our duty, we all felt, to listen and to learn.

We drove on winding, broken roads and skirted the outside of Israeli settlements, some established by religious extremists, but most filled with normal Israelis who moved for the affordable housing and to try to have a decent life. While the Israelis in the outpost settlements were certainly isolated, they had plenty of room. One study stated that Israeli settlers in the West Bank are given eighty-five times more land than the Palestinians, who are crammed into dense urban areas and suffer from the chronic effects of overcrowding.

"Their water always works," George explained, pointing at one of the established settlements as we passed. "Here, the Israelis control our water. Some days you cannot shower. Some days you can. It depends on whether we are given access to the water."

I thought again about the trees I'd seen, the blossoming of the desert all over Israel. The water had to come from somewhere, and that meant that someone controlled it, and that someone else didn't.

A drive that would have taken an hour on Israeli roads took us over four hours on Palestinian ones, and en route we encountered seven checkpoints. The checkpoint is one of the most insidious aspects of Israel's control of the West Bank. Manned by young Israeli soldiers surrounded by a hostile population, they are at best a colossal inconvenience.

At worst they are deadly. Driving a car with Palestinian plates, we joined the line for one checkpoint and waited in the heat for half an hour. We were somewhere near the site where it is believed Jacob lay down and dreamed of the ladder to heaven. The landscape around us was bleak and harsh and undeveloped. I could picture robed shepherds wandering the hills. I could also imagine why the intensely religious would feel called to this place. This was the land Abraham had walked.

We pulled up to the front of the line, and a sniper in a nearby tower kept his rifle trained on us. Sunlight glinted off the scope. Soldiers flanked the car, fingers on their triggers, watching us. A young Israeli took our passports, and, seeing that we were foreigners, he smiled meekly. "Please don't hate me," he said by way of apology, and after a minute of inspecting our vehicle and George's ID, he returned our passports and sent us on our way. What kind of system puts a young man in such a position over civilians? What kind of system creates a soldier who knows that what he is doing needs an apology?

The frustration that this engenders created a place like Nablus. Driving in, we saw a massive parking lot filled with idle taxis, their drivers sitting around waiting for work that would probably not come. We eased down a slope into the city and I saw a familiar logo stenciled on the wall of a building. It looked like the emblem I had seen in Iran: the symbol of Hezbollah. There were graffiti on a lot of walls, symbols of Hamas and Hezbollah, political slogans, mundane tags, whole sentences in Arabic. I later had a friend translate one passage I'd photographed. "You murderers," it read, "if we die in this war, this [city] is our graveyard."

I was uncomfortable in Nablus. Though everyone we met was friendly, there were posters on nearly every wall celebrating militants who fought the Israelis, their martyrdom or their escape. There were ruined houses demolished by Israeli bulldozers as part of a policy meant to break the backs of terrorist organizations but that only seemed to strengthen them. Near the ruins of one demolished building, I met a group of young boys playing with a bicycle. We laughed and joked with each other. Behind us there was a plaque on the wall that caught my attention. It read: "Never Forgive, Never Forget. In Memory of the Israeli Invasion, the Massacre Committed by the Israeli Army, April 2002." Below the text were the names and images of Palestinians who had died. The children were playing against this backdrop. I couldn't help but think that just a few miles away, on the other side of that wall, children their age were leading very different lives, filled with opportunity. But they would one day reach the age of military service, and these boys would one day reach the age where they might want to act on the militant nationalist ideology all around them. Who would break that cycle?

We strolled the old Ottoman market, visited one of the last soap factories in the city, and chatted with merchants. We ate fresh kanafeh, a world-famous Nablusi treat made from crispy pastry threads fried with cheese and butter, then drizzled with honey. Down the narrow street, shops sat empty under the shadow of the Manara Clock Tower in the central square. Business was slow for everyone. Nightly raids by the IDF had frayed people's nerves. When we stopped by the An-Najah National University, we met a young student who had spent hours in a stress position the night before when the IDF raided his apartment building. He cried from the humiliation and the fear, but the university dean on the other side of the room comforted him.

"You'll get used to it," he said. "It has happened to me dozens of time." He looked at us to explain: "This was his first time."

On the wall behind him hung a poster commemorating Rachel Corrie, and a shelf full of copies of a new book that An-Najah National University in Nablus had produced, an oral history of the Nakba. Outside, we passed more ruined buildings. These had been hit by missiles—targeted assassinations, the Israelis said. The buildings had been left in ruins, I think, to reinforce the image of a besieged people. "They raid our homes," George said, "and they call it arrests. We call it kidnapping. It is not the Israeli Defense Force. We call it the Israeli Occupation Force."

What hope was there, I wondered, when the proudest moment in one nation's history is the worst moment in another's, and they are in the exact same space? What happens when two sides can't even agree on the meaning of words? The history they shared meant such radically different things to them that words—*barrier, wall, independence, catastrophe, army, arrest, kidnapping, terror*—meant different things depending on which side you were on. They couldn't even agree on what the contested land was called. Nablus or Shechem? The Occupied Territories or Judea and Samaria? The vocabulary described what you believed more than where you actually were.

Late in the afternoon, when our little group, wandering the run-down Ottoman market in Nablus, passed yet another memorial to Palestinian boys who'd died trying to kill Israeli boys, I thought cynically of Herzl's saying, "If you will it, it is no dream." I was happy to get back in the car and leave Nablus.

Over and over again we ran into checkpoints, and over and over again the guns were leveled at us. Some of the soldiers were friendly, some aloof, and in one case, hostile. There were over two hundred cars in line, and tensions were flaring up as the sun set. We were told to turn back and find another way to go, which would be hours out of our way. The soldier didn't care about our protestations; he didn't care about what we needed to do or where we needed to be. He sent us back because it was in his power to do so. This was the everyday reality for Palestinians, locked inside the West Bank and barely in control of their own lives.

After that checkpoint on the way out of Nablus turned us back, we had to drive out of our way, through small villages and along a road that skirted the sprawling Jenin Refugee Camp. Jan was distraught. Her mother was ill, and she wanted to get home to check on her, but the broken roads and the mercurial decisions of the checkpoint guards had laid waste to our timetable. As we drove, we rumbled past wrecked houses and old goatherds wandering the hills. The biblical landscape mixed with the depressing political landscape, and always in the distance lurked the massive Security Barrier, or Apartheid Wall, or whatever you chose to call it. You could see it from almost anywhere. The wall was a physical divide, but that was only part of its impact. I had never seen neighbors so cut off from each other as the Israelis and the Palestinians.

I thought again about the graffiti near the security gate that led us into Bethlehem. "Is this your dream?" it read. I wondered about the dream of Zionism, the dream of a Jewish state for a beleaguered people, and I couldn't imagine that the anger in Nablus, or the humiliation in Bethlehem, or the ruin throughout the West Bank was part of that dream. Both sides said *Never forget*, but both sides wanted *their* land back, *their* homes. Both sides wanted control. Perhaps this was the dream of Zionism, just as it was the dream of Palestinian nationalism? I'd seen this mentality in Kosovo and Bosnia and Rwanda too. Ethnic national- ism, whatever its form, always ends the same way: with walls and barbed wire and kids growing up in rubble.

This was months before the war in Gaza in early 2009 that would leave thousands of Palestinians and a dozen Israelis dead. That war was waged on the Palestinian side as a retaliation for the frustrations of living behind the blockade of Gaza and an attempt by Hamas to reassert its radi- cal bona fides through violence against Israel. For Israel's part, it could no longer tolerate the threats and the missiles from Hamas, especially with elections looming, and met the Hamas attacks with overwhelming force. The world watched in shock and outrage as Hamas ended the cease-fire with Israel in a hail of rockets, and Israel responded with the bombing and invasion of the Gaza Strip. In cities from New York to Tehran, rallies and protests denounced the Israeli action as the large Jewish organiza- tions tried to circle their wagons and rally to Israel's defense. Anti-Jewish attacks in Europe spiked. A synagogue in Argentina was ransacked and descrated. There were few voices for peace on either side, and those there were—the J Street lobbying organization in the United States, the Holy Land Trust in the West Bank, with which George worked tirelessly—

were quickly condemned and marginalized, made to seem out of touch with reality. Peace, the powerful parties around the world declared, was an unrealistic goal. I watched the news helplessly as the bodies of children were marched through the streets. Even those bodies were a kind of vocabulary that neither side could agree on the meaning of. The seeds of the Gaza violence were there in the fear and anger of the civilians and the soldiers that day in the occupied West Bank. When the war in Gaza erupted, I was not surprised.

ON A LONELY HILLTOP, LONG AFTER the sun went down, as we tried to drive back to the barrier in Bethlehem, we encountered yet another checkpoint. Young soldiers flanked the car. They were on edge, isolated. There were three that we could see. One took our passports while the others stood beside us. There was certainly a sniper somewhere with his sights trained on our car. The soldier next to my window shifted uncomfortably, glancing over his shoulder every few seconds. His cheeks were red, his skin smooth. He was terrified, even though he held the machine gun. He scanned the inside of the car, but he didn't really see any of us. He was not looking for people; he was looking for threats. Hezbollah had just declared its intention to kidnap more Israeli soldiers, and these boys had certainly seen the recent funerals. We were still close to Nablus and to Jenin.

As we left the frightened soldiers behind us in the dark and continued toward the Bethlehem barrier, I couldn't help but think of all that I had gotten wrong in my journey this past year. All this time I had been asking myself that question that Hugo Kahn had put to me: *Ayeka?* Where are you? I had been trying to place myself within the Jewish people and to place the Jewish people within a global context and to figure out how to feel about Israel. But "Where are you?" was not the question that sustained the Jews throughout the Diaspora, and it was not the question that would create a safer and more just future for Israel and Palestine.

When we passed back through the maze of wire and concrete at the Bethlehem crossing—even more intimidating in the dark—and I stood looking at the massive guard towers again and the looming concrete wall that looked so much like a prison gate, I knew that there was another question God asks in the Torah that needed to animate the Jewish people and the Jewish nation. It would be hard, because the violence is real and the dangers are real, and the pain of history is not easily overcome, but the Jews of New Orleans and Bosnia and Uganda had certainly taken the risk of asking this question and were safer because of it.

The question was not "Where are you?" but that other one from the book of Genesis, the one God asks, I think, with a touch of desperation in His voice. "Where is your brother?"

epilogue

Home

Thou hast lifted us above all tongues, and hast hallowed us by Thy
commandments, and hast brought us, O our King, to Thy service.
—SANCTIFICATION OF THE DAY PRAYER

O N ROSH HASHANAH, A year after my visit to Burma, my partner,
Tim, and I went to services together. He was nervous because he
didn't know the songs or what would be expected of him, but he wanted
to share the evening with me. I wasn't a member of any synagogue and,
due to the abnormally high attendance on the High Holidays, most synagogues charged nonmembers to attend. But I found a free, and amazingly
appropriate, Rosh Hashanah service with a Google search.

Congregation Beth Simchat Torah is the country's largest synagogue
for the gay, lesbian, bisexual, and transgendered community. In response
to the historic exclusion of gays and lesbians from participating openly
in most Jewish communities, CBST started the Open Door Fund, which
eliminated the normal admission fees charged by congregations during

the High Holy Days, so that Jews with no synagogue affiliation would have a place to go. Because of that, thousands of New Yorkers with a wide range of connections to Judaism poured through the doors of Town Hall, on Forty-third Street, where the services were being held. Most of the people were High Holidays Jews. This night and Yom Kippur would be their only visits to synagogue for the year. I found it interesting that so many people who usually felt no need for such specific ritualized spirituality would go out of their way for it two days a year. But then again, I had just spent a year going out of my way for it.

It felt wonderful to be surrounded by thousands of people for the holiday, having spent the previous Jewish New Year by myself in Rangoon. It felt even better to share the moment with Tim. As we entered the building, I put on my *kippah* from Uganda. Tim took one of the white communal ones from a basket near the door, but changed his mind about wearing it. Looking around, I saw a variety of styles of head coverings— some Sephardic, some the knitted kind worn by the Orthodox, and even some rainbow "Pride" yarmulkes. Some men chose not to cover their heads at all, and many women chose to wear the yarmulke, claiming what has traditionally been a masculine symbol. This was the most diverse Jewish congregation I had ever seen, as if people from every community I'd visited in the past year had assembled in one room. There were Jews and non-Jews, heterosexual couples and gay couples, single people and families, and every color of skin under the sun.

Rabbi Sharon Kleinbaum, who has been leading CBST since 1992, stood on the bimah, which had been built onstage. She welcomed the community together with a broad smile. She knew that tonight she had massive numbers of new people, and she used the occasion to give a sense of the kind of congregation CBST was. She welcomed the Jews and the non-Jews; she welcomed the gay people and the straight people and the transgendered and everyone else, however they identified themselves. She urged people to bring themselves fully to the space that night with both their minds and their bodies. She hoped that the evening would help those who sought such help to experience a truly meaningful moment together and to experience a meaningful connection with God, however we conceived of such a being.

I was both drawn to the inclusiveness of her welcome and skeptical of it. It was the very specificity of Judaism that differentiated it from vague spirituality—crystals and energies and such.

"Now if you look around and you feel like the person next to you belongs here more than you do," she continued, "like you don't know enough or aren't the right kind of Jew and everyone else here is, you should know that this is a very Jewish feeling, and you are probably in the right place." The congregation laughed. I couldn't believe what I was hearing. Had I not felt that way in every synagogue I'd been to all over the world? She had me hooked again, and she continued with a sharp focus on the Jewish liturgy and the ritual. She explained Jewish custom and made it feel simultaneously unique and universal, and I let go of my doubts. I felt that I had found the kind of Jewish teacher I had hoped I would. The hazan and the cantor at her sides sang passionately, backed up by a talented choir.

The service was cheerful and uplifting. The choir guided us through the songs of the liturgy. The musical arrangements came from different times in Jewish history and from all over the world. There were Portuguese melodies and African melodies and Hasidic melodies mixed with the traditional songs I knew from the Reform congregation of my childhood.

We reached the Shehekianu, the prayer of thanksgiving I'd first spoken aloud in Iran, and this time my voice was not alone in it. The entire theater filled with people lifted their voices in prayer. *Baruch ata Adonai Elohenu Melech ha'olam shehekianu v'kimanu v'higianu lazman hazeh.*

I looked around at the variety of worshippers and listened to the wave of sound washing over us as the choir sang out an "Amen." Tim and I were together with a mixed multitude of people who were committed to building a community of respect and care, as the rabbi called it. There was no question of obedience, as Moses had presented it to the mixed multitude in the desert, though there was a hope for engagement. I thought about what my father had said, how he ran from organized Judaism because it felt empty to him, like a show. The music around me did have a theatrical quality to it, and I had spent the year pantomiming my way through Friday night services. I had brought a desire to let the rituals work on me, revealing themselves as I performed them. The "show," as my father put it, was only worth as much as I brought to it. I had spent much of my life bringing nothing to the services, when I even went, expecting the rabbi to tell me why they mattered. But having spent the past year with a variety of Jews from all over the world, I had a new understanding of the potential of the services. The same prayers could be sung with such joy in Uganda and such solemnity in Iran for the same reason that some wept at the Kol Nidre on Yom Kippur and others smiled, and others felt guilty about its very existence in the liturgy. The rituals were a reflection of ourselves and of the tensions in which we lived.

The rabbi described the congregation as a "place to transform ourselves from a collection of individuals into a spiritual community in which we can create a profound sense of purpose and meaning in our lives and in which we can experience the presence of God."

As we prayed, I felt that sense that I was part of a timeless moment, but not an ancient one, the way I had in Iran. The moment was not a reproduction of the way Jews were supposed to pray but, under Rabbi Kleinbaum's guidance, an immediate moment of engagement and reflection. The experience was not some general spiritual ecstasy, which I had felt looking at amazing views or doing yoga or even standing at the Western Wall, but a specifically Jewish spirituality. The rituals of standing and bending and sitting and standing again were moments that made

Judaism alive. There was nothing abstract about them. They were a kind of psychospiritual technology—like tefillin or the practice of kashruth—that grounded us in ourselves and bound us to each other and to all those who came before us and would come after. Perhaps the Orthodox keep the traditions because they are commanded to, but perhaps an equally compelling reason is because they work. Donning tefillin does center a person. Learning about kashruth (I'd yet to start obeying it) does make a person more sensitive to the means of production of his food, to the suffering of the animals and the earth from which it comes. And being part of a community *does* allow for personal as well as societal transformation. All of these things were commanded by the God of the Torah, but all of them are also gifts of that Torah.

I thought of the sign outside the sanctuary in Rangoon. "A tree may be alone in the field, a man alone in the world, but a Jew is never alone on his holy days." I think I understood it now. As long as we shared in these sacred moments, we could defy distances and time. The moment of prayer is an eternal present.

As we stood for the silent Amidah, which I still hadn't learned in Hebrew, I thought about what Stephen Baer had said to me about his experience telling the story of the Berkley Jewish community, how telling it had made him part of the story. I longed for that feeling. He'd said that it was his way of saying *Hineini*—I am here, which was the answer to the question Hugo Kahn had posed to me in New Orleans. *Where are you?* I thought that telling the stories of all these communities, struggling to answer that persistent question—not Are you Jewish? but *Ayeka?*—Where are you?—might give me that feeling Stephen had had, that feeling of membership and a readiness to serve. I'd seen that the question was necessary but not sufficient. With Tim next to me at services sharing these moments, I thought, for the moment at least, after a year of wandering, *Hineini.* I am here.

I looked down at the English in the prayer book in my hands. It was convenient, at last, to have the English translation along with the Hebrew. I read the special blessing for the holiday Amidah: "Thou hast lifted us above all tongues, and hast hallowed us by Thy commandments, and hast brought us, O our King, to Thy service."

Lifted us above all tongues. I liked that. The blessing itself acknowledged the richness of the Jewish world. There were Ibo-speaking Jews in Nigeria and Malayalam-speaking Jews in Cochin. There were the dozen languages I had encountered in Jewish communities around the world, and countless more I hadn't. During this Amidah, I thought again about my year, and about those communities I'd been privileged to visit.

Each one survived because of a deep commitment to a purpose, to the idea that being part of the Jewish people and of a Jewish community is a duty, a responsibility. They took the concept of *tikkun olam* seriously, and sought connection with each other and with their neighbors. Each had its unique character, touched by the place where it was born and the people who sustained it, but they survived, in a larger sense, because they continually sought to transform themselves into an active and meaningful part of people's lives. Their striving went beyond nation states and borders. It defied history and geography. The traditions were a vehicle to communicate to each other a sense of belonging, a sense of intention and value. *Lifted us above all tongues.* The phrase echoed in my thoughts.

Keeping a synagogue open for traveling Jews was, for Moses Samuels in Rangoon, a way of showing his intent in the continuum of Jewish history. Building a community for their children in Bentonville, Arkansas, assigned a value to Judaism for everyone who had a hand in it. In New Orleans and Bosnia, by using Jewish organizations to help everyone, Jews demonstrated the power of the ancient traditions to become a living, saving ideal. In Uganda, in Iran, in Cuba, each of the communities, by celebrating and mourning together, sent a message that faith, whether in God or in each other, can create rather than destroy. The early Zionists had a slogan, *Livnot v'lehibanot*, "to build and be built." Each of the distant Jewish communities I'd encountered was living out that motto, stripped of its nationalism, and creating a culture of respect, sometimes against strong odds.

While I stood among the worshippers of Congregation Beth Simchat Torah and thought about Jews praying these same prayers all over the world, all renewing their relationship to the divine and to each other, I felt I had learned something. The greatest achievement of the Jewish people was not the long struggle for their own state but the richness of their Diaspora. The state of Israel was necessary, for the time being, as a haven, and it had accomplished many wonderful things, but the lessons that could prevent that necessity and protect that state in the future were being taught by millions of Jews living outside of it.

The model for the future that the stories of these Diaspora communities present lies not in retreating behind borders, not in the promise of any nation state or military arsenal, or even negotiated treaties, but in the promise of a global community of neighbors, one that many small pockets of Jewry are struggling to create. Each of them lives the idea, in its own way, that there is no exile. We are home.

ACKNOWLEDGMENTS

MANY PEOPLE OFFERED THEIR time, advice, insight, and resources while I worked on this book. Although opinions on Judaism, Jews, and Israel outnumber the stars, every one of these people allowed me to pursue my own path to understanding, even as many shared with me (sometimes quite passionately) their unique points of view and often hard-earned expertise. I hope I have been fair, even if I have not arrived where some of them might have hoped or gone further than some of them might have imagined.

This project was made possible by the generous support of Dr. Lynn Maxwell, the Ben and Esther Rosenbloom Foundation, and the Weinman Family Foundation, without whom my intercontinental journey would have come to a grinding halt.

Everywhere I went, I relied on the wisdom and generosity of some remarkable people:

Sammy and Moses Samuels were generous spirits from the start, and I am thrilled to have met Michelle Schaner on that rainy Day of Atonement in Rangoon.

Betsy Rosen in Arkansas was a gracious host, as were the rest of the Etz Chaim family. Ina Davis opened her home in New Orleans to me and shared the many joys of her city.

For my time in Uganda, I am grateful to Jon Kleinman for his easy companionship and vigilant lens, Holly and Ben at Thanksgiving Coffee Company, Harriet Bograd and Laura Wetzler from Kulanu,

Acknowledgments

Rabbi Jeffrey A. Summit at Tufts, Adam Baldachin and his wife, Maital, Elana Kieffer and the other wonderful volunteers in and around Nabugoye Hill, and the indefatigable Aaron Kintu Moses and JJ Keki of the Abayudaya congregation. Samson Shadrak served as an excellent guide.

I never would have made it to Iran if it weren't for the Fellowship of Reconciliation's Leila Zand. I am also grateful to Ethan Vesey-Flad and the rest of the delegation for their activism and insight. For her great wisdom and patience, I cannot express enough gratitude to Rabbi Lynn Gottlieb, whose life is devoted to the path of peace. Su'ad made sense of so much of Iran for me, as did Roya Hakakian and Tanaz Eshaghian, Morteza, Dr. Moresadegh, and Morris Motamed.

I would never have begun this project without the kindness of the Jewish community of Bosnia, specifically Dragica Levi, Dada Papo, and Jakob Finci. I am also indebted to Jasenka Paralija and Ivan Hrkas for their company and their patience, and for many a beer.

In Cuba, thanks go to Monica and Marco, Daniel Motola, Maritza Corrales, and Jose Altschuler, as well as Ruth Behar and Robert Fisher.

In Israel, my gratitude runs in so many directions. For opening his home to me, and trying to knock whatever sense into me that he could, I thank Amos Avgar with all my heart. His wife, my dear friend Jan, was beside me almost every step of this journey, whether she knew it or not, and I am glad I could spend some time with her in her adopted home. George Rishmawi gave greatly of himself and taught me much about the Palestinian struggle, and demonstrated that we don't have to agree on everything to respect each other and work for peace. Orly Rahimian was an amazing teacher and translator, as well as friend.

During my research, I am lucky to have met the enthusiastic Sharon Ungerleider and, briefly, the eminent Rabbi Irwin Kula. For much expertise in the history of Jewish Burma, I am grateful to the work of Ruth Cernea. Rabbi Rex Perlemeter has long been all that one would hope a rabbi could be, and I am happy to have shared so many moments, joyous and painful, with him.

I'm also grateful to my parents, who I am sure never saw this book or this journey coming from me, and to my sister, for paving the way with her hard-earned spiritual skepticism. Stephen Baer shared the history of Berkley, Virginia with me and played a large role in urging me on this journey, more than he knew at the time. Both of us are probably surprised by the impact his research had on me.

I would not have had the chance to write this without the excitement and guidance of Sarah Durand at HarperCollins, and would never have made it to the finish line without the insight, hard work, and kindness of editors David Highfill and Gabe Robinson, who adopted the project with great care. Natalie Robin read more of this than she might care to remember, and I owe most of the good parts, and most of my sanity, to her. Any mistakes or flaws in memory are my own.

My agent, Robert Guinsler, remained enthusiastic when even I wasn't, supported me when I most needed it, and kicked me in the *tuchus* when all else failed. I could not ask for a better agent, and am lucky to have him as a friend.

Lastly, I thank Baxter for the way his snoring tracked the rhythm of my days, and Tim, whose love and support gave those days meaning. God only knows what I'd be without him, my *beshert*.